MONEY, HEART
AND MIND

ALSO BY WILLIAM BLOOM

The Christ Sparks (1995)

The Seeker's Guide (edited with John Button) (1993)

First Steps—An Introduction to Spiritual Practice (1993)

The Sacred Magician (1993)

Meditation in a Changing World (1987; revised edition, 1993)

The New Age (1991)

Personal Identity, National Identity and International Relations (1989)

Sacred Times—A New Approach to Festivals (1989)

Devas, Fairies and Angels (1988)

Ley Lines and Ecology (with Marko Pogacnik) (1978)

MONEY, HEART AND MIND

Financial Well-Being for People and Planet

WILLIAM BLOOM

KODANSHA INTERNATIONAL
New York • Tokyo • London

Kodansha America, Inc.
114 Fifth Avenue, New York, New York 10011, U.S.A.

Kodansha International Ltd.
17-14 Otowa 1-chome, Bunkyo-ku, Tokyo 112, Japan

Published in 1996 by Kodansha America, Inc.
by arrangement with Penguin U.K., London.

Originally published in 1995 by the Penguin Group, London.

Library of Congress Cataloging-in-Publication Data
Bloom, William, 1948–
    Money, heart and mind : financial well-being for people and
planet/ William Bloom.
        p.   cm.
    Includes bibliographical references and index.
    ISBN 1-56836-153-X (hardcover)
        1. Money.   I. Title.
HG221.B5743   1996
332.4—dc20   96-20594

PRINTED IN THE UNITED STATES OF AMERICA

96 97 98 99 00 BER/B 10 9 8 7 6 5 4 3 2 1

For Marika and Marko Pogacnik

CONTENTS

THE CHANGES

ACKNOWLEDGEMENTS

I owe a debt of gratitude to Stiftung Imago Coelestis which funded the original research and to the Lorian Foundation which then supported it.

Allen Gold, friend and financier, inspired and provoked me. The participants in my trainings and workshops stimulated and clarified many things. There were helpful conversations with many people, in particular: Ram Dass, John Clausen, Joshua Mailman, Stewart Boyle, Nick Williams, Bernardette Vallely, Howard Wood, Georg Nicolaus, Dagmar Dietz and Jacob Needleman. Tessa Strickland edited some early chapters and her insightful comments pointed me in a better direction. Several colleagues read early drafts and encouraged me: Giles Chitty, David Lorimer, Wolf Dieter Grossman and, particularly, David Spangler. Also thanks to my editor at Penguin, Janice Brent.

The ongoing support of Sabrina Dearborn and James Bloom, who also plugged me into electronic realities, was loving and essential.

1
BEGINNINGS AND
CONCLUSIONS

The gods only laugh when people ask them for money. (Japanese saying)

Money, which represents the prose of life, and which is hardly spoken of in parlors without an apology, is, in its effects and laws, as beautiful as roses. (Ralph Waldo Emerson)

The Structure of the Book

Money, Heart and Mind is for anyone who needs a better understanding of money.

The problem is not money itself, though it may seem that way. The problem is the limited way that we think and feel about it. There are no clear new strategies or alternatives because we are all caught in the same framework of ideas. Full-time parent or entrepreneur; capitalist, socialist or ecologist; dictator or democrat; rich or poor: we are all using the same set of ideas, the same theories, the same myths and assumptions. Whatever our politics, our background or our role, how can we consider creative alternatives if we are all trapped in the same way of thinking – a way of thinking which has not and is not delivering real solutions?

The whole purpose of this book is to stimulate a new framework for thinking and feeling about money. This framework is not limited to one particular approach. It contains different levels of analysis and is open-structured. It is a transparent scaffolding constructed of the major elements that make up our money world: the anthropology, the psychology, the history, the politics and the metaphysics. In one jargon of our times, this is a *post-modern* approach. In another jargon, it is a *holistic* approach. In yet another jargon, it is to do with *emergence* and *complexity*.

This approach understands that money is not simply the creature of economic and commercial ideas and interests, but is also a creature of individual and mass human emotions, thoughts and actions. Money is intertwined with our material environment, but it is also far more dynamic as an organic actor in our psyches and cultures. The ecology of money is multidimensional. The environment that money influences is obviously physical, but more crucially it is the environment of our psychologies and cultures.

Because money is so much a psychological thing, we cannot avoid looking at our feelings, our emotional financial lives. We need insights into the primal and subtle emotions that hook into, manipulate and manifest through our behaviour with money. This is relevant to us, individually and collectively.

This book, then, has to give attention equally to the different dimensions of money. Excluding one dimension will remove a crucial piece of the overall jigsaw. A limited understanding cannot provide a secure basis for problem-solving. The flow of *Money, Heart and Mind*, therefore, is first to describe and penetrate the various dynamics which create our money world. Then it moves into the realm of possible solutions.

There are two problems which readers may encounter, so let me warn you of them now. I do not want to lose your attention through thoughtless presentation. The first problem arises from the need fully to include all the different elements. This means that domains of information, normally kept a huge distance apart, meet here separated only by a page or two and the reading mind is asked to accommodate them all. This may be painful for those readers who tend usually to stay within one area of interest. Comfortable with psychology, the reader may have trouble with history or politics. Or the political reader may have trouble with the anthropology. Most of all, some people may fidget nervously at the metaphysics. While the metaphysicians may be aghast at having to ground their sensibilities in social and political reality.

What can I say? If we want to understand something, we have to look at it from all angles. We cannot pick, choose and exclude stuff just because of our discomfort.

There is also another problem due to the different types of knowledge. They require different styles of presentation and different kinds of attention. Readers, for example, who do not have a background of enjoying theory may be startled when we begin to look at the anthropological, historical and political background. Here the story is not told through individual experience – easy to relate to on a personal level – but is told through the more general history of humanity as a whole. This may seem less entertaining. And readers who like pure logic and rationality, beware of the metaphysics.

I must also own up to mixing formal theory with personal anecdotes and feelings. Part of my life story is that I am a novelist who became an academic political psychologist, but am now focused on human potential and consciousness. I cannot bear pure theory without personal interludes. I also need anecdote to be backed by theory.

As you will have seen from the contents page, the first part of the book deals with the psychological dynamics. It then looks at the anthropology, history and politics. After which it approaches the metaphysics. It then concludes with strategies and thoughts about change – institutional, political and personal.

The Sources of My Passion

My passion for this subject of money has several sources.

I am, for example, inspired by stories of generosity. There were times of chivalry when the powerful understood that their status went hand in hand with kindness and generosity. Charity was once a word of great honour and power. There have been cultures where the creation of wealth radiated to support beauty and education. There have been times when the spirit of money was proud. As *The Book of Sufi Chivalry* expresses it: 'The best of my people will enter Paradise not because of their achievements, but because of the Mercy of Allah and their quality of being satisfied with little for themselves and their extreme generosity to others.'

I do not experience this chivalry around me now.

In parallel, my passion is also fuelled by the dying children and unforgivable social injustice. We cannot allow this to continue.

Then, as a psychologist and lover of people, I am fascinated by the deep and complex nature of our relationship with money. We love and hate it. We love what it buys and we hate the need, greed and bullying. Mature in most areas of our lives, many of us turn into wimps or bombasts when dealing with money. To exchange money and look fairly and squarely in each other's eyes is a rare event.

We dream that personal wealth will release us into happiness despite the overwhelming evidence to the contrary. Our financial attitudes are confused and neurotic. One weekend I worked with a group in which there was an elegant and well-educated woman in her sixties who began on the Saturday morning to look at the financial attitudes she had inherited from her mother. That evening, to her astonishment, she found that for the first time in forty years she had not used her asthma inhaler but could breathe without it. By Sunday evening she had more understanding about her financial wounding and she said she was breathing in a way that she had never experienced before. Her psychological pain around money had anchored deep into her body, constricting her breath for five decades.

In the same way that this woman needed to breathe, money also needs to breathe more freely. Money is like language. It is a medium of material communication between human beings. It has helped create fantastic material wealth and complexity, but its spirit is emotionally confused and neurotic. It needs to flow and to move.

I am also frustrated to a point of passion by the limitations of our current money and economic theories. We are taught that money is basically a unit of account, a measurable store of value, invented and used to help trade and commerce. We are also taught what it means to be *Homo economicus*, economic human: we are anxious creatures, competitive savages, struggling for survival in an environment of scarcity, using money as a tool for getting what we need in the competitive market. We believe all this for lack of any other explanation.

This idea of money and of economics is limited. It ignores deeper and more interesting perspectives. The relationship between human beings and money is far more juicy than formal economics would allow.

I also have this sense of the true spirit of money. It is far more than a unit of account and a store of value. As an agent, a medium and a language that passes between human beings, it is a creative facilitator of human relationship and human community, a facilitator of ingenuity, productivity and wealth. It is a creative medium that serves human relationship.

And I have this sense of the goodness of money. I experience a great thrill at being part of our complex civilization – and this is a civilization whose material life-blood is money. I know full well about the ecological and humane disasters which have been created by the modern world, and I recognize that we need to reverse immediately the idiocies and greeds which destroy life. Nevertheless I am excited by the technology, by civilization and by money.

I have been rich and poor. I have experienced greed and jealousy in myself, as well as a strong instinct for sharing and social justice. I have enjoyed money and I have resented it. I am also a political creature. I cannot be content with my own wealth while the continual reality of famine and economic despair pull at my heart and conscience. And I remember well, when I was in my twenties, that fellow radicals were suspicious of my easy touch with money, while conservatives were suspicious of my interest in social justice.

Working as a consultant to a philanthropic foundation, therefore, I gladly accepted when the foundation offered to fund me in researching new ways of understanding money. This book is the result of that research. My point of departure was simple: I did not trust the theories about money and economics put forward by mainstream thinkers. Surely there was a different way of understanding money, which could provide a new framework for guiding and motivating our financial attitudes and actions, personally and organizationally?

What I really wanted was an understanding of money which encourages both wealth and economic justice together. Our current financial and economic policies are not working in a creative and beneficent way. We are increasingly confronted with a global economic crisis: the debt crisis, the ecological crisis, urban decay, third world depression, world recession and uncontrollable cycles of growth and depression. We need new ideas.

The collapse of the communist bloc has also created a huge challenge as we try to find ways, theoretical and strategic, for humanizing the free market. We need a money market that incorporates human decency.

Beyond that we have the emerging reality of the electronic global information, trade and finance networks. This new electronic world, accelerating into existence, is dramatically changing the reality of finance itself and is currently beyond the control of any local or international institutions.

There is an imperative, therefore, to find new ways of understanding and working with money. This may seem an ambitious and vain task, for the world is filled with economists and financial thinkers who surely understand the essence of the thing, money itself. But what is their ideological, cultural and theoretical starting point? Are they caught in an abstract, unreal world of models and mathematical equations? New ways of conceptualizing – new worldviews and paradigms – are emerging in many different arenas, but most particularly in psychological and scientific theory. They challenge and dismantle old ways of thinking about money and economics.

Numbers Do Not Work

Because money can be counted, it is easily appraised through the methods of arithmetic, accountancy and mathematical formulae.

Because numerical sums are logical, mechanistic and exact, it seems that money and economics should also be logical, mechanistic and exact, but the figures never tell the whole story and sums are meaningless without the breadth of a more comprehensive understanding.

To approach an understanding of money purely through mathematics and classical economics is misleading.

This book, then, emerges from a framework that is not mathematical but is concerned with the dynamic realities of human nature which create and work with money. There is a wonderful true story which is relevant. It is about a female junior school teacher in London who was young, attractive and, as a teacher, on a low income. She had begun dating a new boyfriend and, three dates into the relationship, they decided to go on a double-date to the theatre. Both couples were to meet in a bar of the Park Lane Hilton Hotel, but the teacher's date was very late. Waiting in the bar she and the other couple got into conversation with a visiting businessman from Australia. Her friends finally left for the theatre and she decided to wait on for her own date, who an hour later had not arrived. She remained chatting with the Australian, who was attractive and charming, passing through London, and she finally accepted his invitation to eat together.

They had an enjoyable meal and then, quite openly, he asked whether she would spend the night with him. He asked so charmingly that she was not upset. In fact, she found him attractive. However, she said, 'No.' He responded by offering her £300. The mood between them was still so good that she took it humorously, but still refused. Five minutes later he upped the price to £1,000. At first she did not believe him, but then took him seriously as the price went up again. He remained friendly and the whole conversation was amusing. By the end of the meal, he had offered her £3,000 and she agreed to spend the night with him.

They had an enjoyable night. When she woke in the morning, she looked around the room and he was gone. She cursed and then she smiled. She rarely went for a one-night stand, but this had been a very pleasant experience. He had been considerate, careful and exciting. Her only worry was that she might have to pay the hotel bill. She got up and then noticed a message for her on the table. 'Thank you for a beautiful night. Enclosed is a gift. I hope it helps.' It was a cheque for £30,000. She laughed, certain that it would bounce.

The cheque did not bounce and it provided her with the down payment on a mortgage for a small house that, on her teacher's salary, she would never otherwise have been able to afford. She never saw the man again.

Many issues are raised by this story, to do with sex, gender, power, luck, prostitution, empowerment and paradox. It is a story about money and it is a story about many other dimensions as well. Most of all it is a story that would not be well told in the language of economics or accountancy, for the cash figure of £30,000 on its own says nothing. The cash figures on any invoice, receipt, budget or set of accounts – personal, commercial or governmental – are always only a tiny part of the story.

To understand money we need to know far more than the bottom line of the figures.

Playful Thought

There is, in fact, a tradition of wisdom and exploration which does not admire, and never has admired, certainty in relation to knowledge. Certainty is useful for particular operations, like counting and measuring, but is not useful for wise thought, because knowledge is relative and always unfolding and changing. This is obvious, for example, in pure science where we see clearly how knowledge changes as new instruments and theories are developed. As the methods of research change, so we see and understand life in new and different ways.

We are also always passing through a historical process, and the essence of history, or time, is that things themselves – not just our perceptions of them – are always changing. Some things may appear to remain the same, but the observer and the observed are always in transition and flux. Our understanding of money is mainly caught in a particular set of assumptions which catch only one temporary reality.

And there is the famous problem that we are trapped by the actual way in which our minds think and understand. To pursue a total investigation, we need to understand and be detached about the way we think, but to become detached from our own way of thinking requires that we use our minds! To free ourselves from our thoughts we have to use our thoughts. The method that we use to escape is the method we are also escaping.

How, then, can we trust our investigations and conclusions? How can we trust economists, financiers or politicians to explain money to us? They themselves are trapped within the boundary of their own customary thinking. Classically, Plato suggested that we need to accept that the search for wisdom has no complete end and conclusion. One thought provokes another, which provokes another. Life itself is like this: one action triggering another, which in turn triggers another. This is *dialectic* and it is an attitude of wisdom about the process of knowledge. Ideas about money or anything else, therefore, cannot be static and fixed.

The dialectical approach is particularly associated with the contemporary school of *critical theory* which suggests that we recognize two important realms that determine how we think and how we identify ourselves. The first is the socio-economic and political world, and the second is the psychological and the psychoanalytic. To liberate our thinking we need to understand the power of our backgrounds and our unconscious assumptions. Critical theory suggests that in order to understand how we think, we need to keep a constant and revealing eye on our backgrounds and upon our psychologies. Most importantly this approach advises us never to trust the accepted view of things, but always to try and unveil new and different meanings.

Surely the essence of good thinking is a playfulness of the mind.

Theory, Sex and Complexity

My favourite economics teacher, a mid-European refugee, at the London School of Economics, began his introductory lectures on macro-economics in the following way:

'Ladies and gentlemen, do not be frightened by economics. It is all highly logical. It is like sex. People say that it is men who are always pursuing women and men who are always having sex. But I ask you this: with whom are the men having sex? With women, of course. This is logical. It is an equal interaction – numerically. This is like economics. What goes in must come out.'

Just as his approach to sex was numerical, so was his approach to economics. Neither is realistic or humane. Our general behaviour with money is not logical and numerical. It is, in fact, full of eccentricity and extraordinary actions. Economists, chasing the nineteenth-century illusion that they can analyse and understand economics with the same precision as 'real' scientists in chemistry or physics, are stuck in an intellectual world whose very existence is now dubious. Sub-atomic physics has clearly demonstrated the fluid dance of energy in all forms, from matter through to consciousness. The mechanical approach does not work in the sub-atomic world of modern science, so how can it work for the kaleidoscopic pattern of the millions involved in a working economy?

The recent sciences of complexity, chaos and fractals are also directing us into new ways of thinking. They show that life is in a continuous state of emergence, with innumerable elements continually coming into creation, whether in the creation of a universe or a simple biological organism. Organization occurs as a self-catalysing process between many thousands of variables, and professors of complexity, meeting mainly in the Santa Fe Institute of New Mexico, have pointed out the similarities here with the economic world. M. Mitchell Waldrop described it in this way:

Think of the quadrillions of chemically reacting proteins, lipids and nucleic acids that make up a living cell, or the billions of interconnected neurons that make up the brain, or the millions of mutually interdependent individuals who make up human society. In every case . . . the very richness of these interactions allows the system as a whole to undergo *spontaneous self-organization*. Thus, people trying to satisfy material needs unconsciously organize themselves into an economy through myriad individual acts of buying and selling; it happens without anyone being in charge or consciously planning it. . . In every case, groups of agents seeking mutual accommodation and self-consistency somehow manage to transcend themselves, acquiring collective properties such as life, thought, and purpose that they might never have possessed individually. (Waldrop, p.11)

Outlining the ideas stimulated by chaos and complexity theory of the economist Brian Arthur, Waldrop lists the differences between the 'Old Economics' and a 'New Economics'. One of the most startling oppositions in the list is that of: 'Old model – *No real dynamics in the sense that everything is at equilibrium*. New model – *The economy is constantly on the edge of time. It rushes forward, structures constantly coalescing, decaying, changing*' (Waldrop, p.37).

To understand money we must, therefore, approach it in many different ways.

Some Conclusions at the Beginning

In my twenties I made a living for a while from writing novels and thrillers, so I like to tell a story. One of the first rules of good story-telling is not to tell the listener how it ends. But when I went to college and university as a mature student, and then began teaching, I began to dislike the style of teaching which withholds conclusions and truths until the end of the class when they are revealed like a rabbit from a magician's top hat. I want this book to be entertaining, but more than that I want to be persuasive. So let me change gear and immediately present a few of my basic conclusions.

The Origin of Money

The whole way in which we are taught to understand money is a complete fabrication. This fabrication appears in the first few paragraphs of any formal economics course. We are told that money first appeared when barter in a market became so complex that we needed tokens to facilitate the various exchanges. We are taught that money emerged in order to help barter, trade and the market. *This is not true.*

The anthropological and historical evidence shows that there are, in fact, many ways in which money emerged, but the basis of all of them is that a certain type of object became commonly used to signify an important relationship or moment in time. Beads, teeth, cattle, shells and so on were given or exchanged to mark an important relationship or moment: marriages, visits, rites of passage, political alliances, ceremonial sacrifices and so on. The objects that were commonly used in this way *also* became used to help trade, but in the first place the role of these forms of money was to mark and help human relationships and ceremonies.

Making trade easier is only one of several reasons why money emerged in the first place. In the tribal communities where money first emerged, the gifting and exchanging that created money was mainly to do with building relationships, signifying social solidarity, making gestures to nature and the gods, signifying a recognition of something important.

The simple truth, therefore, is that *money emerged in order to facilitate human relationships – not to facilitate trade and business.*

Even in bartering and in the market, the underlying reality is that producers and consumers, whether in a village market or in the global electronics commodity markets, are human beings in relationship with each other. Without money, these relationships would not be possible.

This perspective can stimulate a very interesting new way of assessing money, or financial and economic policies. Instead of asking the simplistic questions about profit and loss, we can ask more meaningfully of any money situation: how well is this facilitating relationship?

Homo Economicus

Our understanding of money and economics is based on another fundamental proposition which is also severely flawed. This proposition classically states that the economy – and the money flowing through and around it – is made up of savage (occasionally cooperative) human beings chasing scarce resources. This simplistic and partial perspective informs most economic and much political thought, and it ignores other fundamental features about human beings: *People are social. People are creative. People have a basic instinct for sharing and generosity.*

People love to be in relationship and to have contact with each other. Hardly anyone opts for the Robinson Crusoe or hermit's life. We like talking, touching, relating. We are animals of relationship. We are also animals who like being creative and making things. Very few of us like to be constantly idle and when we are not idle we like to do things together. If someone makes something, the next natural thing is to show it to someone else. A child makes something and then shows it. This is a very basic instinct. *The human economic animal creates and relates.* To put it another way, this is to say that people do not work and create the economy because they want to support the economy. They create and relate – and this, in turn, creates the economy. We need to get this idea the right way round and dismantle the power of the accepted economic idea.

Generosity, Sharing and Financial Specialists

Sometimes we are savage and sometimes resources are scarce and we fight over them, but this is only one aspect. Looking at the lives of small communities, tribal societies and our own families and love lives, we can see that generosity and sharing are natural human values. We can also see that small-scale societies and families possess checks and balances that prevent bullying and injustice. In small communities, bound by kinship or shared belief, sharing and generosity are normal. It begins with a parent's willingness to sacrifice on behalf of children and can run all the way through a small-scale society.

As small communities, however, historically became complex societies – from a village of 150 souls, to a megalopolis of 20 million – so the pressures changed and monitoring systems that prevented and penalized bullying and unfair exchanges disappeared. At the same time, as production and trading became more complex, a class of specialists arose who were more interested in the game of finance than in the game of culture and society.

Because societies became larger and more complex, these financial and commercial specialists, and their way of thinking, became separated from the normal rules that keep small communities fair and just. In fact societies and markets became so complex and so big that the ideas of the trading and financial specialists began to become accepted wisdom. The accepted wisdom of financial specialists is that economic behaviour is essentially self-centred and competitive – because that is how they themselves behave.

A Humane Society

To re-create a humane economic society we need to recognize that financial wisdom has become separate from the natural instincts and values of the human family and community. We need to reintroduce our own monitoring systems, at a personal and at an institutional level. In practice, this means that every time, for example, we have a money transaction – from buying a newspaper, through to making a billion dollar trade deal – we need to do so with certain clear awarenesses. I find it easiest to list three basic awarenesses:

First, we need to remember in every transaction that we are dealing with human beings. So, in every financial transaction, we need to pause and give attention to the people as people.

Second, because we want a humane and fair world, we need to assess whether the transaction feels good and fair.

Third, we need to give awareness to the implications of the transaction. Who and what else, not immediately visible, is involved? Do we fully recognize the knock-on effects? Does this financial transaction hurt or benefit?

Fear and Anxiety

Because money is the medium for achieving food, shelter and warmth, it is the target for primal fears about survival. Once we were frightened of nature, but today we are frightened of the economy. We may appear to have control over her, but the economy can move into forceful periods which, like a hurricane or tidal wave, cannot be controlled.

Money is also the medium that buys all the material images we use to achieve our psychological sense of identity. Our sense of identity is such a crucial element of our psychological health that any threat to our identity can lead ultimately to complete nervous breakdown.

Money is, therefore, both materially and psychologically entwined with our most primal senses of survival. We need to develop strategies for dealing with this ongoing threat. In particular, we need to begin a healing process of wise understanding.

The Creativity of Money, Adding Value

This book is about the creativity of money, how money facilitates creative, complex and ever-changing human activities and relations. At a certain very physical and material level, it is money that allows all this complexity to occur. *Money is a way of communicating and clarifying the energy that goes into material creativity and relationship.* In a large and complex world money allows strangers to come into material relationship, thereby expanding the chances of creativity for everyone.

In our complex world money is as necessary as human language. Like language it can be a medium for almost any quality of behaviour, from prostitution to morally inspiring exchange. To build a more creative and loving economy, we need to recognize, encourage and appreciate innovators, entrepreneurs and cash creators. And we need to be more cynical about those of us who, as financiers, merely manage and manipulate cash.

The Agony and the Ecstasy

Psychologically, there is immense confusion around money and wealth. People want to feel safe, wealthy and prosperous, but make the mistake of thinking that cash wealth will deliver those feelings. *The feelings of safety, wealth and prosperity do not come from cash possessions.* There are tens of thousands of millionaires suffering deep personal anxiety. The emaciated Howard Hughes dying of malnutrition in the midst of millions is image enough to demonstrate that cash does not equal true wealth.

In the psychological experience two primal archetypes govern how we feel about money, wealth and prosperity. These two great psychological forces sit at either end of a wide spectrum. I name them:

The Black Hole of Primal Anxiety ←→ The Golden Flow of Solar Abundance.

It is interesting for each of us to ask where we are located on this spectrum. There are paupers who experience a deep sense of prosperity. There are billionaires who live in anxious despair.

We need to learn how to distinguish between a genuine sense of safety and fulfilment, and a financial wealth that merely covers and hides our insecurity and anxiety.

Archetypal Realities

The activity, emotions and thoughts around money have been, and are, so intense and powerful that I am prepared to suggest that they exist – in a Platonic, Jungian or occult sense – as energy realities in their own right. Millennia of anxiety and greed, as well as millennia of inspiration and fulfilment, have created a money entity – a thought form or archetype – which exists in humanity's mass psychic experience. This *Zeitgeist* is the collective inner life of our psychological attitudes.

This metaphysical perspective suggests that this archetypal energy field contains two great extremes. These, again, are the Black Hole of Primal Anxiety and the Golden Flow of Solar Abundance. They affect many of our financial attitudes and feelings. It also suggests that what humanity has created with thoughts and feelings it can also re-create in a form that is more agreeable and cooperative.

Even if these ideas are fanciful, they nevertheless – along, for example, with fables of finding lost treasure – are a mythic reality which has real psychological effects.

The Economy is Not Simple but is Complex

Nobody can understand economics. We need to realize that the economic world, as we know it, is very recent. It exploded into existence only over the last 150 years. The world population explosion, the industrial-technological-electronic-communications revolutions and electronic financial complexity all emerged in recent decades. Some people love this new world. Others are deeply alienated by it. But one thing is certain, love it or hate it, no one fully understands the new financial world. It is still emerging!

There is always wisdom in acknowledging our ignorance, for it allows an attitude of real investigative thinking. The economists and financiers who claim knowledge or truth about the economy are hanging on to the tail of a dragon, a dragon with many tails. If there were a commonly acknowledged truth, there would be a commonly accepted strategy for managing economies. There is not. The reality is that financial and economic realities are continually emerging as 5 billion human beings interact on this planet. The real issue is not to understand how certain figures add up (old economics), but to grasp the patterns of emergence (new economics).

Individual Behaviour, Government and Organizational Policy

At an individual level, I argue that people need to understand their own psychological relationship with money. We then need to use that understanding to support our own self-fulfilment and how we behave with creativity and responsibility in our many environments and communities – home, business, nation, globe. I believe that individual awareness and action *can* change national and global economics in the same way that the ecological movement has been powered by individual responsibility as much as by organized pressure groups. The slogan of *think globally, act locally* is as relevant to financial as it is to environmental behaviour.

Cyber Cash

Over the coming years money is going to become increasingly electronic. Computer-based transactions in cyberspace are going to become the usual way of doing business. Despite appearances, this will not create a more inhumane and robotic culture, but will facilitate a new economic culture in which there is increased human connection and more open information. Some vested interests may try to block this, but the nature of the global electronic communications medium is such that decentralized individuals and groups will gain increasing power. *E-cash* will be a crucial ally in transforming money and economics into something more humane.

The Fifty-million-dollar Sting

A few years ago I was involved in a business deal that profoundly affected me. My oldest friend, Allen Gold, runs a finance company which launched a major ecologically based investment fund. This fund would finance leasing heavy industrial equipment for pollution control and cleansing, and it was an exciting and original project.

Allen was under various pressures at the time – financial and emotional – so I became involved almost on a daily basis in supporting him as he launched this fund. Because the source of any investor's profit was not interest repayment but came from a share of the leasing income, the fund was potentially very attractive to Middle Eastern money because Islamic law forbids profiting from interest and usury. There was also increasing talk in financial circles of green and ethical investments, and it seemed time for some Arab petro-dollars to flow in this direction. So, through his merchant bankers, Allen began negotiations with a Middle Eastern banking group which indicated that it was willing to invest 50 million dollars in the fund.

This was exciting, but even more exciting was the quality of relationship that Allen was building with these bankers. They seemed fully to understand the idealism lying behind the whole project and they greeted Allen like a long-lost brother. At least, they greeted him like a long-lost brother when they actually saw him. When there was geographical distance between them everything was more tortuous.

The relationship and negotiations became very difficult and sometimes strange. It was difficult to read the messages. Something was agreed and then two days later taken back. Bit by bit, piece by piece, every part of the deal had to be unpacked, rewoven. Every slice of the action had to be accounted for in ways that kept changing. A little sliver of one quarter per cent had to be greased in this direction or that direction.

Allen then had a series of meetings with these investors in New York, in London, in Amsterdam and in the Middle East. Slowly the deal got closer and closer. The whole fund now depended on this initial large injection of capital. A signing date was agreed. It was put back. Finally agreed again. The great meeting happened. The goal posts were moved again and some extra changes made.

Then, fifteen months after the first negotiations, it was signed and sealed. The deal was closed. The 50 million dollars were coming! The fund was up and away. The team's jobs were safe. The business had a future. There was celebration and happiness.

It seemed a considerable coup, 50 million dollars committed to environmental leasing. The green and ethical forces were winning.

A few hours after the final signing, Allen and I were talking. The conversation was understandably emotional and elated, and then there were a few seconds of silence. After the lull we began to talk about how the deal actually felt in that moment. The jubilation gave way to a grey realism. Yes, the money was going in the right direction, was being liberated for useful and visible service, yes the business would survive, yes money was going to be made all round, but the whole process, the whole negotiation sucked.

If we were to assess the quality of relationship, the feelings of goodwill, the whole atmosphere and resonance of the deal, it was all unpleasant.

This realization had a profound impact on me as I realized that what I really wanted was not simply to liberate the money to good and creative works, but that I wanted the whole process to be redemptive. I did not want greed, cleverness, ambition, manipulation and games. I wanted chivalry, goodwill, open negotiation and dignity.

Certainly I wanted the cash money liberated to be creatively active, but more than that I wanted the spirit of the money liberated from selfishness and released to goodwill. And this could only happen if the actual process of any financial transaction was conducted with goodwill – whether the transaction was a multibillion international deal, or simply buying a newspaper, or giving your children their allowance.

Beam Me Up

There is a scene from *Startrek-2* which haunts me. The Starship Enterprise picks up an abandoned pod which contains some folk who, threatened by terminal illness, have chosen to be frozen and sent into space until cures for their illnesses are discovered. One of these sleepers, now brought back to life and cured, is a wealthy financier. Within minutes of regaining consciousness he asks to be put in touch with his bankers and brokers. Three hundred years on, he smugly knows that he will be even richer because of his investments and ownership.

He is consistently pushy with the patient Starship Captain Jean-Luc Picard, insisting that he be allowed to make his radio calls. Finally, Captain Picard can no longer contain his impatience. As if talking to an ignorant child, Picard explains that humanity has evolved a way of managing its affairs so that money, food and survival are no longer major issues. There is enough of everything and it is simply a matter of distributing it properly. Human beings, Picard explains, are now free to get on with doing what they are really meant to do: develop themselves and fulfil their potential. Money and profit, wealth and power, are primitive and long past.

I am haunted by this scene because I perceive the seed of true realities in it. We have enough for everyone. The new technologies are gradually lifting the mass of humanity into unimagined qualities of life. Money itself is transforming from centrally issued notes, coins and tokens into decentralized networked transfers that exist only as electronic information and not as material cash objects.

We are on a new wave of history, but whether its unfoldment is a collective nightmare or a collective advance will depend on our attitudes and consciousness. In particular, it will depend on how we understand and use money.

WHY WE FEEL THIS WAY
ABOUT MONEY

2

THE PSYCHOLOGY OF
NEED AND DEPRIVATION

In a shipwreck one of the passengers fastened a belt about him with two hundred pounds of gold in it, with which he was afterwards found at the bottom. Now, as he was sinking – had he the gold? Or had the gold him?
(Ruskin)

Primal Realities

There seems to be a primal fear, a haunting anxiety underlying our economic feelings. It is fair to describe much of our individual and collective behaviour towards money as neurotic. We have uncontrollable feelings around money and these feelings guide and stimulate our actions. It can be as small as ignoring a bill. It can be as big as the obsessive compulsion which leads to corruption, theft and murder. Collectively the neurosis can be seen in the raging behaviour of dealers in the money market burning themselves out and in the mountains of food awaiting legislation before they can be liberated to feed the starving.

As human creatures – natural animals of flesh and blood – we have in our civilization become separated from a primal experience of nature and in certain ways we now live in a false and alien environment. This is not a new insight. Many writers, poets and philosophers have described and decried this alienation. At a deep unconscious level, located in our biologies, in our cellular consciousness, this separation from nature creates a form of primal disorientation. Our minds are happy in our constructed civilization, but our bodies, our creatures, lack a natural anchor in the earth and we, as creatures, are disoriented.

This disorientation has been much discussed, but I believe that there is another primal reality caused by this disconnection which has a profound influence on our economic behaviour. In our separation from nature, I believe it possible that we have transferred our natural and primal fear of her and her powers on to money and the economy. We are no longer frightened of nature but are frightened of the economy and money. Money and the economy have replaced nature in our biological unconscious.

Nature, of course, still feeds us, but not through response to our own direct labour. Between us and nature are a thousand producers, distributors and retailers.

When our relationship with nature was direct, there was no ignoring her power. Famine and plague came directly from her. Her moods, subtle and terrible, were to be attentively noticed: storm, famine, pestilence, earth movements, the elements unbound. We stood tiny in the face of her elemental power – and her beneficence and blessing.

Our progress through history has changed all that. Slowly at first, as the hunter-gatherers settled in the gentle river valleys, then faster, and finally with an accelerated fury, we have conquered nature. For us, born into modern culture, into our rooms with beds and running water and power at a switch, she is beneath our threshold of consciousness. Nature herself has not of course disappeared, but we have lost the sense of awe, vulnerability and proportion that accompanied the primal relationship with her.

Yet in our cells, in our biology and our unconscious, I believe that we still carry that natural sense of awe and fear. But for what shall we feel it? Nature apparently conquered, our vulnerable relationship is now with this other creature, the economy. If nature is no longer the danger, it is intuitively coherent that we should carry this feeling over to money.

In reality, money mediates between us and nature.

When I buy my bread, how many thousands of people have in one way or another been involved in the process of bringing food to me? Shopkeeper, delivery-person, wholesaler, baker, warehouse people, shipper, commodity buyer, farmer, grain-merchant, fertilizer-merchant ... sales staff and accountants, bankers and shareholders. Once it was just me, my local community and nature.

Each part of this long economic chain, which finally brings me my bread, is linked by a money transaction. Each transaction, each stage of the chain is made possible by the exchange of money. Within this system money is the medium of communication without which nothing happens. Our biological needs and anxieties, once related to nature, are now related to the economic system.

The economic world is now our natural environment and like nature the economy is a powerful and temperamental being. Money can be a nurturing friend, but may also turn uncontrollably against us. We may carefully tend our financial garden and if we do everything right and if the elements are with us, then we shall reap the profits of our production.

But here is the great resemblance to nature. Even if we do everything right, we are still subject to the uncontrollable forces of the economy. Who knows which way the great waves of recession, depression, boom and bust will flow? When they come our way, we may not be able to withstand them, any more than our house can withstand the hurricane or the harvest can survive flood. The economy has moods like nature. All of this is daily evident in the changing and mercurial movements of the stock market, of the various financial indices and of the changing states of the world economy. Graphs, like flashes of lightning, contain the stories of great success and abysmal failure. Individuals and institutions go bankrupt. A commodity price falls like a stone in a bottomless well and some developing country collapses into economic stagnation.

The Great Depression of the thirties swept across the western world like the black death of medieval times. Country by country there is a struggle with the beast of inflation, sometimes tamed, always shifting, and sometimes raging beyond all control halving the value of money day by day. People once took wheelbarrows to the German banks to pick up their bundles of cash notes; a few days later the paper itself was worth more than their stated value. The crash of the world stock market on the Black Monday of 1987 hit like an unforecast storm, and people in Britain remember the strange synchronicity of that night's actual winds which pulled out great old trees all across the country.

Money and the economy, seen as wild nature, can take on a mythic appearance.

Do we unconsciously experience money and the economy in the same way that our ancestors experienced nature? Are our economists and financial specialists seen as priests and voodoo artistes because *at least* they appear to be doing something in the face of the uncontrollable?

There are also a few great wizards, international financiers, who seem fully to understand money and the world economy – but, even then, there is no surprise when they fall helplessly into total financial loss. The economy is beyond our full comprehension and people who play with the economy successfully are like magnificent surfers riding waves which are bound finally to reach a safe shore – or fatal rocks.

The world economy, like weather patterns, is made up of thousands of millions of separate endeavours and actions. It is impossible, therefore, fully to grasp its dynamics. When we are faced with an environment that we cannot understand or control, our normal reaction is anxiety.

The Biology of Need

There are still people on our planet who are hunter-gatherers, moving through nature living simply off what she directly provides. There are many other folk who make their living from farming and working the land. A few hundred years ago most of humanity lived directly on and from the land. Today we receive nature's bounty through a visit to the supermarket or local shop.

We are also many hundred of years past being able to go to our local shop and barter for our food. We have no choice but to use money. In accepted theory, money is this useful unit of account or storage of value, but this is an idea which works only at a very specific level of understanding. It takes no account, for instance, of the primal psychological realities, the biological needs, that are satisfied by money. Those things which we need for survival are, in our culture, bought by money: food, warmth, shelter. The primal reality is that without money we may die.

We are also, most of us, many years away from the tribal community or clan which we know will support us in times of our failure and poverty. The modern state, however, has replaced the solidarity of kinship with the safety net of social security benefits, but who knows if we will fall through its uncertain and often broken fabric. It is possible that any one of us might end up in the gutter, starving, begging, barely surviving.

It is no wonder that whatever fears we have about our survival may be psychologically projected on to money – for it is money that seems to ensure our survival. This aspect of our relationship with money is very obvious – that money is intimately connected with food, warmth, life and death, primal realities – but even so, we often fail to remember it and recognize its influence.

To achieve clarity we need first to focus on these biological realities. We are all of us born as vulnerable infants, incapable of survival on our own. The human infant is sensitive and demanding. It screams when it needs nurture and nourishment. Very rarely are its needs fully and consistently met and, even if they are, the child must sooner or later become detached from the warmth of maternal comfort to learn independence. To grow up is to lose primal gratification.

Young humans are a strange mixture of needy flesh and emotion, and they become hysterical when their needs are not met. It is fair that these basic needs are called 'primal needs' and our fear of them not being met 'primal anxiety'. In a very real way these needs and anxieties are genetically programmed into the cellular and nervous system. They ensure survival. When humans become anxious about their physical survival, fuelled by a rush of adrenalin, we slip into extreme physiological and psychological states.

To one degree or another we all suffer insecurity about our survival and this level of anxiety is reflected in our basic financial attitudes. At worst we experience a panicked rush of anxious adrenalin in our financial behaviour. We are clinging, desperate and needy. At best we have an inner sense of safety and, with our money, we are secure, generous and stable.

The primitive fear lives in most of us. I knew an aristocrat who lived lavishly and was one of Europe's richest men. Talking about him to a friend, I commented on how relaxed and generous he was. 'Do not believe it,' she replied. 'Remove his fur coat and you will find a dangerous screaming animal.' A while later I saw him when he was involved in a legal dispute that might have lost him one of his castles and estates. His anxiety was tragic.

The Psychology of Need

Money provides for physical survival, but we need to look at how money also delivers what we need for psychological survival. It is clear to me that the relationship between money and psychological survival is the most powerful human dynamic in economic behaviour. The major purpose of this chapter is to spell out the exact nature of that relationship.

To understand this area wisely it is not enough to talk about greed, consumerism or materialism – or envy, or jealousy, or keeping up with the Joneses. We need insight into the real psychological forces that are playing through and controlling our attitudes and behaviour. An attempt to understand money that does not incorporate a realistic and analytical examination of our psychological motivation is bound to be shallow. It is this precise lack of psychological insight which has led, I believe, to so much naïveté about economic behaviour and reality.

For individuals to have a clear understanding of their attitudes to money they must understand some basic unconscious processes. I am going to describe these in some detail, drawing on research I did a while ago on why people get so attached to their nationality that they are prepared to die for their country rather than betray it (Bloom). Patriotism always fascinated me, especially the spectacle of regimented soldiers marching, singing, into battle. Normally people will do anything to avoid death.

The psychological fuel that drives people cheerfully to patriotic death is the same fuel that drives our financial behaviour.

Money pays for the lifestyle and cultural symbols that give us psychological identity and safety. This structure of psychological identity is no casual affair. People will sometimes do almost anything to retain their lifestyle, so fused is it with their sense of self. A threat to identity, a breakdown of lifestyle, can lead to nervous breakdown and total psychological collapse.

Destroy the style and the self is also fatally wounded. In a culture where money appears to be able to buy anything and everything, money becomes mainly a tool for sustaining a sense of self.

So there is the greed and anxiety about money that directly reflects our sense of biological security. This is fairly obvious. But there is also this dynamic of psychological identity which is just as powerful. This dynamic has its roots in our earliest infantile needs for social acceptance, for without social acceptance we would lose warmth, nurture and succour. Without social acceptance, we would die.

The Identification Imperative

Most people know something about our need to maintain self-esteem and to bolster our sense of identity, but there is little realization about how fundamental it is to our psychological health and how powerful and elemental a dynamic it is.

This need for psychological safety is not a conscious mental function, but is an instinctual drive. When satisfied, we feel good to the point of euphoria. When it is threatened, we may suffer complete breakdown.

The basic feature of this psychological safety is to have a clear sense of who we are in relation to the people and the social situation around us. As infants it is crudely obvious that we adapt our behaviour and attitude so that we get fed and nurtured. Right behaviour, right identity, achieves the breast, food and warmth. Wrong behaviour, a different identity, achieves punishment, cold and threat. The right behaviour – behaviour that matches what important people around us want – equals survival. Wrong behaviour equals death. The two major schools of mainstream psychology, the behaviourist and the psychoanalytic, usually at loggerheads, agree about this basic feature of human nature and they also agree on how we achieve this psychological safety.

They both describe how our basic strategy as infants for achieving physical and psychological safety, so that we survive, is unconsciously to internalize the behaviour of the important people around us. To put it more plainly: we unconsciously copy them and become like them. We obey the signals not to bite the breast. We notice the voice tone, body language and attitude of these important giants – known in the jargon of social theory as 'significant others'. We adapt who we are to their signals. As Freud wrote in *Group Psychology and the Analysis of the Ego*, 'Identification is the original form of emotional tie with an object' (Freud, p. 107). This adaptation is not done consciously. We unconsciously become like those around us in order to survive and feel safe. We unconsciously become our social identities. This whole process of copying and becoming like the people around us is called 'identification' and it is a crucial process in our development as human beings. It is a behavioural imperative that none of us can avoid.

Our identity which we build in order to survive in our family and community is something we present to the outside world. But it is also how we recognize ourselves. In a very fundamental manner we know who we are in relation only to our family and community. George Herbert Mead, one of the fathers of behaviourist psychology, stated it meticulously:

The individual experiences himself as such, not directly, but only indirectly, from the particular standpoints of other individual members of the same social group, or from the generalized standpoint of the social group as a whole to which he belongs. For he enters his own experience as a self or individual, not directly or immediately, not by becoming a subject to himself, but only insofar as he first becomes an object to himself ... and he becomes an object to himself only by taking the attitudes of other individuals toward himself within a social environment or context of experience and behavior in which both he and they are involved. (Mead, p. 138)

In words that are less maze-like, we discover who we are by reference to how others experience us and by how we experience ourselves in reference to them. We all of us have a sense of how we are and who we need to be in the world, and we achieve and sustain this by monitoring how we fit. When everything fits and matches, it's great! When who we think we are does not match our presentation in the world, it is a crisis, catastrophe and depression. When everything fits, our unconscious inner child feels safe and reassured about its survival; it celebrates. When the inner sense of identity does not fit external realities, the inner child is profoundly threatened to the point of trauma and collapse.

This collapse can be terrible. Without a clear sense of self, people can sink into a state of non-being and meaninglessness, a state called 'anomie'. It is a much-observed phenomenon, for example, that people who lose their jobs can lose all sense of who they are and slip into depression, suicide or early death. They no longer possess the reliable outside terms of reference to know who they are. Anything, even death, for some folk is better than having no sense of identity. Peter Berger, in his study of religion *The Sacred Canopy*, wrote movingly: 'To be in society is to be "sane" precisely in the sense of being shielded from the ultimate "insanity" of such anomic terror. Anomie is unbearable to the point where the individual may seek death in preference to it.'

People are often prepared to do almost anything to enhance

or maintain their sense of identity. This works out in simple and also in very extreme ways. Talk to a football supporter and tell him that his team is rubbish. His identification with his team means that a threat to his team is a threat to him. Beware, therefore, of his reaction. If his team does badly, he will get depressed, finding solace in the solidarity perhaps of a group ritual of depression at the nearest bar. Tell someone addicted to shopping that consumerism is unhealthy and, again, beware. Ask a twelve-year-old to go to a party in clothes that do not suit her peer group and the threat to her psychological safety may also be so great that she will throw a tantrum to get her way.

Threatening a person's social identity is a threat to their very self. We need to appreciate how early these social identities, these identifications, are made. I described how babies begin to copy the giants around them. This copying is not just in behaviour but also in attitudes. There have been studies of child psychology which demonstrate, for example, how a clear sense of nationality can already be present in children by the age of seven; at this age, children may already be prepared to argue and fight for their national identity. Other studies have shown how patterns of consumerist behaviour are also already well anchored in young children.

It is obvious how this all affects our relationship with money. In my own case, I thieved as a teenager in order to maintain and pay for my sense of identity. Other folk shop every day or week to maintain theirs. In modern society, our sense of identity is often intimately tied up in the image we present to the world, an image that is bought and sustained by money. In its deepest form it dominates how we feel about our careers, education, family, mortgage, house, clothes . . .

In my teens my family lived in the West End of London and one of the city's most respectable gaming clubs was only a few hundred yards away. My father strolled round there to play roulette, sometimes five nights a week. This was his hobby and relaxation. He never gambled a great deal of money and over a week he would never win or lose more than a hundred pounds. His gambling life was private and only once, one Christmas, did he take our whole family into the casino. I was fourteen years old and I remember being surprised, as we walked across the deep-pile carpets, at how many people, staff and players, knew him. Three years later, I began gambling myself, mainly blackjack in the small back rooms of discotheques. I once surfed a winning streak that kept me fed and in cigarettes for three months. You can catch from all this something more about my own financial background.

I was also a thief.

When I was five years old or so, I noticed that my father's wallet was always thick with money and I thought that he was a millionaire. When talking with other children, I always told them that he was a millionaire. I also noticed that he always left his wallet, from the time he undressed at night to the time he dressed in the morning, in the top left-hand drawer of a bureau in his study. And when I was fourteen I began regularly stealing from it. With no guilt, nor the slightest sense of wrong-doing, I would slip into his study, open the drawer and quickly remove a note or two. I did this every week for three years.

Using this weekly wage, I took cabs to school, took my girlfriend to the cinema and bought her clothes. Till the day he died my father and I never talked about the thefts. I do not know whether he knew what was happening. I assume that he was ignorant and that his casual relationship with money prevented him keeping accurate tabs on his cash flow.

With the money that I stole from him and with the money that I began to steal wherever I saw it, I managed to sustain a comfortable lifestyle. No one noticed this or thought it unusual because I went to a private school in London and I was surrounded by boys who maintained even more lavish lifestyles on allowances from their genuinely millionaire parents. From my perspective, I was only achieving the same lifestyle as many of my friends. It seemed normal to me.

I identified myself with a lifestyle that I could not achieve with the resources given to me by my parents. The power of my identification – my need to fulfil this unconscious sense of being like the rich boys – was so great that I stole. It was not a matter of mental logic. My unconscious drive to fulfil my sense of identity was more powerful than other aspects of my psychology. Our prisons all over the world are filled with people who have followed the same path.

We have certain identities and an integral part of these modern identities is fused with our wage packet and social status. In the modern world money is a universal medium for buying what we need to maintain our sense of self. Money, therefore, becomes a fluid extension of our psychologies. Unconsciously we rely upon it to fulfil our identifications. Lord Toff, as my friend said, might scream in primal terror on losing his fur coat. This scream of terror is known also to all those who feel their jobs are threatened, their earning capacity and status at risk. Workers, especially careerists, who find themselves wageless and jobless are not happy creatures. They need a careful process of transition into a new sense of personal reality and identity.

Not to fulfil our sense of identity is a form of death and my friend Allen Gold talks about the near-death experience of people who are self-employed or who run their own businesses. This happens when bankruptcy and closure are imminent because there simply is not enough cash to meet demands. In these situations, the business person experiences terrible psychological pressure and distress. This distress can usually be felt physically, with headaches, general pressure around the skull, a sense of lightheadedness, near fainting, a sinking or gnawing feeling in the stomach, a dry mouth and cold sweats.

This, in fact, is a universal psychological-physical experience when we are faced with a real threat to our deepest sense of identity. The physical sensation accompanies, at worst, complete psychological breakdown.

But there is also the opposite of anxiety and identity crisis. When we are successful, when external realities match our inner sense of self, we experience great happiness and even euphoria. As a teenager I felt this way swanning around town with my money. *This was the real me!*

In small-scale, less complex societies, self-esteem and identity come almost purely through intimate, obvious and simple identifications: through age, gender, clan and so on. In the modern world, how we know ourselves, how we maintain our identities, is more to do with complex images than immediate relationships. In a desert, tribal ways of dress may not have changed in a thousand years. In Tokyo or Paris or Lagos, fashions change season by season. People's sense of self, presented through clothes, changes season by season. Would I rather die, I ask myself, than wear denim bell-bottoms? Would you?

Insomuch as our need to maintain identity is driven by a primal instinct and anxiety, this completely influences how we relate to money, how we relate to the medium that can gratify our primal need. Money buys both secure and adaptable images.

It is a sobering exercise to examine everything for which we are paying money and to ask: am I buying this because it fits my sense of identity? Our homes, clothes, hobbies, gadgets, leisure pastimes, children's education, holidays – all these reflect who we believe we are. All these are bought by cash. Our lives can be purely focused on achieving the money to fulfil the lifestyle dictated by our sense of identity. *And we think it is completely normal.* Remove the money that pays for this lifestyle and the psychological distress can be overwhelming if not fatal. As members of complex economic societies we are driven, as individuals and as groups and whole cultures, to fulfil our sense of self and to achieve the necessary money to pay for it. This is as primal and as basic as the need to find succour on the breast, except that now we are all adults and we all think it is normal. The prophet or idealist who complains about our consumerism is considered naïve and romantic.

Relative Deprivation and Self-esteem

Our sense of identity develops in relation to our social surroundings and responds throughout our lives to changing images and realities. We find psychological comfort and encouragement when our unconscious sense of who we are, our sense of identity, matches our relationship with the outside world. Over and over again, however, people are presented with images and realities that do not match their unconscious sense of identity.

As a teenager the images and identities I found meaningful and unconsciously took into my own psyche were images that required money to fulfil them. I stole in order to keep up appearances. But the appearance was not a superficial thing for me. It was a matter of psychological survival. I did not need the money for its own sake. I needed it as the tool that allowed me to be me. If I had not been able to behave like the other young men with whom I identified, I would have had to endure an unbearable inner tension.

From a psychological perspective – not a moral perspective – I was, compared to my rich schoolfriends, deprived. I was not wise or mature enough to know otherwise. I mentioned earlier the tantrum of a young child who does not have the right clothes for a party. This is not simply a spoilt child; it is the drama of a life or death threat to her psychological survival.

What we need to appreciate is the terrible unconscious power of internalizing an identity that other people have, but which we ourselves cannot financially afford.

There are, of course, several ways in which a family, or friends, or society generally, can help to guide a young person out of this obsessive psychological trap. They include supportive love, alternative images of fulfilment, education into non-materialistic values and clear moral guidelines – but if these are missing or the child is simply bloody-minded then the thieving or tantruming will continue. And this applies not only to children. As adults we too are firmly caught in our sense of identity and need to fulfil it. We are addicts of consumerism, status and image, rather than devotees of psychological or spiritual substance. My car may be older and smaller than yours, and this can be deeply wounding. My old friend from school earns 500,000 dollars a year and all I might feel, instead of encouraging support, is stinging jealousy or rumbling disempowerment

Within a tribal society or within a coherent family these issues of relative deprivation do not arise so easily, because people's roles are simple and very clear, because there is a natural spirit of sharing and generosity, and because there are checks and balances to prevent power manipulation or material accumulation. The Bushmen of the Kalahari will do anything to prevent jealousy. There is a tribal wisdom that fully understands the terrible psychological force and social disruption of relative deprivation.

In a complex society, however, disengaged from these fundamental guidelines and where individual roles are complex, relative deprivation is normal. In fact, we could almost say that one of the most consistent features of modern civilization, one of its pillars, is relative deprivation. Road by road, apartment block by apartment block, house by house, people live with competing images of wealth and poverty. In one house a family faces financial destitution, while their neighbours next door are prospering. One house has children without shoes; the next has smart clothes. One home has fruit, the next has none. One man has a job; the other does not. There is awful psychological pain in these situations.

It is often difficult to take relative deprivation seriously because the issues may seem so superficial. It is not a world-shattering problem if a young girl does not have the clothes she wants or a company executive is not given the appropriate car for his status. Psychologically, however, the experience of deprivation and its threat to identity *is* shattering. It is shattering for individuals and destructive for communities.

Throughout the modern economic world, people in general are irritated or shattered by their relative deprivation. Much of this deprivation is not so superficial. For one extended period of my life I existed on a very low income and lived in a situation with three young children. In this situation the fruit for the children was rationed. In other houses I visited during the same period fruit was not rationed but lay abundantly on the kitchen table. I felt irritated, inadequate and jealous. But beyond my own egocentric feelings was the reality that the children with whom I lived were deprived. If fruit and its vitamins helped the physical health of children, then the deprivation was very real.

The difficulty with this whole issue is precisely its relativity. Because it all seems so relative, we have a tendency not to take it seriously. One person's need is another's luxury. But human beings are creatures of consciousness just as much as they are creatures of flesh and blood, and psychological suffering is as cruel as any physical pain. Often psychological and physical pain are indistinguishable. These issues of relative deprivation eat away at individuals and at communities. Obvious disparity, huge gaps between the haves and the have-nots, even subtle differences: create immense psychological pressures.

In communities, relative deprivation can literally be fatal. In its most dramatic form, an excess of relative deprivation leads to revolution, when a mass of people can no longer tolerate their inability to achieve that which they identify as theirs. The German philosopher, Jurgen Habermas, talks about *identity-securing interpretative systems* which are shared by groups of people. When a whole class of people are dispossessed and cannot relate to the official identity-securing interpretative system, there is bound to be immense social instability. For example, if the main ideology of a society is about material success and material possessions, then this is the official identity-securing interpretative system. But if there is a large number of people whose personal reality does not match the interpretative system, then beware of angry revolution and dangerous streets. We can all see this historically in many of the great revolutions that overthrew complete systems of government and social structure. We can also see it in the danger of our inner cities, where an underclass is continually provoked with images of the good life which, for them, is virtually unachievable. There is bound to be anger and danger. The psychological volcano of the sum total of all the individual unconscious needs and drives rumbles through the whole social fabric, exploding into our streets and squares the world over. As President Sukarno of Indonesia once remarked, 'In my country the refrigerator is a potent political symbol.'

It is not so difficult to understand the emotional outrage of the dispossessed when they are surrounded by images of glamour and material well-being. These people are born into a world which projects as normal for everyone: good food, alcohol, cigarettes, clean and smart clothes, clean and smart children, literacy, access to education and electronics, a comfortable home, cars and travel. This is the lifestyle, the identity, which people have little choice but to absorb and internalize. It is easy to understand the psychological confusion, anger and disempowerment that comes from being in this modern world, but unable actually to live its lifestyle.

We can also understand the psychological dynamics that lead the child without the right party clothes to throw a tantrum. We can also understand the psychology of relative deprivation that leads people to thieving. But we need to appreciate that these powerful psychological dynamics run through all of us. No matter how flimsy, weak or self-indulgent the actual issues may appear to be, we are still driven by the same need to fulfil our identifications. The psychological force here is as powerful for the habitual consumer *born to shop* or the family that needs a better house, better car, better job as it is for the dispossessed revolutionary or the city slum-dweller or street gang member. The appearances are different, but the underlying psychology is precisely the same.

In a tribal society there are few choices of social identity. In today's world, there are thousands – and most of them need money. In the developed world an educated person expects a certain professional responsibility and standard of living. Take that away and you may expose a neurotic creature as desperate to maintain self-image, status and identity as any begging child in the undeveloped world, hands outstretched tugging frantically at the tourists.

One of the other similarities that binds us all together as part of the same human race and as part of the same psychological package is that we always find our behaviour perfectly normal. Our need for new clothes, a better job, a house like the Joneses', feels completely normal. In fact, it feels so normal that we never examine its validity or usefulness. But if we want to understand our financial behaviour, we have no alternative but to understand this powerful aspect of ourselves.

I Know But I Cannot Help Myself

In my study I have on the wall over my desk a picture from *Newsweek* magazine of a three-year-old Asian child, grimacing and carrying bricks. This child is a slave. The rough bricks are directly against his bare skin. He can only just carry the weight and his eyes are brave but holding tears. I have his picture close to where I work so that I remember the realities of life, so that my heart stays open and so that I can put my own situation in perspective.

Even with this image constantly with me, even while I work professionally on the problems of social justice, I can still, however, be tempted by a seventh pair of shoes. I can justify this temptation because, I tell myself, I need certain clothes for teaching and public speaking. Even to talk about this as a temptation has a puritanical ring about it. But the reality is that while I hold an awareness of child slavery and malnutrition, I still hold just as important psychological images of myself in these new shoes. It is a good investment buying that extra pair of shoes while there is still the child slave to feed and save. When I bother to think carefully about it, this is an awful and embarrassing situation. I care about the starving child, but I also care about my self-image. My food budget for one week would feed that child for a year.

In our world we live in this terrible paradox of relative deprivation. It seems so normal to buy that extra shirt or frozen meal, yet the money could feed or mobilize action for the helpless child victim. This is a painful situation. It is so painful that I can hardly hold my awareness fully open to it.

I often watch one of my friends, on a grander scale, justifying his purchases, that as a businessman he needs to look rich to help his business. Once, passing through London, he bought £1,500 worth of clothes in one afternoon and solemnly informed a group how sensible this was because in his home town, the same purchases would have been twice the price.

His solemnity – the appearance of a shrewd businessman

making a shrewd purchase – covered an insecure child. This insecure child needed regularly to buy the images to bolster his sense of identity. To stop consuming would be as challenging for him as coming off drugs.

Both he and I are still children throwing tantrums wanting the right clothes for the party. To hell with the real starving child! We need our clothes and cars. Without them, we face the trauma of psychological death.

I also cannot bear to focus too clearly on the child slave, for if I do, I will very soon find resonances with my own inner wounded child. It would be wonderful to be more secure, more mature, to possess real wealth.

Facing the Psychological Realities

When we study the human relationship with money, we are touching primal feelings. It is very dangerous. Let us list the dynamics.

To the degree that we are savage, elemental and frightened, so is our relationship with money. The rich are not in any way saved from this primal anxiety. They are just more thickly cushioned against the triggers and irritations. Many of the richest people I know are desperately insecure. I have sat with million-aires who scoop food anxiously into their mouths, eating as if it were about to be snatched from them; communicating to restaur-ant staff with snarls. The actual possession of money has done nothing to soothe or heal their basic wounding. They are still frightened infants grabbing the security of nourishment. They are a typical part of our human family; we are linked by the bond of insecurity.

This basic insecurity and anxiety comes from the earliest woundings we receive as children, when our basic needs are not met or are actually hurt or punished. The infant who is thought-lessly removed from the breast, the infant who experiences its father's anger from its earliest days – these kinds of wounding, if never healed, leave us permanently insecure, ready to cling to what we have, often desperately trying to suck in more. In our nurseries and playgrounds there are always insecure children, some aggressive and others manipulative, who cling on or seek more.

This psychological wounding sits on top of our biological anxiety about physical survival. And then we have the whole terrible and confusing business of identity, self-esteem and relative deprivation which I have just described.

It is quite a personal load which we carry.

It is also a social and political load, for these personal dynamics affect the attitudes and behaviour of all of us in the real world. When I write 'all of us', I mean all of us. Human beings do not lose their human nature just because they take on a certain role or image. These human factors are working just as much through political leaders, economists, financiers and business people as they are through addicted consumers, dispossessed revolutionaries and inner city muggers.

But I am hopeful and I do not want others to feel hopeless. Although I am outraged and confused by economic realities, I am also optimistic. I am cheerful because, although humans are capable of senseless acts of cruelty and destruction, we are creative and sociable beings. Give us half a chance and we are friendly and funny, and we care for each other.

I believe in and have experienced much psychological transformation and healing. The process of self-understanding, self-honesty and self-change hurts, but people go for it when they know they have to. Any one of us who has ever spotted a pattern of destructive behaviour in our lives and changed it knows exactly what I am writing about. Most of us, over time, as we grow older, have these minor and major revelations, and slowly and often begrudgingly we change ourselves. Afterwards, it feels better. It serves us to heal and change. It also serves those closest to us and our communities in general. The economic situation may seem overwhelming, but it is we who create and we who can change it.

3

PROSPERITY-CONSCIOUSNESS, POVERTY-CONSCIOUSNESS AND WEALTH

I'm rich because I have a lot of money. (Joseph Kennedy, when asked why he was so rich)

Real Life, Real Feelings

At a deep personal level we are all, to one degree or another, affected in our attitude to money by our insecurity and sense of deprivation. We are also caught in a culture where ideas about prosperity and poverty, and the nature of wealth, are confusing. This confusing culture can subtly and grossly influence us. In this chapter, I look first at the difference between being and feeling, *being* rich or poor and *feeling* rich or poor. I then look at false ideas concerning wealth and wealth creation.

We live in a complex world of great extremes. One of the most obvious extremes is the division between the very rich and the very poor. On the day, for example, that I wrote the first draft of this chapter, the London *Sunday Times* carried two features which illustrate this divide. The first story contained an extract from a book on the Iraqi situation; the second concerned the Queen of England.

It was our wedding anniversary, and it seemed as if we were going to die together, slow, agonizing deaths with our grandsons in our arms. Or worse still, Assiz would go first, leaving me alone to look after the children on the mountain, a task I was now too weak to manage on my own . . . I didn't even have enough supplies left to make a pot of tea to warm their sick stomachs. Hunger and thirst were gnawing at our insides, the pain mixing with the diseases and poisons which were now gripping us all. (Francis and Crofts, *Nowhere to Hide*)

The Duchy of Lancaster, which provides her with an income of £3.7m a year, had investments of £22m in September 1992 and the Duchy of Cornwall had another £35m – a total of £57m between them. Her investment portfolio must, on the same basis, be worth at least £150m. Then there is the jewellery . . . if she had to sell it tomorrow it would fetch at least £100m. The Queen personally owns Balmoral and Sandringham . . . £80m . . . She has a private art collection worth £20–£30m . . . To value it all, and the palaces, at £5 billion is to be conservative, even in a recession.

The difference between the two realities – the starving family and the Queen of England – is a physical and existential fact. Some people are wallowing in surplus. Others are starving. There is a real experience here that is physical and immediate. At the same time there is also a very interesting psychological dimension here which requires attention.

This dimension is about whether we feel rich or poor, and it is about our attitude to prosperity and poverty.

There are billionaires who, beneath their layers of style and luxury, feel terrible poverty. And there are beggars – people who have completely abandoned and rejected materialism – who feel prosperous.

There is, therefore, psychological and inner wealth, distinct from material wealth. And there is psychological and inner poverty, distinct from material poverty. People can feel prosperous and generous, regardless of their material circumstances. People can feel mean and poor, whether they are paupers or emperors.

Equally, people carry particular mindsets and expectations about wealth and poverty. There are people for whom poverty is an unimaginable and distasteful state. They can hardly bring themselves to see the humanity in a poor person; at worst, they let people starve. They do not like poverty.

Then there are people for whom wealth is a totally distasteful state. They can hardly bring themselves to see the humanity in a wealthy person; at worst, they assassinate the rich. They do not like wealth.

There are also, of course, the people of goodwill who try to be tolerant and see good in all their fellows, regardless of material status. If their goodwill is running at full volume, they wish prosperity and abundance, both inner and material, for everyone.

In new age, human development and get-rich-quick circles, the phrases *poverty-consciousness* and *prosperity-consciousness* are often used. They are usually used in relation to how well someone is doing materially and how well they are going to do in the future. I remember a rich friend emerging from visiting a commune, literally shuddering with distaste as he commented on the poverty-consciousness of the community. It was as if he were shaking off their attitude lest it contaminated him. But, although he visited in his luxury car and luxury clothes, his own prosperity-consciousness was skin-deep. He did not possess the sense of inner abundance either to wish them well or even simply to tolerate them. His own inner psychological poverty was triggered by the external images of poverty which frightened him.

This man's inner attitude was anxious and frightened of poverty, despite his great wealth. It is worth aiming for the ambitious goal of feeling psychological security and abundance regardless of our actual financial situation.

Lord Bountiful, My Anxiety and the Tibetan

I bought a house once that was a dump with much potential. In the large lounge, for instance, there was textured wallpaper which had been painted over so many times that it felt like industrial sandpaper. Simply brushing against a wall could tear your clothes.

It took us over two years to bring the house into some order and in the middle of this restoration process I collapsed with a back injury. I still had to work, however, and I was making early connections with a new educational trust that was being financed by one of Britain's nicer aristocrats. It was agreed that he and I needed to meet in order to sort out the format for future management meetings and, because I was ill, we agreed to meet at my house.

I desperately tried to get at least one room into a reasonable state before 'Lord Bountiful' came round. Five minutes before he was due, however, I had a spinal spasm, could not bear to be in a chair and was carted back to the bedroom. The bedroom was a complete tip – especially because everything from the lounge had been dumped into it. I looked round the room: peeling wallpaper, bare bulbs. My feelings became hysterical.

Lord Bountiful, multimillionaire, arrived. The discreet Mercedes sat outside my house and he sat in my slum. He was a good sport and took no notice of the environment. We discussed the coming meetings and their structure. Then, somehow or other, the subject of this book on money cropped up and that I ran weekend workshops about money. 'You run workshops on money?' he asked. His eyes slowly travelled around the room: bare floorboards, broken furniture, piles of rubbish. One of his nostrils involuntarily rose. 'Really? You do not seem to know much about it.'

In that moment, I completely lost my composure and confidence. I could not resist the dynamics of the situation and I slipped temporarily into a deep experience of poverty-consciousness. I felt poor. I felt disempowered. I felt defeated. And I wanted everyone else to feel the same way.

A few months later, when the house was looking reasonable, we gave a party for a Tibetan who was passing through London, who offered to give an informal slide-show and talk on the history and predicament of Tibet. We invited about twenty people, a nice crowd of friends including a Member of Parliament and some effective campaigners for ecological and tribal rights. In the midst of preparing for this politically correct event, my poverty-consciousness surfaced and I became neurotically obsessed with one of the guests who was bringing her mother, a powerful American matron and estate agent. She was bound to notice everything in the house that indicated poverty: badly painted floorboards, chipped wood, cracked sink ... At the same time I was anxious about her, I also displaced my infantile irritation on to her son-in-law, another rich man. I remembered him bragging about the amazing deal he had just made, saving himself several thousand pounds, and then expressing how sad he was because his mother, having lost two husbands and having made bad financial decisions, was now broke and could not do the only thing that gave her pleasure, which was to travel. Because it would not give him any direct pleasure, he could not even think of giving her some of his money to travel. He swanned around in his St-Laurent kaftan while his mother sat alone and depressed in her kitchen. My irritation was pathetic.

On the evening of the party the great matron could not actually come, but I received another lesson from our Tibetan guest. He was in his sixties and had seen his home city of Lhasa shelled and destroyed by the invading Chinese. From his status as a monk and as an academic he had been forced into exile, and now he travelled, raising people's awareness about his country's situation. He was a distinguished and handsome-looking man, and all he asked for when travelling was floor space, a sleeping-bag and some grain to eat.

After his slide-show and talk, I brought him a plate of vegetables and grain. There was too much on the plate for him and he was visibly shocked. The abundance, to him, was grotesque waste. I should have taken the plate away and brought him one with less on it, but like a good host I wanted him to eat well and enjoy. Two hours later he was still picking over the same plate and would not let me take it away. 'I hate waste. I must eat it, even if it is slowly and over time.' He also did not want a proper bed and was cross with me when I made him up one that was too comfortable. He could only tolerate simplicity.

I was confused by him because his ideas were pure, but his attitude was aggressive and narrow. His spiritual and physical exile, however, touched my heart and made my own anxieties seem preposterous.

Prosperity and Success

The ideas of prosperity- and poverty-consciousness often accompany another belief, that we are completely responsible for the lives that we create and that we live. As one modern saying goes: *we create our own reality*. Part of this philosophy of life is based in the idea that our core beliefs determine how our lives turn out. If deep down, for instance, I expect to be abused, then I will create situations in which I actually am abused. Or if deep down I expect to be valued, I will equally create situations that empower and support me. To become materially prosperous, then, we need a core belief that we deserve to be prosperous. If, unconsciously, we believe that we are worthless and deserving of nothing, then that is what we will create.

In most of the programmes and books for achieving financial success, a clear relationship is drawn between motivation and success. The fundamental attitude of *I deserve it and I can get it* is necessary because dedicated hard work does not necessarily deliver the goods. There are many millions of folk who are dedicated and work hard, but who are not rich.

In *How to Think Like a Millionaire* Charles-Albert Poissant advises his readers:

Believe you can get rich ... Our education, society and intellectual conditioning, are all unfortunately more pessimistic than optimistic, and lead us to believe that wealth is meant for others, but not ourselves. How often does someone tell you not to waste your time on pipe dreams, that you have to be 'realistic'? Because most people think like this, success always seems reserved for the fortunate few and wealth seems to be an exclusive club. That is just not true. If affluence is an exclusive club, it is because it seems to be so in the minds of people whose attitudes bar their own entry. In fact every wealthy person started out believing that one day they would be rich and famous ... You must completely convince yourself that not only is it possible for you to become as wealthy as you would like, but also that *it is easy*, much easier than you had ever dreamed possible. (Poissant, pp. 15–16)

This idea that wealth can be naturally and rightly ours is interestingly expressed by a maverick spiritual teacher, Stuart Wilde:

Poverty is restriction and, as such, is the greatest injustice you can perpetrate upon yourself. Yet when you look at nature and you see the abundance and flow that are naturally a part of our environment, it is hard to understand why people take up poverty as a way of life. It seems that in order to be poor a person has to work so hard. It takes a constant effort of mind to avoid the abundance that life offers naturally. In the same way that joy is natural and God given, so too is abundance; everything else is a drag ... How are you going to change your feelings so that you make lots of money quickly, reclaim your power and trot off into the sunset absolutely free? (Wilde, pp. 1–2)

I wonder what the great spiritual renunciates would make of those ideas. Anticipating such a puritanical and precious question, Wilde considered the case of Mother Theresa of Calcutta:

The fact is that Mother Theresa is sold in the P.R. package as this little ol' dear who hasn't got any money but is doing good things for the Lord and the indigent of India ... But if truth be known, Mother Theresa is a multi-million-dollar business that is supported by the massive wealth and power of the Catholic Church. She forms a pivotal part in the merchandising of their philosophy and the solicitation of money. She is a business.

This gung-ho materialism has a certain joyfulness about it and I am quite happy to see sacred cows questioned, but I am worried about it papering over real problems.

Not surprisingly, there are many books and educational programmes designed to help people become prosperous and successful. Most of these programmes deal with this business of altering our core beliefs and provide strategies for doing this, but I have become increasingly worried by three of the core beliefs common to these programmes which they do not make clear.

These unspoken beliefs are:

1. Success equals material success and material prosperity.
2. Material success and prosperity equal happiness.
3. Material success is the goal of every normal human being.

51

These beliefs are obviously shallow and untrue. They sell a false happiness.

My biggest worry is that people turn to these programmes for a quick fix to problems that simply cannot be quickly fixed. They make no distinction between material and psychological poverty.

Prescribing material wealth is akin to prescribing anti-depressants or tranquillizers. The symptoms of psychological unease may disappear, but at what cost to genuine healing and personal integrity? What is actually going on underneath the anaesthetic of material wealth? (To be fair, though, many of these programmes do also give people the encouragement, the skills and strategies, and the motivating boot, to overcome timid inertia and lack of confidence.)

My own suspicion of the mindless search for material success is lightweight compared to the people who feel a roaring anger against social injustice and economic thoughtlessness. One of the most cogent recent attacks on financial thoughtlessness came from the American social thinker Philip Slater. I recommend his book *Wealth Addiction* to anyone who has romantic and naïve notions around wealth. He is at his most cynical when he describes the attitudinal motivation that leads people to becoming rich, where there is material prosperity but spiritual poverty:

Great fortunes can almost never be acquired ethically for a very simple reason: *money is an instrument of trade and in an ethical trade everyone would come out at the end relatively equal* ... Apologists for our system claim that making a few people rich in this way brings benefits for everyone. People work hard to get rich and the rich spend their money and keep everything moving. This is the well-known 'trickle-down' theory. The name itself is refutation enough: we don't call it the 'pour-down' theory. The basic problem with the whole idea is that the rich *don't* spend in proportion to their wealth. That's why they are rich. They take more than they give and they save more than they spend and they buy cheap and sell dear ... They feel compelled to take more than their share because their addiction is always competitive: what they have is not satisfying if others have it, too. Taking seems to be gratifying for them only if it involves taking *away* from others. This is the only way we can make sense of the frequency with which wealthy people hoard or overconsume during a shortage. (Slater, pp.20–23)

I do not completely share this cynical perspective, but the critique has a realistic bite.

Are We Asking the Right Questions?

In discussing poverty- and prosperity-consciousness, spiritual wealth as opposed to material wealth, we are challenged to look at the whole way in which we create our working lives. In particular, if we are chasing material wealth, we have to ask: how much am I actually sacrificing my true well-being? And beyond my own well-being, in fulfilling my ambition to be rich, how much am I sacrificing my natural solidarity with other people, with other life?

There are also other questions, such as: do we understand the *expectations*, conscious and unconscious, we have of ourselves that lead to us pursuing financial success? Do we understand how much we are motivated by the unconscious need to satisfy the anxiety of a threatened cultural-social identity? Do we accept that financial wealth does not bring psychological well-being? If so, why are we still pursuing it?

These are not easy questions, but they are worth asking if we are to free ourselves from blind materialism. We have to conduct this kind of self-inquiry if we are to avoid deepening psychological wounds in our compulsive quest for financial success. There will be no real happiness until we are mature enough to accept that, even after financial success, the old wounds remain.

In a culture that has lost its humaneness, people do not attend to their genuine needs because they are distracted, in the most overwhelming way, by their apparent financial and material needs.

Tracking Down Inner Prosperity

It seems obvious, therefore, in the midst of these paradoxes, that we need to have some better understanding of what this inner prosperity feels like. To start, it is not a sense of moral or spiritual superiority, which may just be another cover for deeper wounds and anxieties. It is also not an attitude that requires a spiritual or religious belief about the world.

Inner prosperity, or inner wealth, *feels good*. It feels psychologically and physically comfortable. It is emotionally reassuring. We can tangibly feel it in our bodies. From where does this feeling come?

Since Wilhelm Reich, there has been a school of psychotherapy which recognizes that emotional and mental states are felt and anchor down in the physical body. Emotional and mental moods, attitudes and disturbances anchor down into the body creating areas of physical tension and cellular-muscular 'armour'. As most of us know and experience, our bodies carry stiffness and pain directly caused by psychological anxiety and tension.

There are many different psychological patterns which can create anxiety, but in the context of this book the most serious tension arises from a mismatch between our inner image of ourselves and the outer reality, between our inner identity and outward personality show, between our material expectations and the material reality of our lives. This mismatch can work in both the conscious and the unconscious mind. An executive can experience *conscious* anxiety about her image and status when she has to drive an ordinary saloon, but wants a luxury car. But another person can experience the same anxiety without being aware of the real reason. To one degree or another all of us suffer from these mismatches.

In an important way, this is all another example of the power of relative deprivation. Here, we are focusing on how this psychological dynamic of inner deprivation anchors down into our physical being and determines how we physically feel. The point is very simple. An experience of relative deprivation, a mismatch between inner want and outer reality, creates tension and anxiety which anchor down through the psyche and into the body.

A true sense of prosperity, then, is an attitude which feels good and sits comfortably in the whole personality and body. This inner wealth can only belong to people who have healed any sense of relative deprivation and who no longer feel disempowered and put down if, to put it bluntly, they have not got what they want. This form of true wealth belongs to people who, for one reason or another, are not overwhelmed or influenced by their sense of identity in material terms. This requires a general level of relaxation and self-acceptance. Perhaps people like this come from enormously stable and emotionally supportive families. Perhaps they come from cultures where materialism is despised and chivalry admired. Perhaps they have made conscious decisions for this particular path of personal liberation.

The simple decision of material renunciation may not work. There are nuns and monks who have renounced materialism and embraced poverty, but are nevertheless bitter and resentful creatures. There are socialists and green activists who chose poverty and despise richer lifestyles. Their attitude is also not generous. A sense of prosperity creates a generous attitude, even to enemies.

In a later chapter I look at strategies for working on a personal sense of wealth.

Let Them Eat Cake

Our psychological need for material prosperity can change as our lives and expectations change. A young person's frantic 'needs' become realistic with time. Also our general mood can change. In my twenties I was rich and happy. Later I became poor and was also happy. I used to boast that I might be broke, but I was never poor. Then later, living in London and remarried, planning children, I broke into a cold sweat one day as I realized that my income would not be able to support a child. If we were to have children in London, I could not bear the idea of doing it in a small apartment with no garden and without the cash to meet any special needs for schooling or attention.

After months of intermittently experiencing this anxiety provoked by the idea of having a child while I was on too low an income, I finally started to become calmly self-reflective about my feelings. I began to look at what was truly bothering me. I watched thoughts surface about other children not being able to visit us because our apartment was too small, of longing for green countryside or at least a backyard in which the child could play, of special needs unmet at the cruel school. But beneath all these images was a deep and uncontrollable fury.

I slowly took my awareness into the fury and found beneath it a deep shame. A middle-class man, I could not fulfil my own inner images of parenting and family. I looked like a loser. I looked poor. I was ashamed of myself. My inner image of the financial status needed for parenting a child in the city was not matched by my outer realities.

In Chapter 10 I will look specifically at strategies for healing inadequacy and poverty-consciousness, but to end that story, let me just add that I began more consistent and serious therapeutic work on myself. It was with some success that I dealt with the poverty of my inner child. I could have stayed in the small apartment and started a new family, but I also made a clear decision that I wanted to increase my income and buy a larger home if I were to parent again. And – a happy conclusion – I was successful in earning more money.

I like to think, though, that, having done the therapeutic work, if I had failed to achieve my financial goals I would nevertheless have remained happy.

Years later, as I look back at that whole episode, there is a memory that stays with me. When we moved out of the small flat and into a spacious house, a close relative and a close friend, both well off, both said exactly the same thing: 'It will be so nice for you, now that you have a proper home.' They meant *home* and not house. Through their lens they had never seen our little flat, in which we lived for six years, as a proper home. I was stung at the time by their insensitivity, their inability to honour our actual home. Two-thirds of the people on our planet live in homes that are one room.

Wealth Creation, Adding Value

To understand more fully how we feel about prosperity and poverty, we also need to look at our ideas around wealth and wealth creation. There is an assumption through most of our society that wealth creation can be recognized when someone is making more money. But money does not equal real wealth. If a government simply prints and issues more money, no real wealth has been created. There is just more money – devalued money – circulating, but no other reality has changed. It is a basic error to confuse wealth creation with money.

In essence, wealth is created by any human action which enhances, amplifies or transforms anything into something better or more interesting than it was before. 'Better' or 'more interesting' may be a subjective judgement, but by and large people tend to agree that when value has been added to something, then wealth has been created. A branch is carved into a walking stick. Value has been added to the raw wood and wealth has been created. Wool turned into yarn is added value and the creation of wealth. More wealth is created when the yarn becomes cloth, which in turn becomes clothing. Value is added, wealth is created, when the clothing is then carried from an inaccessible warehouse into a shop around the corner. All along a manufacturing and distribution process, human ingenuity and labour add value and create wealth.

Ideas and information also create wealth. This is obvious in art, or writing, or the production of a newspaper. The whole entertainment and computer industries are based mainly in the added value and wealth of creative ideas. Rudolf Steiner, the German philosopher, asserted that all wealth was created by the human *spirit* engaged in productive labour – mental, physical, inspirational and practical. Human spirit expresses itself through the work of the hand and the mind, and in cooperation with the fruits of the earth, and the fruits of other women and men, wealth is created. In more modern language, wealth is created every time that human energy engages in some process to create a different and valued outcome.

Money enters the equation only as a necessary symbol and token of this wealth-creating human energy – necessary because people can use it as a way of trading the things that they find valuable.

If, then, we consider the proposition that the purpose of money is to facilitate human relationship and creativity, we can see that money is simply the fluid that allows this new wealth and added value to flow between people. For example, in my creativity, I can produce a wonderful magazine, but I need there to be money, so that people can use it to receive my magazine.

The more wealth that is created, then the more money there must be in circulation, in order to allow everything to flow around. It would be no good having a productive society if there was not the money there to allow the basic communication of exchanges and commerce to take place. *Money allows wealth to be exchanged and moved. Money is not in itself wealth.*

Accumulating money and the creation of wealth are two distinct processes. Thinking that they are the same damages our psychological health and the health of our societies. It is unhealthy and self-destructive if we confuse our instinct for creativity with a need to make money; or if we do not value our natural creativity because it is not financially rewarded.

It is easier to perceive all this more clearly in a tribal or commerce-free society where all work is valued for its own sake. Giving work cash value simply does not happen. Cooking food, rearing children, keeping house, are obvious creative labour which bring wealth and value into the community. Making pots, gathering or hunting food, trading, are all also valuable labour but not more valuable in themselves than the domestic creativity.

In a money economy, however, the only work that is recognized – and paid for – is that which is in some way intermeshed with the manufacturing, trading and financial community. Housework, because it is not paid for, appears, therefore, not to be about wealth creation. Because housework and child-rearing apparently have no cash value, they can be considered, thoughtlessly, as having no value. This, obviously, is a warping of humane realities. It can warp the whole of a society away from the meaningfulness of humane connection to a confused cul-de-sac of money addiction and psychological materialism.

We need, therefore, to be realistic about our society and recognize that it has produced two levels of value: humane and financial. Because of the way in which finance dances across our planet and through our cities, it is possible to accumulate a great deal of money by doing things that are not humane and that do not add real value. Equally, labour of great humanity and real value may attract little or no financial gain. That is the way it is.

Psychologically, the best that we can do is to pull our ostrich heads out of the sand and give full recognition to the fact that this is simply the way the world works. In opening our awareness fully to the idea that there are two levels of value and wealth, we can begin the process of liberating and refining what it is that we choose truly to value. There are certain things that, indeed, we do for the money, because we need it to engage in many forms of everyday practical relationship. But there are also many things we do for their intrinsic creativity and humane value. Just because they have no or little cash value means nothing. We need to be able to assess true wealth as opposed to material wealth, and we need to value it with our hearts and not with our wallets.

HOW WE GOT INTO THIS
SITUATION

4

WAMPUM, DOGS' TEETH
AND EDIBLE RATS

The Origins of Money, Economic Behaviour
and the Market

The worse thing is not giving presents. If people do not like each other but one gives a gift and the other must accept, this brings a peace between them. We give what we have. That is the way we live together. (Kalahari Bushman)

We are brought up with certain fixed ideas about money, economic behaviour and the competitive market. These accepted notions – by their very nature – severely limit how we can think and imagine our economic lives. Anthropological facts, however, dramatically contradict these accepted ideas, releasing us to a new and more creative understanding.

Mainstream economic and financial thinking is based on the idea that money is essentially a unit of account invented to help trade and business: *a standard of value, a medium of exchange* and *a store of wealth*. I assert, on the other hand, that the essential role of money is to facilitate human relationship, community and culture. There is overwhelming anthropological and historical evidence for this.

Economic and financial thinking is based mainly in the idea that the prime drive in economic behaviour is that humans are savage and competing for scarce resources. This is not borne out by either family or tribal behaviour.

It is also accepted that the market should be a place of competition, but all over the world small-scale markets are, in fact, environments of enjoyable human communication.

Wampum

First, let us look at the origins of money and get it absolutely clear that the idea that money emerged to serve the market is inaccurate. Let me begin by listing some of the chapter headings in Paul Einzig's classic study *Primitive Money*. They give an immediate and useful picture of its diverse origins.

Mat and Bark Cloth of Samoa
Stone Money of Yap
Pig Exchange in New Hebrides
Shell and Teeth of Solomon Islands
Shell and Yam of Trobriand Islands
Drums of Alor
Bronze Guns, Bees' Wax and Buffaloes in Borneo
Tin Ingots and Gold Dust in Malaya
Tea Bricks in Mongolia
Reindeer and Cattle in Asiatic Russia
Salt in Ethiopia
Whales' Teeth of Fiji
Beads of Pelew
Feather Money of Santa Cruz
Dogs' Teeth of Admiralty Islands
Rice in the Philippines
Gambling Counters in Siam
Silver and Lead in Burma
Coconuts in the Nicobars
Iron in Sudan

Brass Rods of the Congo
Cowries, Slaves, Cloth and Gin in Nigeria
Shell, Fur and Blankets in Canada
Wampum and Shells in the United States
Arrows and Guns in Brazil
Barley and Silver of Babylonia and Assyria
Bronze Axes and Wheels in Gaul
Cattle, Cloth and Fish of Iceland
Leather Currency of Italy and France
Butter in Norway
Fur in Alaska
Cocoa Bean in Mexico
Maize of Guatemala
Snail Shells of Brazil
Sheep and Silver of the Hittites
Slave Girls of Ireland
Fur in Russia
Rings in Denmark

Einzig's full list of objects used as money is, in fact, far longer. Under the discrete title, for example, of 'Other Currencies of the Eastern Pacific' he includes 'edible rats', which are, he tells us, 'considered a delicacy and eaten raw'. This is an interesting economic fact not often taught in our colleges and universities, no doubt because the information is difficult to digest. I can hardly stomach it myself.

This long and, to me, rather beautiful list of different objects helps us to disengage from our usual idea about money being coins or notes, book entries or electronic transfers. From the list we get a sense of real things, real objects, that have some meaning in themselves. The cows or the beads or teeth are things to which we can be attached or, at least, for which we can have some sentiment and feeling. Whereas a fifty-dollar note is an anonymous and alienated object, we can have real relationships with the objects originally used as money in tribal societies.

The Wrong Myth

In our schools, however, we are taught that the first money was the minted coins of the Middle East (Egypt and Babylonia) which appeared some time around 3000 BC. We are given the impression that the emergence of centrally minted coins to help trade and accounting is the full history of money. The meaningfulness of all the other diverse objects used as currency is ignored, thereby obscuring many dimensions of money. Why are we not taught the full picture?

It is well known that people rewrite history in order to justify their own position – and this is precisely what has happened to the history and understanding of money. By the time anyone was writing about the history or meaning of money, they were already doing so in a situation that experienced trade and commerce as the major realities of economic life. They could not see, or ignored, the other dynamics. Today, as we move into the twenty-first century, we casually take for granted this incomplete

HOW WE GOT INTO THIS SITUATION

and superficial history which teaches us that money was invented to facilitate trade in a complex market and to keep account of who owes what to whom.

We partly accept this information because it has been put forward by such wise men and because their argument seems to be so plausible. In fact, of course, this understanding of money does make sense and is partially true. The problem is that, not knowing any other theories about the origin of money, we easily accept the only one told to us. The most famous and classical statement about money being invented for trade and commerce comes from Aristotle in *The Nichomachean Ethics*:

All commodities exchanged must be able to be compared in some way. It is to meet this requirement that men have introduced money; money constitutes in a manner a middle term, for it is a measure of all things, and so of their superior or inferior value, that is to say, how many shoes are equivalent to a house or to a given quantity of food. As therefore a builder is to a shoemaker, so must such a number of shoes be to a house, or to a given amount of food; for without this reciprocal proportion, there can be no exchange and association; and it cannot be secured unless the commodities in question be equal in a sense.

It is therefore necessary that all commodities shall be measured by some one standard, as was said before. And this standard is in reality demand, which is what holds everything together, since, either if men cease to have wants or if wants alter, exchange will go on no longer, or will be on different lines. But demand has come to be conventionally represented by money; this is why money is called nomisma (customary money) because it does not exist by nature but by custom (nosmos), and can be altered and rendered useless at will.

The second most famous argument is John Stuart Mill's much-quoted imaginary instance: 'A tailor who has nothing but coats might starve before he could find any person having bread to sell who wanted a coat; besides he would not want as much bread at a time as would be worth a coat, and the coat could not be divided' (Mill, p.4).

In anthropological circles there is also a charming and much-quoted story about a French chanteuse, Mademoiselle Zélie of

Paris, who after giving a concert on one of the Society Islands received in payment three pigs, twenty-three turkeys, forty-four chickens, 5,000 coconuts and a large quantity of bananas, lemons and oranges. She, of course, had trouble banking her fee.

Stories such as these are used to explain the emergence and the *need* for money as a unit of account. If they are thoughtlessly accepted, we are also left with the impression that coins and notes are tools of sophisticated and civilized peoples. Anything less than money would simply be primitive.

In our contemporary education system Aristotle and the whole gang of classical western philosophers and economic thinkers have more sway, of course, than a Kalahari Bushman or Australian Aborigine. So it is not surprising that this utilitarian and commercial view of money predominates. Focusing, however, on the use of natural objects as currency helps us to gain a wider perspective. If we can perceive the 'natural' dimensions of money, it is possible to transfer this perspective across to paper and electronic money.

Other Theories about the Origins of Money

We have to nail Aristotle's simple idea that money is a child of commerce, and it is important, therefore, to understand the full range of theories that exist concerning its origins. Earlier in this chapter I quoted from Paul Einzig's *Primitive Money*, and I am happy again to rely heavily upon his research because his book is a superb work of universally acknowledged scholarship; there is nothing else in the field that compares with it. Again, for those readers who are not academically inclined I apologize for the density of the information that is about to follow – skim it if you need to – but I want to be fully persuasive. I particularly want to persuade thoughtful folk who like to hold on to old ideas until they are overwhelmed with new and different knowledge. At least, having read the next few pages, the reader will be in no doubt that there are sound contending theories about the origins of money. For all its dryness, the academic approach is thorough and it is often best to have as complete a picture as possible.

Einzig lists eleven theories about the origins of money. At the very least they provide academically respectable alternatives to the commercial approach:

Origin through medium of exchange.
Origin through external trade.
Origin through internal trade.
The standard of value theory.
The store of value theory.
Origin from the standard of deferred payments.
Origin through ornamental and ceremonial functions.
Religious origin.
Political origin.
Matrimonial origin.
Origin through status symbol function.

THE MEDIUM OF EXCHANGE THEORY is very straightforward and is the major theory which we all tend to assume is correct, stating that money is basically a tool of business people. It suggests that in the process of bartering, one particular type of object is used more than others and becomes a standard. Paul Einzig states it clearly in one sentence: 'The increasingly frequent use of one particular medium of barter and its gradual standardization tended to raise its status gradually and imperceptibly to that of a medium of exchange.' Addressing the idea that some 'lazy genius' could not be bothered with the complications of barter and therefore *invented* money, he comments: 'While it is just possible that some communities out of untold thousands may have adopted money through the deliberate invention of one person or the deliberate decision of the community, in all probability in the overwhelming majority of instances the evolution of money was an unconscious and gradual process.'

ORIGIN THROUGH EXTERNAL TRADE. The main evidence for this theory is that objects such as shell, amber instruments and weapons have been found great distances away from their source. It was assumed that when it came to exchanging with outside tribes, only particular types of goods would be in demand. These goods might be ornamental or sacred objects, or they might be staples such as salt or spices that were not available within one of the communities. These particular goods then took on the status of money. The original purpose of external exchanges was not commercial, but the creation of good relations.

ORIGIN THROUGH INTERNAL TRADE suggests that certain products are such basic staples of the community that people are prepared to hold on to more than they actually need because they know that they will always be able to exchange it in the future. This is clear, for example, in a community where the main staple is wheat, for which there will always be demand. Another well-known example of a staple of this kind are the communities in Africa where cattle serve as money; this emerges from the fact that cattle are their basic source of life and livelihood.

THE STANDARD OF VALUE THEORY suggests that the major reason money came into existence was not to facilitate barter and exchange as a form of human reciprocity; but its major purpose is to act as a unit of value so that when goods are exchanged there is a sense of parity.

THE STORE OF VALUE THEORY is also straightforward. Stanley Jevons stated it succinctly: 'The use of esteemed articles as a medium for conserving value may in some cases precede their employment as currency. Historically speaking, such a generally esteemed substance as gold seems to have served firstly as a commodity valuable for ornamental purposes; secondly as a store of wealth; thirdly as a medium of exchange, and lastly as a measure of value' (Jevons, p.16). Originally valued for its look, the object used as money, when stored, serves as some guarantee of safety for the future; it provides a medium for future transactions.

ORIGIN FROM STANDARD OF DEFERRED PAYMENTS. Paul Einzig lists five ways in which deferred payments originate in a pre-monetary community: 1. A discrepancy in the value of goods exchanged. 2. Late delivery of goods exchanged. 3. Loans for fines, tribute, blood money, bride money, etc. 4. Rents fixed in advance for long periods. 5. Loans granted for trading purposes. Some theorists have even suggested that debts arose before money. F.M. Taylor suggested that 'Some one money (e.g. wheat, salt, shells) will become the standard money of debts and then take for itself also the place of standard money in prices. This follows because the standard means of payment is free to move while that of debts is not' (Taylor, p.158).

ORIGIN THROUGH ORNAMENTAL AND CEREMONIAL FUNCTIONS. There are two separate theories here. The first states that people enjoy collecting and displaying attractive objects – such as shells, beads, feathers, animal teeth, articles of clothing, etc. – and that steady demand for these objects made them acceptable as a medium of exchange. The second states that objects which became valued possessions because of their monetary use came subsequently to be regarded as ornamental objects. Whether the first or second theory is true, what is certainly real is that people like to display their wealth and 'One of the few forms in which he (primitive human) could hoard wealth without being accused of meanness is through the display of ornaments' (Einzig, p.367).

RELIGIOUS ORIGIN. It is worth quoting Einzig:

The Religious aspects of money may be summed up under the following headings:

1. Money may have originated in many instances through regular requirements for specific standardized objects for the purpose of sacrifice to deities.

2. In many communities the creation of money is attributed to supernatural powers.

3. In other communities the (admittedly) human producers of money have to observe certain religious rites or rules in executing their 'sacred' task.

4. Magic qualities attributed to certain objects have led to their adoption for monetary use.

5. The use of certain objects in connection with religious purposes other than sacrifices, such as death rites, may have contributed towards their adoption for monetary use.

6. The fixing of fines for breaking taboos, and of fees for performers of religious rites, gave rise to the need for a standardized unit. (Einzig, p.370)

What I find particularly interesting here is the notion that money comes into being in order to facilitate relationships with the sacred and the spiritual. Money is not simply a communication between two people, but also a communication between people and the gods.

POLITICAL ORIGIN. These are fairly straightforward again. They include payments to or from the central political authority, such as fines, rewards, tributes, dowries, compensations and subscriptions. All these 'payments' are, of course, offerings to significant social figures and mark a significant social transaction.

MATRIMONIAL ORIGIN. This theory suggests that where dowries were paid for brides, the payments had to be in objects and goods that were of particular value; and that these objects and goods then became used as a standard unit for other exchanges.

ORIGIN THROUGH STATUS SYMBOL FUNCTION. This theory suggests that the strongest social driving force is the ambition to achieve importance. The drive of social ambition leads people to need to display their prosperity and, therefore, their success and power. This display is made through accumulating and distributing objects and goods that are communally valued; these objects and goods then become accepted for trade.

Einzig finally comments that, of course, 'The origin and evolution of money must have varied from community to community and it is always dangerous to generalize about its origin' (Einzig, p.387).

I Do Not Want to Eat You

The way in which we understand the origin of money directly affects how we understand the nature and psychology of economic behaviour. If we limit our understanding of its origins to barter and the market-place, we do not even possess a conceptual framework for thinking about other psychological dynamics in financial behaviour. When we look at the evidence and theories of a historian and anthropologist like Paul Einzig, we have no choice but to expand our framework and comprehension. We are not dealing here with accountancy or shrewd planning. We are dealing with flesh and blood tribal peoples leading multi-faceted lives in which repeatedly used objects become accepted as relevant and meaningful tokens for different types of situation.

These different theories point to certain general conclusions. The first is that money did not simply appear because some monarch, trader or high priest decided to invent it to help trade. Money, in its many various forms, emerged organically out of different situations. It emerged because it served a practical human function in certain types of situation which frequently recurred. Certainly, facilitating exchange was one such situation, but only one of many. But, whatever type of situation, it involved human relationships – with each other, with chiefs, with strangers and with spirits and gods. Money always accompanies and facilitates human relationship.

In all of the different theories about the origin of money what we have is tribal people in relationship. They are giving or exchanging something in order to help that relationship. And certain objects that people became accustomed to giving became used in other situations, such as trade. To put it very simply: objects that were habitually gifted or exchanged became what we call 'money'. And, without exception, this 'money' served human relationships. We need to understand this better.

Universally, we know what a good human relationship feels

like. It contains trust, safety and affection. Gifting evokes trust, safety and affection.

When strangers from different tribes meet in the desert or jungle, for example, they cannot know in the first instance whether the meeting will be friendly or hostile. One of the most obvious displays of friendly intention – like a smile or an open extended hand – is a gift. In gifting, we say to a stranger, 'I am not hostile. I do not intend to eat you.' The gifting creates relationship. It helps to make the encounter more meaningful and significant in a humane way. One of the very first lessons of any first-year student of social anthropology is that the giving or exchange of gifts is always a significant transaction, denoting the building of relationship and social solidarity. The gift, in some way, contains a part of the person. In some traditions a gift is said to contain a fragment of one's own soul, freely given. At the very least it carries the charisma of goodwill. At the very least it is a universally recognized symbol of a reaching out for relationship.

You can, if you want, call this 'trading', but the very word 'trading' has a meaning and limitation that holds it to a materialistic perspective. In tribal societies exchanges were never important for their material value, but for their significance and symbolism.

When, nowadays, we take flowers to a friend or relative, there is a significance in the gift. The cash value of the flowers is irrelevant, yet the flowers are a currency of affection, respect and relationship. It does not matter what they cost. They carry a message that makes the moment of the gifting significant. The explorers who carry gifts for strangers are not patronizing, nor manipulative, nor bribing. These explorers are sensible, for they do not wish to be eaten and are seeking relationship. Gifts at significant moments in people's lives – birthday, coming of age, marriage – signify respect, support and affection.

Significant and important gift-giving has a piece of anthropological jargon all of its own. It is called *prestation*. Prestation is the presentation of significant gifts and they are significant because they express a clear communication from the giver to the receiver. These gifts are not casual. They say a number of things: mainly they say, *You are important to me. This moment is important. I want you to know that. I want you to feel good about this.* Money, in its basic form, always arose and had its origin in gifting. In one tribe it became customary to give sharks' teeth. In another tribe, they got into the habit of giving beads or shells or cattle. In its early and 'primitive' form these types of money are always a prestation, a significant communication. In all its origins money arose from the instinct to give, exchange and make safe relationship. And throughout this book I will argue that in order to make sense of our current directionless economic system, we need to come back to an awareness in which we again regard each of our financial transactions as a form of prestation.

A stark example of how early money is used for prestation can be seen in the fines paid to the tribal chief for 'criminal' activity. The fines of tribal societies are not the same as the fines in our courts. If a tribal member breaks the local law, he has placed himself outside his culture. By giving something to the chief, the criminal symbolically demonstrates that he still values his culture's rules. The gift, the prestation of cattle or shells or beads (or edible rats), represents an apology, a balancing and a continued respect. The fine, paid as a tooth or cow or coinage, is not a cash penalty. Its payment is the way in which the culprit demonstrates a desire for continued relationship.

In some instances significant transactions and prestations build up into elaborate rituals of exchange which take place over great distances and over great cycles of time. The most famous of these, in the Trobriand Islands of the Pacific, was described by the anthropologist Malinowski. Here in the South Seas two sets of gifts, coral necklaces and armbands, circle clockwise and anticlockwise around the islands, carried by canoe and presented gracefully and ritualistically. The full cycle of a necklace around the islands takes thirty years. Through this cycle social relations between the different islands are maintained. No seagoing canoe need ever be afraid of meeting strangers or being marooned. They stay in relationship through the ongoing ritual of cyclic gifting. Again, it would be stupid and limiting to call this careful exchanging 'trade'.

In small-scale societies, the historical roots of all culture and society today, there is no such thing as a gift or exchange that does not have social and psychological significance. Money, as it emerged in these tribal settings, was always only an object that had become habitually used for gifting and exchange. The historical and social origin of money is in human relationship.

Generosity and Sharing

The other great pillar of economic theory is that people are naturally competitive in a dangerous world of scarce resources. The opposing idea that people are, in fact, instinctively generous and sharing is often greeted with cynicism. It is true that people often behave savagely, but that in itself does not negate the existence of our other powerful instincts.

Within the primal family unit we can see everywhere the naturalness of sharing and generosity. Except for pathological and tragic cases, there is a natural instinct for parents to share with their children. It begins with the flow of milk from a mother's breast. It is normal for parents to make sacrifices for their children. The financial affairs of a family do not work in the same way as a competitive business. There are many more families than businesses on our planet, which is evidence enough that, in general, caring is more widespread than material competition. Our financial ethics, within our families, are very different from those of the modern business world. This is clear evidence of a financial attitude different from that of greed, anxiety and competition.

Economists, financiers and politicians – when they consider the world of money – rarely look beyond the commercial systems into family life. Perhaps it would be too embarrassing for them to try to square their understanding of economic man with normal family instincts. In fact, some politicians have become so disengaged from understanding instinctive family values that they deliberately encourage competitive and aggressive financial attitudes as being the *only* sensible and normal way to behave.

But it is not only families which demonstrate sharing and generosity. All across the world, *without exception*, tribal peoples – the 'primitives' and 'savages' – demonstrate a similar attitude of instinctive sharing and generosity. The anthropological evidence is one hundred per cent consistent that tribal communities possess an inherent social and psychological attitude of sharing. These peoples display it not only person to person within a tight nuclear family but also through their communities in general. Moreover, this ethic of sharing manifests in situations of both scarcity and plenty. Every single tribal society investigated by social anthropologists displays internal sharing, generosity and material solidarity. (This solidarity, however, breaks down when confronted with modern society.)

There is the question, of course, about why tribal peoples behave in such a way. Is it love, or a biological instinct of solidarity, or realistic common sense? The anthropologist Evans-Pritchard went for common sense when he wrote:

This habit of share and share alike is easily understandable in a community where everyone is likely to find himself in difficulties from time to time, for it is scarcity and not sufficiency that makes people generous, since everybody is thereby ensured against hunger. He who is in need today receives help from him who may be in like need tomorrow. (Evans-Pritchard, p.85)

Even if it is just common sense, this strategy of sharing in times of scarcity is in startling contrast to the basic academic premise that people *always* compete for scarce resources. Let us look at a clear example. Elizabeth Thomas in her study of the Bushmen of the Kalahari wrote:

A Bushman will go to any lengths to avoid making other Bushmen jealous of him, and for this reason the few possessions the Bushmen have are constantly circling among members of their group. No one cares to keep a particularly good knife too long, even though he may

want it desperately, because he will become the object of envy ...
Their culture insists that they share with each other, and it has never
happened that a Bushman failed to share objects, food or water with
other members of his band ... (Thomas, p.22)

The classic work on tribal economics is Marshall Sahlins's
Stone Age Economics, and I warmly recommend it to anyone
seeking to alter their fundamental notions about economics and
money. Sahlins writes at one point:

The observation is frequently made that any accumulation of wealth –
among such and such people – is followed hard upon by its disburse-
ment. The *objective* of gathering wealth, indeed, is often that of giving
it away. So for example, Barnett writes of Northwest Coast Indians
that, 'Accumulation in any quantity by borrowing or otherwise is, in
fact, unthinkable unless it be for the purpose of immediate redistribution.' The general proposition may be allowed that the general drift in
primitive societies tends on the whole away from accumulation towards
insufficiency. Thus: 'In general it may be said that no one in a Nuer
village starves unless all are starving.'

But what, for example, happens during a famine? Sahlins is
not naïve about the limits to a culture of sharing. He goes on to
say:

Yet the reaction to depression 'all depends': it depends on the social
structure put to test ... the tendency for compassion to be more-than-
proportionately expended on close kin in need than on distant kin in
the same straits. Probably every primitive organization has its breaking
point, or at least its turning point. Every one might see the time when
cooperation is overwhelmed by the scale of disaster and chicanery
becomes the order of the day. The range of assistance contracts progres-
sively to the family level; perhaps even these bonds dissolve and,
washed away, reveal an inhuman, yet most human, self-interest. (Sahlins, pp.213–14)

There are examples, though, where even this form of self-
interest is not true. As is well known, in the Eskimo culture
when times are tight and the clan is on the move, elderly

members may voluntarily walk out into the ice landscape, discreetly committing suicide so as no longer to burden their people.

There is evidence from tribal peoples all over the world of a natural culture of sharing. One of its most distinctive features is the role and behaviour of leaders, chiefs and leading warrior-hunters. A general trait, for example, is that leadership and political authority are only given to those people who *accumulate and then distribute* their goods and wealth. This fact is often unbelievable to folk who have never studied anthropology: that monarchs, tribal leaders, 'big' men and 'big' women retain their position and status not because they wield power over their people but because they are effective conduits of goods and wealth. To be a leader is to distribute all you have to your people. One of the marks of these leaders is that they display no personal interest in wealth at all. Describing the Kuma big men of the New Guinea Highlands, the anthropologist Marie Reay wrote, 'The aim is not simply to be wealthy, nor even to act as only the wealthy can act: it is to be *known* as wealthy. Further, a man does not really achieve his ambition until he can be seen to act as if wealth itself were of no account' (Reay, p.96).

There is a classic description of this, again in the Trobriand Islands, by Malinowski:

Wealth is the indispensable appanage of social rank and attribute of personal virtue. But the important point is that with them *to possess is to give* ... A man who owns a thing is naturally expected to share it, to distribute it, to be its trustee and dispenser. And the higher the rank the greater the obligation ... Meanness, indeed, is the most despised vice, and the only thing about which the natives have strong moral views, while generosity is the essence of goodness. (Malinowski, p.27, my italics)

Isn't this an extraordinary statement about a group of human beings, apparently savage and primitive: that meanness is the only thing about which they have strong moral views!

In these cultures the handing over of wealth, the giving away of possessions, expresses superiority. The retention of wealth is considered the action of a mean man unworthy of any status. This is not the same as the generosity of a contemporary millionaire, because in the tribal situation, in the eyes of the whole community, the chief gives *everything*. This is not to say that some 'big' people do not abuse or manipulate their political situation, but it does throw a completely different light on economic relations and the nature of true leadership. The true tribal leader finds legitimation in giving everything to the tribe, in being the selfless parent to the family, in a natural generosity and sharing.

This generosity also has a mythic aspect to it. James Frazer in *The Golden Bough* wrote much about the mystical relationship between the monarch or chief, seen as a representative of spirit, and the prosperity of their people and the fertility of their land. There have been many cultures in which good crops and and successful hunting were considered to be directly related to the quality of the monarch. A lousy season and low harvest, unsuccessful hunting, could lead to the ritual assassination of the chief who was not doing a real job of channelling abundance through to the people.

In these cultures, leadership and chieftainship is a parental role of providing prosperity. The chief is the maternal breast that succours the community. The chief is the good parent. The generosity of these tribal leaders can sometimes be so great that it seems to approach a form of madness. All across the world there is evidence, much of it contemporary, of a generosity that has apparently become crazy. In these situations, the leaders and chiefs of the clans and tribes destroy great quantities of wealth. Goods and produce are thrown into ocean, river or lake, or on to ceremonial fires. The most frequently described instances of this behaviour are among the north-west American tribes of the Pacific, who have regular gatherings and ceremonies where 'big' men ceremonially destroy their possessions. Blankets and food, and beautiful copper and brass plates are destroyed. Houses are burnt. Food is allowed to perish. Ceremonial objects are broken and thrown into the sea.

These events are called potlatches, a word which Marcel Mauss translated as both 'to nourish' and 'to consume'. Lewis

Hyde reports that one of the potlatch tribes, the Haida, called their feasting 'killing wealth'. In these cultures a leader's status and authority is maintained not only by distributing everything he has, but also by making ostentatious displays of unconcern about his wealth. The destruction of products and goods, including those that act as money, is done not only as a great gesture to their communities, but also as a sacrifice to the gods and spirits.

This ethic of sharing is not simply held by the chief but permeates the whole community even to include the most likely rebels, the young and successful hunter-warriors. Lest anyone think that primitive generosity is a wimpish cultural attribute, let me quote from Robert Spencer's study of the north Alaskan Eskimo: 'In times of food shortage, it was the successful hunter and his family who might go hungry, since in his generosity he gave away whatever he had at hand' (Spencer, p.164). In these Eskimo villages, it was easy to recognize the hut of the most successful hunter, for it was his hut that was the poorest.

Also, all across the world there are rituals for sharing the hunt with the community, different organs and cuts of the animal going by custom to different families and individuals.

Within the contemporary family, the ethos of being the good provider remains intact. But once we move beyond the family into wider society, there is no longer that equation between leadership and generosity. The macho free market of our contemporary world may need courage and daring in order to achieve success, but I wonder about the far greater courage needed to remain sharing and generous.

When money first emerged, it did so in these tribal situations. It was created in a culture of meaningful gifting and instinctive sharing and generosity. These are good roots to remember.

The Joys of the Market

The tribal culture of sharing contrasts starkly with that of modern commercial business. There is also a stark contrast between the modern large-scale commercial market and other smaller markets.

The usually accepted image of a business person working in the modern market is dark-suited and deadly serious. Men and women power-dress in sombre blacks and greys to go into business. Their briefcases and umbrellas are like swords and shields. The mobile phone is the insignia of the communications officer, ready with the latest intelligence to do battle. This is all an affair of survival. Only the fittest will succeed. Economic man, we are taught, is on a mission to survive in a world of scarcity. This is serious business. Business is serious.

All of this colours the way we think of the market and of business. There is no room here for relationship and human joys. The free market of contemporary society is a harsh environment and we, therefore, assume that it is natural for our business and financial relations to be harsh.

But is this image true to how we originally entered the market-place?

Every day, all across the world, there are other real markets which are very different – colourful and exciting. I lived for two years in southern Morocco, in a valley high in the Atlas Mountains, and my home was a mile and a half from a plot set aside for the local market. Every week, under the benevolent and snow-capped gaze of Mount Toupkal, a thousand people would gather to trade and to meet. In the early hours of the morning we would be woken by the extraordinary sound of a thousand baying donkeys and mules, while their masters and mistresses carried their wares into the market and set up their sites and stalls. People came from all over the surrounding valleys and mountains, bringing food and crafts, clothing and kitchenware. There were even tribesfolk who travelled up from the Sahara.

Entering this market, like entering open-air markets in all places and at all times, the immediate impression is not of objects and goods being bartered, but of people in all kinds of communication and relationship, people window-shopping and watching the theatre of the market. There were many people there, not necessarily for the trading, but for the communication, the gossip and human contact. The magic of the environment was enhanced by entertainers such as story-tellers and jugglers, by the women dressed only in black, flaming eyes inviting us to sit with them for a psychic reading through a crystal ball or tarot pack.

Here, in the market, people from the isolated villages tasted the outside world, listened to the various levels of gossip from family through to clan and national politics. This was a world of eyes, seeking relationship, seeking contact. Buying something was not a brief encounter, eyes shaded. Eyes met and hands shook, perhaps a sharing of sweet coffee and tea, and then into business. Bargaining and negotiation was not a hard-nosed competition between cut-throat entrepreneurs, but ordinary folk coming to a mutually acceptable agreement. The bargaining was enjoyable human communication, bringing folk who might be isolated for much of their lives into creative contact. In the culture of this particular market in the Atlas Mountains, the morality of Islam was also present, ordering that no person take advantage of another, but that the trade be fair and to the common good.

In Marrakech, sixty miles away, there were also markets which contained this same throbbing atmosphere of human communication and entertainment. Even the covered market in the colonial area of the city, the market for the French and Spanish settlers, held this bubbling atmosphere. But this is not strange or unusual. Street markets all over the world contain this atmosphere of many people in magical interaction. Almost every city on this planet has its open-air market of antiques and bric-à-brac, old clothes and crafts, food and plants. A visit to the flea markets of the great capital cities is not simply a search for a bargain but an adventure out into an enjoyable human community. Even the local vegetable market carries an aura very different from a shop or supermarket. And to stay within the theme of this book, we need to remember again that it is money which facilitates the interaction and transactions of these markets.

The open-air markets provide a very different picture from the financial markets of the great metropolitan cities. The open-air markets are fun and socially cohesive. In them we see people in a humane and earthy way enjoying their lives. Yes, they come to buy and sell for material needs, but the psychological and social realities are far deeper.

It is the human enjoyment of creation, exchange, communication and relationship which creates the market – *not* the need to trade.

People love to make things and to be in contact with other people. People are naturally creative and naturally social. It is the attributes of creativity and sociability which have built and driven the historical process of trade from isolated tribal groupings into our current global culture.

In the true markets we express the creative energies of our true humanity. In the market of academic theory, in the market of modern large-scale capitalism, humans are disengaged from their roots and their humaneness. How and why this disengagement happened is the subject of the next two chapters. For the moment it is healthy and balancing to remember the enjoyment of the natural market-place, and to contemplate the possibility of recovering those feelings in the markets of the dark suits, computer screens and cellular phones.

It's a Different Game

There is a game we play in my money seminars called the Barter Game. Its purpose is to give people a direct taste of the dynamics of a market. I ask everyone to bring to these seminars three objects that they would like to barter and exchange. People bring an assortment of things: books, clothing, wine, toys, jewellery, plants and so on. They play this game early on in the seminar, when they are still strangers to each other. All I ask them to do is to walk around and to look at what everybody is offering. Then, when they are ready, they can begin to exchange and barter their objects.

The interaction always begins slowly and carefully, as they

suspiciously sniff each other and their gifts. Things then begin to warm up and in a little while this group of strangers – between a dozen and several hundred people – is involved in a noisy and enjoyable game, with the full atmosphere of a market, trading, examining, bargaining, getting and giving. Often, this is the first time that people have experienced the fun and contact of bargaining, assessing and rejecting or accepting.

I let the Barter Game run for about fifteen minutes before I intervene with another dynamic. There are usually one or two people in these workshops who have forgotten to bring objects with which to barter and I use this as an opportunity to stimulate a discussion.

I ask them all to stop and I point out that we have some folk who cannot play. I then produce a few wooden beads (from one of those beaded car seats) and suggest that the newcomers be allowed to trade with these. There are always immediate and different reactions. Some folk are happy for them to join in. Others want them excluded. Some people are sympathetic and feel sorry for the excluded folk. Others aggressively reject them and say that it is their fault for forgetting to bring gifts. Others in the group are confused or apathetic. Others get into a discussion about whether the beads have any value at all.

'Supposing,' I suggest, 'we trust that these new people will become good and valuable members of our community. If we expand to include them now, their contribution later will make it completely worthwhile to let them trade with the beads.'

'Bullshit!' responded a woman in one group. 'These are human beings. They're here, so they should be part of our community regardless of what they do for us. They should not be left out in the cold.'

'Why not?' came a voice of cynicism. 'They didn't bring anything. And the beads aren't worth a fig.'

'They brought themselves.'

'I don't like the look of them anyway.'

'I'll feel ripped off,' says someone else, 'if all I get is beads for my gifts.'

'Supposing,' I suggest again, 'that we pretend we are a clan or a tribe and that we recognize these folk as cousins.'

'The forgetful, lazy cousins!' came the cynical voice.

'Let them starve,' someone else giggled.

'They can have my gifts anyway,' comes the voice of the soft-hearted and sympathetic creature. 'I just want them to join in.'

'Here is another option,' I intervene. 'Let us imagine that these beads have been given to us by spiritual authorities and that they have great power. Is there anyone here who would like to be a great spiritual being and bless these beads?' I ask.

There are usually one or more folk who, in this kind of psychodrama, volunteer to play the priestesses. 'In the name of the most high being of our tribe we bless these sacred beads as tokens of wondrous power and magic.'

I then ask again whether the people can play with the beads.

'They're still not worth anything. You're conning us.'

'I really want one of the sacred beads. It will remind me of today.'

'They are sacred and holy. They will bless us.'

'I just want the people to be able to play with us. I'm very happy to let them trade with the beads.'

The newcomers are then allowed, with their beads, to participate in the game.

At the end of these Barter Games, the folk who started with beads have invariably been able to exchange them for goods. And the people who have accepted the beads feel very good about the exchange. Once there was a woman who ended up with three beads and no goods at all. She was as happy as all the other folk. She was clear about the fact that she felt good possessing three beads, rather than a book, a bottle of wine and a scarf. I asked why she felt good and she could not put it into words. Other people who have ended up with the wooden beads have said that it felt good to *trust* that the beads were worth something. Or it felt good to make this gesture of faith to another person. Or it felt good to bring into the game the people who had forgotten to bring bartering objects. But most people say that, in the end, it was not the gifts that mattered but it was the human contact which was important.

What cannot be denied by anyone, including the most cynical, is that over a half-hour and sometimes even less time, a group of strangers in a cold and uncertain atmosphere have become friends in a now enjoyable and friendly atmosphere.

There are several obvious points that can be drawn from the way the Barter Game unfolds. The first is that people enjoy the contact and creativity of the exchanges. Then by introducing the beads, we can actually expand the game. But first there is confusion, a similar confusion to that which people often have over money. The introduction of the beads, however, integrates the new people and allows everything to keep flowing. There is no sense of scarcity, but instead there is a sense of trust and confidence. We can see very clearly that trading is fun, humane and creative. Finally, we can see that the beads, which in the game have become money, are facilitating relationships between people. That is their primary function, even though they may also be deemed to have value and are units of trade.

We can also see that trading and bartering simple objects is easy and uncomplicated. As soon as we introduced the beads – which have symbolic meaning – a whole load of arguments began about their value and worth, the nature of the game and so on. This, as the participants often notice, is like economic life. Gifting is simple, but as soon as we get involved with money – symbolic tokens – things get more complicated. The complications evaporate, however, once people relax and let the game flow to enjoy the exchanges and contact.

Essentially, of course, the game underlines how barter and financial (the beads) exchange are about human connection. When the beads were just sitting in my pocket, they were meaningless. An act of the imagination turned them into a medium of communication which people could use. This is the nature of money; it is like language. Samuel Butler wrote in his *Notebooks*: 'Gold and silver coins are only the tokens, symbols, outward and visible signs and sacraments of money. When not in the actual process of being applied in purchase, they are no more money than words not in use are language.'

The acceptance of the beads into the Barter Game, the acceptance of their value, is very similar to how modern citizens accept the value of their national currency. In the game, the beads are acceptable currency simply because people agree that they are. In a modern country, our money is also acceptable currency simply because we agree, with the overarching help of our government and treasury, that it be acceptable. If the people lose faith, then the money becomes worthless.

The anthropological perspective, looking at what people actually do in less complicated circumstances – the small tribe, the family, the open-air market – provides a completely different perspective on what is 'natural' economic behaviour. We are not savages competing for scarce resources. Money is not just a unit of cash value invented to make the commercial market efficient.

We are naturally sharing and generous.

Economic success need not mean personal accumulation but, like tribal chiefs and leaders, can mean letting it flow to everyone. Economic success can mean distributing everything. In tribal cultures accumulation is considered a laughable and moral error.

We also see that the idea of the competitive market is very limited. Markets are for fun and energy. The modern financial markets have become frantic places of conflict, a nightmare. The purpose of money is to bring people into relationship. Without human relationship money itself is worthless.

5

FROM CARING TO
COMPETITION

To be noble is to be generous. To be generous is to be noble. (Anon., tribal)

Our parents have trained us to admire gold and silver, and the love of it has grown up with us to such a degree that when we need to show our gratitude to Heaven, we make presents of these metals.

It is this that makes poverty look like a curse and a reproach, and the poets have perpetuated this: the chariot of the Sun must be of gold; the best of the times must be the golden age; and thus they turn the greatest misery of mankind into the greatest blessing. (Seneca, *Morals*, first century)

Paradox, Contrast and Conflict

If there is overwhelming evidence that families and tribes demonstrate material generosity and sharing, how come it does not look that way in society generally? How on earth did we create our current economic and money culture? In fact, the money culture in which we live is so overwhelmingly dominated by commercial competition that it is almost impossible to believe that there could be another type of economic life. The competitive domination is so great that it seems almost naïve to imagine that our family or clan values could be relevant.

It is crucial, therefore, to understand exactly why it is that our general economic culture is so different from the relaxed sharing of a close family. The primal bonds of family and tribe ensure cooperation and support. A complex society no longer has those bonds. Does this mean that a large-scale complex society is bound to be economically heartless and savage, that money be purely a cash instrument? Is a complex community bound to lose its sense of humane values?

If we can understand what has happened to us, we can then begin to work our way out of it. In this chapter I discuss nine factors which I identify to be the major influences in creating an inhumane economy in large-scale societies.

Background

We live in an extraordinary world of paradox, contrast and conflict. This is reflected, for example, in my own attitudes. I want wealth and at the same time I want economic justice. I want to be part of an inventive and creative financial flow, and I want every child fed and nurtured. I want a world that is ecologically healthy and I want the excitement of new technology.

In financial attitudes generally, there are extreme contrasts. On one side, for example, are the people who care for the earth and for social justice. These people may be passionate about an inhumane economic system which seems to be slipping us into inevitable catastrophe. On the other side are the folk who are enjoying the fruits of the economy, living well, enjoying life. At best these people create wealth and innovation for all of us. At worst, they are selfish with an enthusiasm for aggressive economic competition.

In between these two extremes – the caring and the careless – are the rest of us, just getting on with our lives, sometimes caring, sometimes careless.

We also live alongside a world of people for whom poverty and subsistence are normal. Half of the world's population has not been through the industrial revolution, while we in the other half are beginning to enjoy the benefits of a further post-industrial electronics revolution.

There are still tribal peoples who are completely disengaged and separate from the modern world. There are still isolated communities who live in a stone-age social and economic system and, without exception, these tribal communities still display a natural and socially encouraged generosity and spirit of sharing. The money they use – the shells or cattle (or edible rats) – is transferred between them always in the context of a meaningful and significant relationship.

A thousand miles away, though, in the electronic dealing rooms of New York, London or Tokyo, millions of dollars are being traded by computers. These electronic brains watch the ebb and flow of the global currency, commodity and futures markets, and they monitor minute opportunities for profit. For a few seconds there may be a disparity between the levels at which a currency is being traded. The computer, in that instant, will buy and then sell. The amount of money moved in the deal is so great that a profit of only a fraction of a per cent still yields a high figure. A half of one per cent of a billion dollars is still 5 million dollars. Not bad for ten seconds of work by a computer.

In the jargon of the electronic business world, the boffins who invent the software that can make these fantastic electronic deals are called 'quants'. One of these quants, a PhD from MIT, personally earned 23 million dollars in 1990 trading for the firm of Salomon Brothers. In these huge electronic and lightning flash deals, by their very nature, there is no attention to anything beyond the immediate opportunity for profit. When the dealing was done purely by human decision, there had to be at least a consideration of the investment. As Joel Kurtzman says in his book *The Death of Money*, 'Almost all markets are now driven not so much by investment opportunities – the way they were in the past – as by transaction opportunities.'

We have here, in stark relief, the problem. On one side, we have small groups of 'stone-age' humans carefully interacting with each other and using their money, or tokens of value, with awareness. On the other side, we have internationally networked computers, programmed to work faster than the human brain, jumping into financial opportunities without any awareness of the humane or other ramifications.

Faced with this paradox, do we groan, cheer or just look stunned? No wonder many of us are confused. Even if we could begin to sort out our own inner contradictions, we live in this external world of overwhelming contradictions. There is stunning wealth alongside pathetic poverty. There is tender and caring human relationship alongside brilliant but heartless technologies.

We have produced a gargantuan world economy, and I think most of us believe that very large organizations are bound to lose their humanity and produce alienated human beings for whom there is no meaningful relationship. In social theory this is reflected in the interesting debate about the difference between 'society' and 'community', both words intuitively possessing very different qualities. Society is organizational, structured and cold. Community is humane, flowing and warm. Large groups of people create societies, whereas small groups create communities. E.F. Schumacher's ringing and evocative social slogan, 'small is beautiful', also sounds out a note of truth that seems to be self-evident. But why is this so?

If we are trying to get at the facts of what actually happened to our financial attitudes during the transition from small-scale to large-scale communities, the problem is that we simply do not have clear historical evidence. Historically, we seemingly have this simple and flowing story of the growth of modern civilization: from small hunter-gatherer communities to our contemporary global village of 6 billion. It seems that we also have a simple history of a continuous and huge increase in the use of money.

It is also evident that as the *quantity* of money transactions increased, at the same time their humane *quality* decreased.

But even the idea that there was a universal trend from humane small communities to inhumane large communities is not absolutely true. In *The Chalice and the Blade* Riane Eisler reminds us that there is, in fact, clear evidence of at least one large-scale complex society that retained humane values, the society of ancient Crete. She quotes Platon as writing:

The whole of life was pervaded by an ardent faith in the goddess Nature, the source of all creation and harmony. This led to a love of peace, a horror of tyranny, and a respect for the law. Even among the ruling classes personal ambition seems to have been unknown; nowhere do we find the name of an author attached to a work of art nor a record of the deeds of a ruler. (Eisler, p.34)

It also led to a society in which wealth was shared, even the peasants were well off and the rulers were not ostentatious.

Eisler's book suggests that the whole of Europe, in fact, was a landscape of peaceful and cooperative human communities, their culture coloured by a model of behaviour which she calls the 'partnership model'. Archaeological digs have found villages and communities all across Europe without defences, in vulnerable strategic landscapes, and without weaponry. It seems that there was then an invasion of peoples with a far different model of behaviour, which she calls the 'dominator model', in which power hierarchies, competition and cruelty were the major features.

The evidence from Crete, also from the Incas, Egyptians, Chaldeans, Africans, Indians and Chinese, is that it is possible to have large-scale societies which are beneficent and humane. Most of us, I hope, have that experience in our own lives – perhaps on a weekend or a bank holiday – when it feels good to be alive and part of the human community. I have often walked in cities early in the morning or during holidays and felt a deep contentment at being part of their magic. In fact, it can often seem that a sense of community and partnership can exist even while the aggressive dominator model controls politics and finance.

The question, therefore, is how the caring culture turned aggressive. Let me identify and discuss the nine elements which I believe to be fundamental.

One – The Great Enchantment

On the wall opposite where I am writing, there is a painting by the Moroccan artist Hamri. In primal colours of orange, green and yellow, the painting depicts a sorcerer who, with the help of a magic fish and five female apprentices, is conjuring up a daemon, while some flowers look on and applaud. In the glass of the frame, I can regularly see the reflection of aeroplanes as they make their long circle round east London towards Heathrow airport.

Hamri gave me this painting at the end of my two-year stay in Morocco. During those two years in the High Atlas Mountains I lived in a small house two miles from the nearest road. When I first moved there I heard about a local healer and sorcerer who lived in the village a mile away. I had a clear intuition to send him a prestation, as a gesture of greeting and respect, and I sent him three large cones of sugar, a customary gift. This was a diplomatic gesture as I was taking retreat in his spiritual backyard.

One day I actually met this healer, and he was a sad man who treated me with a humility that I found uncomfortable. I was expecting to be in awe of him, but in fact he was disempowered and overawed. I did not fully understand his story until I had spoken to a few local people, who told me that he came from a line of healers and herbalists who had always been well-respected. With the coming of modern medicine and a health clinic twenty kilometres away, he had begun to lose his clients and his income. His family owned no land, always relying upon their skills, reputation and tradition – and now he was facing poverty. His own life had been overwhelmed by the new culture. The attraction to the magical powers of the local clinic was so great that people would travel hundreds of miles and queue perhaps for days to treat an ailment their local healer could in fact well handle. (The irony, of course, was that while the healer was losing ground to western medicine, back in Europe and America the alternative methods of healers and herbalists were resurfacing.)

Modern technology, modern ways, often possess a charisma

that englamours newcomers. It is certainly true that modern medicine has miraculous effects for a culture that has never previously experienced it. Faced with miracles, faced with dazzling new technology, people easily lose discrimination. We accept everything new, reject everything old, lose our sense of proportion and balance.

In certain ways the whole of humanity has fallen enchanted to the dazzling ways of complex economies and emerging technologies. My point here is so simple as to be almost naïve. *The changes brought about by technology and international commerce have been so great and so overwhelming that humanity is quite simply bedazzled by them.* We do not see through them to other values and realities which, although less dazzling, may yet possess a profound relevance and meaning for us.

Less than a hundred years ago, in the time of our grandparents and great-grandparents, there were no cars, televisions, radios, washing-machines, phones ... Look at what we have now. It is little wonder that we have been enchanted.

We should remember that human beings literally can be hypnotized, seduced into another form of consciousness, so that they give up all personal will. Hypnotherapists do this professionally in their consulting-rooms. Other hypnotists work in theatres and cabaret.

But we are also often hypnotized and beguiled by other forces and images. When we see something beautiful, erotically attractive, potentially gratifying of our desires, it is wonderfully easy to lose ourselves in the enchantment of a dream of possibilities. In these dreams our shallowest and deepest needs can be touched, caressed and gratified. Like magpies we can be attracted to anything that glitters.

Money glitters for us, not just in itself, but because of its fantastic promises. It glitters with the possibility of fulfilling our most extraordinary dreams.

When tribal peoples and small communities meet the complexities of modern technology and the world of money, the imagination is overwhelmed. All previous dreams are shocked by the power and forceful abilities of this new reality.

This new reality, we need to remember, is incredibly recent. Most of us are still hypnotized and enchanted.

Two – Future Shock

We have not only been enchanted by the dazzling new things, but we have also been overwhelmed by the suddenness of it all. This jewel of a beautiful planet was once host to only a few human beings. These humans were in small clan groups, who travelled across their landscape, hunting and gathering as the seasons drew them to the best locations, and their impact on the planet was minimal.

How many humans were there altogether? How can we know? Not a lot. But, as we know only too well, our species did remarkably well. Its adaptability and intelligence far outstretched other animals. Our use of fire, of the wheel, of horticulture were fantastic inventions. We flourished and our population grew. Our inventiveness also continued. Since the time that some of our ancestors stopped hunting and gathering, and started the great river basin civilizations, we have been inventing and innovating, adapting and expanding. Although the pace of innovation and invention was relatively slow, over the last 1,000 years it has accelerated, and in the last two centuries change has exploded.

Walt Disney's image of Mickey Mouse as the sorcerer's apprentice unleashing uncontrollable forces – forces that at first delight Mickey and then trigger him into frenetic panic – is a useful metaphor and symbol for the whole history of the growth of invention, innovation and what we call civilization. But the very nature of an invention or innovation is that it is *new* and being new *we cannot have a real idea of its effects and ramifications.*

Since the first valley civilizations some 10,000 years ago our species has been rushing forward inventing and innovating. There is an elemental fury here, a tidal wave of change rolling through history, building up decade by decade. These innovations and inventions are not simply technological. We have also been inventing new ways of living together and organizing our communities.

In the fabric of any city, for example, are a myriad different social and communication systems which hold the urban community together. All these systems were once innovations: partnerships, working communities, police, courts, messengers, managers, government ... System by system, innovation by innovation, humanity was innocent as to its ramifications. When the first settlements of only a few hundred people began, who could have possibly foreseen a city of 20 million souls? When the first court messengers were instituted to carry communications and gifts between distant palaces, who would have prophesied satellite conferencing or cyberspace?

The international economic system and the more local national economies are all part of this haphazard unfoldment. We never knew that they would turn out the way they have.

This tidal wave of human invention, of which the monetary system is but a part, has two features today that make it particularly uncontrollable. The first is the population explosion. The second is the increasing acceleration of change. As Alvin Toffler put it, we are living in a state of *future shock*. Everything has happened, and is still happening, too fast. Look at some of the statistics for world population.

> 10,000 BC—10 million people
> 1,000 AD—340 million
> 1650—545 million
> 1800—900 million
> 1900—1,600 million
> 1950—2,500 million
> 1990—5,000 million – and still growing.

Our civilization is also very recent. The first horticultural settlers were only 10,000 years ago. The industrial revolution only began to take off 200 years ago. The electronics and communications revolution happened in the last decade. In fact, the vast majority of all the inventions and technology we know happened in the last few decades.

Yet born into the twentieth century we take it all for granted. Peter Russell graphically describes how recent it all is in his book *The White Hole in Time*. He charts the evolution of life on our planet against New York's tallest building, the quarter-mile-high World Trade Center:

If we make street level the formation of our planet 4,600 million years ago, then the process of physical evolution which preceded it stretches down as foundations some two-thirds of a mile deep.

Above ground, the simplest living cells appeared about 3,500 million years ago, on the twenty-fifth floor of the building's 108 storeys. Photosynthesis evolved around the fiftieth floor, and bacteria that breathed oxygen came another ten floors later – more than half-way up. More complex cells, capable of sexual reproduction and with a central nucleus, appeared around the seventieth floor. Multicellular organisms came another ten floors above that – and crustaceans ruled the waves on the ninety-fourth floor.

Fish appeared on the ninety-seventh floor, and crawled out of the sea on the ninety-ninth. Dinosaurs reigned on floors 104 to 107. And mammals live on the top floor. But *Homo erectus* first walked on two legs only a few inches from the top. It had taken 99.99 per cent of life's journey so far to reach this step – and humanity was only just beginning.

The Neanderthals with their enlarged brains, simple tools and tribal culture appeared in the last quarter of an inch. Then came Cro-Magnon people with clothes, painting, language, and perhaps religion. The Pharaohs ruled Egypt a fiftieth of an inch from the top. And the Greek and Roman empires thrived a hundredth of an inch above that.

The Renaissance occurred in the top one-thousandth of an inch: less than the thickness of a layer of paint. The whole of modern history occupies but the thickness of a microscopic bacterium. And the age of the microchip, rock 'n' roll, global telecommunications, nuclear power, moon-walks, and global warming is a layer almost too thin to measure. (Russell, pp. 16–17)

This acceleration in cultural change and technological innovation is even more rapid in the world of finance and money. The amount of money in circulation and the number of transactions have increased beyond imagination. In the electronic money market, for instance, 'every two weeks the annual product of the world passes through the network in New York – trillions and trillions of ones and zeros' (Kurtzman, p.17). And sums of similar magnitude pass through the networks of all the major financial centres. As Kurtzman wryly notes, 'It is now far easier and faster to move $1 billion from New York to Tokyo than to move a truckload of lettuce or grapes across the California–Arizona line' (p.18).

It is not just that changes in life have accelerated. They have exploded. In the previous section I suggested that we have been bedazzled by all the innovations and changes. I want to add another factor to that bedazzlement. It is one of innocence. We have had no control over what has been happening. Individual by individual we may have some authority over our actions and decisions, but collectively we have created and been part of a mammoth explosion of population, growth and change. We did not know – and still do not know – what we are doing. We stand innocent in the midst of a volcanic emerging system.

This innocence in the face of change is a source of great hope. The hope lies in the idea that a lack of caring and a lack of humaneness are not built into the system we have created. The lack of humane values, the destructiveness of it, are due to the fact that we are in a state of bedazzled and innocent shock because it has all happened too big and too fast.

Three and Four – Reaction to Threat and Accumulation Instead of Sharing

Social anthropologists are clear about the culture of sharing in tribal communities. They are also realistic, perhaps even cynical, about the ecological necessity for clan cooperation. The mutual dependence is so great that generous cooperation is crucial for survival. If one dies, all die. But there are bound to be moments of pressure when the solidarity is vulnerable and open to rupture. Even without the historical process of increasing population and contact with alien cultures, there are bound to be internal and external pressures.

The major *internal* pressure will come from alienated individuals who, to achieve psychological comfort, put their individual needs before others. The major *external* pressure will come from an environmental threat such as famine or a cultural threat such as meeting a more advanced society; both threaten community and individuals. It is easy to understand how in these situations the solidarity of a tribal group breaks down and the insecure aggression of individuals begin to take hold.

This tendency towards fracture is bound to increase as foreign cultures come into contact with each other. What one community holds sacred may be a source of amusement for another culture. We need only to look at the dietary habits of different peoples to see how dangerous a clash of cultures can be. A Jew or Muslim might rather die than eat a pig. A Hindu might rather die than eat a cow. There are even some tribes where a smile is considered to be the body language of a threat. A wave of greeting can be seen as a gesture of obscenity.

In these situations where strange customs meet each other, it takes tolerance and patience to maintain stability. Tribal peoples, just like us, may often lack strength of character, especially in the face of environmental or cultural threat. Insecurity, intolerance and impatience become widespread. Partnership gives way to domination and competition.

When tribal peoples meet modernized man and modernized technology, the threat is even greater, is overwhelming. Over and over again tribal solidarity has collapsed in the face of a more modern culture, the modern culture always possessing more effective and fatal weapons. Sometimes these weapons are rifles; sometimes they are the enchantment of the first transistor radio or addictive cola. In brutal and existential terms, the modern culture has greater power.

Obviously, with the growth of population and communications, the opportunities for psychological threat increase immensely. In fact, hardly anywhere has managed to remain isolated from 'civilized' influence. Tribal peoples in the most remote deserts, mountains and forests have been touched and affected. Aid workers and anthropologists working in these regions have universally written of how modern culture destroys the solidarity and ethos of these peoples. A happy coherent group descends into social decay. It is only different when the first and ensuing contacts are made by explorers with a clear sensitivity to the inherent problems.

Meeting modern civilization, tribal societies become unsafe at the edges and then the threat begins to permeate the whole social fabric. This lack of safety, this threat, reaches even into the atomic and clan family. Unless a very clear effort is made to restore the previous set of values and morals in which sharing and generosity are normal, then the community will slide into relative states of internal savagery and competition. The elders may not be strong or authoritative enough, or there may simply not be enough of them, to restore the tribal culture. Sharing and generosity as community values die. Gifting and bartering lose their charisma of prestation, and become only transactions of material value. Money loses its charm as a creator of relationship and as a supporter of innovation, and becomes coldly and competitively functional.

The Maori of New Zealand have a particularly evocative word for when times are tight, such as in winter, and families hide their food: *bisa-basa*. *Bisa-basa* is an attitude with which we are all familiar. The hunter, whose pride and self-esteem came from sacrificing his share for the good of his clan, will now turn his pride and his skills against the threat. The ruler who maintained her position by gifting and recycling all her goods to her people now needs to turn her attention against an enemy. The priestess or big man hides some of the grain that was intended for redistribution. One trader exercises some extra muscle to achieve a better deal. Fines or bride prices are manipulated in favour of a particular family.

Thus it is that as complexity, size and anxiety developed, goods, resources and money stopped circulating freely and generously and began to accumulate in specific hands. This broke the natural sense of community and began a social fragmentation based on possessions rather than who we are as actual people.

Five and Six – No One Watching and the Money Specialists

All of the above suggests that it is the inherent social and cultural *process* of modernization, not the modern world itself, which creates the problems and which seduces peoples away from communal solidarity into social competition. The process of meeting new ways and cultures is threatening and, in our reaction to the threat, we create an aggressive social and economic system. In this process money becomes a servant of competition rather than a servant of creative human relationship.

But in a large society there is also, as we have already noted, a far greater possibility of getting away with theft, bullying and manipulation. In a small community everyone's eyes are upon you. In a complex society, most people are strangers and they do not give attention to what you are doing. They mind their own business. In a small community, in a family, everything is everyone's business. A large community releases individuals to a new freedom. Nobody-watching is a liberation. It is also a licence for selfishness and abuse.

We have discussed how money evolved out of frequently repeated transactions, transactions whose purpose was to help people be in creative relationships. The types of relationship and the types of situation vary from simple gifts to acknowledge a family event, through prestations for rites of passage, to sacrifices to the gods and spirits. The quality of the transactions and the relationships is positive. In the swapping, gifting and trading, everybody comes out feeling good. This way of life is encouraged and supported by the community. Acts of selfishness are monitored, discouraged and penalized. Children are educated and socialized into this behaviour.

I know many people who work with large groups or have lived in communities. In conversation over and over again I have heard that people in a community can be familiar with each other up until a threshold of about 300 people. Beyond that figure some people are bound to become strangers. Two things can then easily happen.

The first is that individuals can begin to behave selfishly or bullyingly without being punished or sanctioned by their community. This is either because no one responsible notices or because everyone thinks that it is someone else's responsibility. In large communities social responsibility can give way to laziness.

The second thing that happens as a community grows is that a class of money specialists can arise who have no primal connection with their community. This is very bad news for an expanding or modernizing group which has no strong legal or political structures that support humane community values.

Some societies, as they grew, very definitely held on to their sense of community and caring, and this was reflected all the way through their social, economic and political structures. This was clearly evident in the Eden of Crete. This same ideal is also clearly evident, even though not fully achieved, in the aspirations of both the westernized democracies as well as the socialist states. Historically, though, we can see this ongoing tension between the good and the bad guys, between the partners and the dominators. Some cultures have been effective in maintaining a base of humaneness. Others have lost it completely.

As we emerged from tribal groupings and as our communities expanded, we released rogue elements. Many of these rogues went into politics, or religion, or finance. Sometimes they were – and are – constrained by a cultural solidarity or by law that will not tolerate their abuses. Sometimes these rogues win everything. The problem with a large system is that it is bound to contain some rogues. If the system contains some rogues, then we are bound – to a greater or lesser extent – to play their game, if only to defeat them. This, surely, is partly what happened to the financial world: as humanity created more complex societies, we released these darker elements into a system without clear and maintained moral boundaries. To a degree, they dominate the money world.

Even if we did not release rogues, as society became larger and more complex with an ever-increasing number of trades and financial transactions, so a class of trading and money specialists emerged. These were women and men who enjoyed trading, could understand the new complex nature of the larger market and had an instinctive skill with financial arrangements. These were folk who had found a new way of enjoying themselves.

Provided that they remained psychologically attached to the humane morality of their tribal communities or families, there was no problem; they would live their lives of trade and finance with decency. If they disengaged, however, from the spirit of sharing and generosity of the primal family, they too became rogue elements in society. We have on the one side, then, the entrepreneurial merchant travelling the world's markets seeking a fair price and an equitable deal. On the other side, we have the carpetbagger stroking his oily moustache as he seeks to manipulate the situation to his own advantage.

There is also another powerful factor at work here. Whether a culture created rogue or humane financiers, the reality of the money world, of the commercial world, is that people cannot continue to play their enjoyable game if they run out of money. Built into the money game is the necessity always to have some money. If you go broke you cannot play the money game. And if you want to play a bigger and more interesting (or ego-gratifying) money game, you need even more money. Historically, the need to hang on to money and to accumulate was completely new to tribal peoples. In tribal societies status was maintained by giving away. Moreover, in tribal societies relationships and transactions continued whether or not there was formal money. At the very least, there was always something natural – a piece of wood, a stone, clay – to be fashioned into a gift.

In the money world, however, in the world of commerce, it is simply impossible to play if you have no money. This means that the trader must always hold on to money and, whenever possible, increase his stash. This is the direct opposite to the absolute need of tribal leaders to show generosity and sharing, and to keep commodities and valuables flowing evenly around the community. Even if a trader has a naturally generous instinct, she nevertheless must accumulate and hold on to money in order to stay in the game.

Look now at the various elements we have here.

- We have a commercial world where there are bound to be some rogues.
- We have a commercial world where you must always have money to survive.
- We have a commercial world which is disengaged from tribal and family values.

All of this is bound to lead to a set of ideas about money which is completely separate from small community values. At the very least money loses its obvious role as a respected medium of communication and relationship between people. It loses all its charisma as a prestation, as a marker of significant moments. It becomes instead a token in the game of traders and financiers.

Seven – From Relationship to Legal Contract

We can understand that in the days of early money, most of the transactions contained the same ease and familiarity that exist within most everyday family transactions. In many families there is great elasticity about loaning, gifting and repayment. An unreturned loan may easily be forgiven and forgotten. It is in the nature of intimate relationships to recognize that energy flows back and forth between us, and that money is only one aspect of this reciprocating flow.

Once, however, the transactions begin to involve people whom we do not know, the mood can change. Once the transactions involve several people in chains of *commercial* relationship, then any non-payment has serious ramifications and cannot be simply forgiven and forgotten. In a complex society the payment and repayment of money, therefore, becomes a mechanical obligation outside of the warmth of family relationships. In our contemporary world, we know about this only too well.

The non-payment of debt begins with the unopened envelopes, and can end in court and with the loss of our home. In lawless societies it can end with the cruel reprisals of gangsters and organized crime. (If we want to observe the very opposite of tribal attitudes to money, look at the reaction of Mafiosi to unpaid debts.)

This is not a warm family culture. On the other hand it provides a reliable framework for negotiation and contract. This contractual nature of money is good and useful for providing a reliable and predictable basis for people to do business in a complex society. But it also removes the warmth from money as a flowing and easy, a natural, prestation.

This whole business of loans losing their informality and becoming contractual powerfully reinforces any culture whose basic ethos is harsh and competetive. The financial specialists who are also militaristic in their attitude – the open market is a form of war – become heartless in their use of the law to ensure repayment and, if there is no repayment, the legal punishment. There is, in fact, within this whole economic business now the creeping smell of human evil as the law and money are used to victimize and abuse.

Eight – Money Separates from Natural Life

In the previous chapter we covered the organic process by which money emerged in the first place. It happened in thousands of different places all across the earth and is reflected in all the different types of object that became accepted as money. But as societies grew, became complex and a trading class emerged, money became simply a token for exchange and accounting.

As the most important token used in trade, money began to be seen as an *object of value in itself* – money itself is seen as valuable – and, therefore, it no longer possesses a basis in either natural or sacred life. Previously the shell or bead as money was something that emerged out of local natural life and was used between people who knew each other. Objects used as money possessed a certain natural charm or charisma both because of what they actually were and because of their symbolic nature in communicating significance and relationship.

In the new commercial situation, people who trade do not care about the nature or charisma of money. Traders need something which is purely *functional* as a generally agreed unit of value. It is not relevant that the object used as currency is a natural thing, a part of natural life, to which they can relate. It is also not relevant whether these objects are in any way sacred or considered special by their societies. Traders just need something that can be used. Money, therefore, becomes disengaged from nature and from humane relationship. Today in our culture many people find money more important than nature or relationship.

In the primal community, money's only function is to serve as a medium of relationship. In the complex community, money is an important thing in itself. In a primal community, money may have no intrinsic value. In a complex society, money has value simply because it is money and people can make money simply out of trading money.

Nine – The Authoritative Issue of Money

It is obvious, then, that a real problem emerges when a society grows large and complex, one in which there are many thousands of players and daily transactions. People, especially merchants, need general agreements about the nature and quality of money in order to make trading reliable. It is obviously no good if some maverick turns up trading with fake money. Is a one-year-old cow as good as a ten-year-old cow? Are the cowrie shells worth anything, if anyone can just go and pick them off the beach? There is an obvious need for some kind of authority to state clearly what is and what is not money.

Complex societies need central authorities – priest, warrior or monarch – to place their stamp of legitimation upon the objects used as money. And it is only too obvious that there are great opportunities for corruption around the production of currency. Whoever issues currency has real power. A central authority can work towards the common benefit or towards vested interests. Money can be issued in a spirit of service towards the community, or it can be issued to maintain and increase centralized power. The temptation for a government in power, but frightened of losing power, is simply to issue more money and buy off whomever needs to be bought. In crisis a government can produce more currency and pay soldiers to repress the crisis. Equally, a government in crisis can produce more currency and pay more money to social services, thereby lowering the general value of money in the land and informally taxing everyone without permission.

It can be clearly seen, then, that to control the issue of money is a situation of great temptation, leading to gentle corruption or sadistic repression.

The Nine Elements in the Cauldron

We can now put together the various reasons why we have moved away from a humane to a competitive money culture.

First, we are bewitched and hypnotized by the glitter and power of the new economy.

Second, it has all happened so fast that we are in a state of shock.

Third, as population grew and societies became more complex, people from alien cultures met, felt threatened and reacted aggressively. We can write this as an equation:

Primal community = Solidarity and Trust = Sharing and Generosity.

Larger Community = External Threats and Internal Strangers = Anxiety and Accumulation.

Fourth, sharing stopped and accumulation began, triggering a social fragmentation based on possessions rather than who we are as actual people.

Fifth, as societies grew, we could no longer keep a family eye on everyone and unrestrained rogue elements could surface.

Sixth, we created a group of money and trade specialists, separated from the values of their primal communities and creating their own money values.

Seventh, informal and fluid loans and arrangements become legalized and contractualized.

Eighth, as more and more money enters circulation it becomes separated from its association with natural life and relationship.

Ninth, the centralized and authoritative issue of currency can easily become a tool of power political games more interested in domination than community.

These nine elements make for a real cauldron of stewing difficulties and challenges. It is hardly surprising, therefore, that we have a dysfunctional money system. But what is becoming evident is that the essential problem, the foundation of our difficulties, is not in the system itself, is not in money itself, but is in our own very human attitudes and actions.

Wabuwabo and Peace-making

I began this chapter by noting the paradoxes and conflicts in our financial attitudes, and I mentioned that these paradoxes also manifested in our societies generally. Let me end this chapter by focusing on one particular paradox, in which money is a trigger both for warfare and for harmony. There are two contrasting realities, one negative, one beneficent.

The negative reality is that every day we can watch men and women getting into their power clothes – dark and angular – going to work, going on to the battlefield of commerce. It's jungle out there. It's full of cannibals and the sharks are out to get you too.

Nations, too, are at economic war. There are trade wars and embargoes, balance of payment deficits and surpluses. It is economic warfare. This is the very nature of trade, commerce and finance: savage competition.

Indeed, some tribal societies, as they come into contact with alien cultures, move immediately into a form of tribal economic warfare. The Kung people, for example, do not enter into commerce among themselves because they consider the procedure undignified and too likely to stir up bad feelings. They are, however, prepared to trade with other peoples, recognizing them as less than human and opponents in competition. The anthropologist Douglas Oliver also noted, for instance, that native moralists of the Solomon Islands assert that neighbours are friendly and mutually trustful, whereas people from far off are dangerous and unworthy of morally just consideration (Oliver, p.82). Veblen, quoted in *Stone Age Economics*, stated clearly, 'Gain at the cost of other communities, particularly communities at a distance, and more especially such as are felt to be aliens, is not obnoxious to the standards of homebred use and wont.'

Even the Bible has its own ideas about what can be done to strangers. Deuteronomy 23:20: 'Unto a stranger thou mayest lend upon usury; but unto thy brother thou shalt not lend usury.'

And I like very much the word for sharp practice from the Dobu tribe: *wabuwabo*. Wabuwabo is okay for strangers, but not for family.

According to a Marxist analysis most, if not all, war is the result of economic competition or a competition for productive resources. Historically we have certainly seen that this is often the case. In the 1990s, for instance, the western response to Iraqi aggression could be interpreted mainly as a war to protect western resources – oil – rather than an ideological conflict. Great powers are prepared to stick their necks out if economic resources, such as oil, are threatened, but ignore more humane threats. Many other analysts have pointed out the dangerously close ties in all countries between industrial-commercial interests and military interests. Tied together they are known as the *industrial-military* complex, and it is certainly true that the objects of these folk are served by war. They get power and make money out of war.

In general, then, if we are suspicious of money, it is very easy to see this sinister connection between money and aggression, between financial interests and warfare. If we do not have a friendly relationship with money, money can appear to be clearly coupled with greed leading to a conflict that kills.

But there is also a beneficent reality.

Trading, commerce and financial transactions are often the only safe occupation and relationship in otherwise dangerous situations. When strangers meet, if they are interested in trading and exchanging, they can ignore the cultural differences and get on with business which is mutually beneficial.

Imagine two hostile tribes meeting. It is easy to guess the attitudes of the leaders and warrior-hunters. It is also easy to guess the attitudes of those who are interested in trading. The traders want peace and tolerance. They want to make relationships that serve all the parties concerned. Even in wartime, money may flow creatively across borders otherwise cruelly defended in blood.

In these situations of hostility, commerce can be redemptive and peace-making. I appreciate that these traders may be insensitive to some of the realities around them and ignore the ramifications of their trade, but nevertheless something creative is happening. At the very least – even in selfish ignorance or total self-interest – they are getting on with a more humane attitude and relationship than the fear, insecurity and fatal hostility of cruel war.

Money allows total strangers, instead of being alienated and anxious, to come into relationship. From one perspective, therefore, as human society has become larger and more complex, money has been an element saving society from falling into further confusion and savagery. Winston Churchill once said, in relation to the international peace-keeping process, 'Jaw, jaw. Not war, war.' We equally might add, 'Trade, trade.' The French social theorist Claude Lévi-Strauss also focused on this exact issue: 'There is a link, a continuity, between hostile relations and the provision of reciprocal prestations. Exchanges are peacefully resolved wars and wars are the result of unsuccessful transactions' (Lévi-Strauss, p.67).

In this whole contradiction, that money can stimulate both war and peace, we see once again a paradox of our financial lives. We can see also once again that it is not money or commerce as such that is damaging but the context, awareness and the culture of the transactions. I am absolutely clear, for myself, that there is nothing intrinsically negative about the size of the money system, other than that it allows human beings – if they choose – to lose their sense of humanity and responsibility. It is not surprising, given the speed with which its size and complexity have grown, that we should be in a state of dazed shock. The speed with which it has grown has been too fast for us to hold on to our true humane values.

Our problem is a lack of awareness, which is due to our being unable to see the whole beast and have a perspective on it. Indeed, for several centuries the great economic beast seemed to be serving us well, so there was no need for a better perspective. But today, faced with various crises, we need to expand our awareness so that we do not carry on being overwhelmed and bedazzled. A wise understanding, even if admitting past faults, is a necessary step towards wise strategies for the future.

6

FROM TRIBE TO WORLD
ECONOMY

International Political Realities

Money is not, properly speaking, one of the subjects of commerce, but only the instrument which men have agreed upon to facilitate the exchange of one commodity for another. It is none of the wheels of trade; it is the oil which renders the motion of the wheels more smooth and easy. (David Hume)

Apathy, Ignorance and Discomfort

One of our tragedies – not exclusive, I am sure, to our age – is a weariness with politics. It sometimes seems as if a whole generation, perhaps three generations, have turned their back on political engagement. The people who were touched by, or part of, the sixties counter-culture movement seem interested only in the personal dynamics of human potential or in the movements of art, literature and media. The generation after that has been described as ex-yuppies looking for meaning. And the generation after that, Generation X, is surfing into the electronic media revolution interested, it seems, in only one form of politics, that of computer-based communications.

These, of course, are wild generalizations, but when I survey the apathy and ignorance surrounding the interdependence of our world economy, I despair.

We live in, we affect and we are affected by an intimately interdependent world economy.

It is not possible to understand our relationship with money unless we understand its general environment, the history and the structure of the world economy. Not one of us can say we are detached from it. What we are wearing and eating, or driving or watching, makes us part of it. The purpose of this chapter, therefore, is to outline how the world economy became the way it is and how it is structured.

In the last chapter we surveyed the nine factors that contribute to the rawness and inhumanity of contemporary financial behaviour. In the following pages we look at the actual events and the actual political situation which intertwine with the competitive culture. My intention is that, by the end of this chapter, readers with no previous education in history or economics shall have a general understanding of some of the real dynamics running behind and through the world economy. When what happened a thousand miles away was not relevant to us, we could afford ignorance. Today in our contemporary reality we cannot afford that ignorance.

I know only too well how tempting it is to look away from these realities, to forget them and get on with our lives. Earlier in this book I described how I could contemplate a seventh pair of shoes while at the same time looking at the image of a three-year-old slave. I also once interviewed a well-known philosopher who had himself written about money and said that for commerce to be redeemed economics had to possess a new awareness. I talked to him about this and queried how this might actually look in people's personal lives. I asked him directly what such an awareness might look like in his own life. In response, he became defensive and evasive.

I was not trying to provoke him, but I asked if he gave awareness to individual purchases to monitor, for example, whether a carpet might have been woven by enslaved children. At this suggestion he lost his temper, accusing me of trying to introduce a new form of fascism. He himself had been a refugee from Nazi Germany.

'One of my great freedoms,' he exclaimed forcefully, 'is to go shopping! You are suggesting a fascist control of my private life.'

'I am only discussing,' I replied, 'putting economic consciousness into practice.'

'I do not want to think every time I go shopping! This is an infringement of my freedom.'

He became increasingly agitated and I beat a hasty retreat from his house, from a barbed and unpleasant encounter. I felt compassion for his escape from Nazi Germany, but almost fifty years on I was not convinced that his love of free shopping was simply a reaction to totalitarianism. I suspected, I was certain, that consumerism had become an addiction. The emotionality and the irrationality of his reaction, though, was steeped in deep patterns and insecurities.

To one degree or another, most of us wish to ignore the political and social realities of our world economy. We pretend to trust experts or we say that it belongs to a sphere of politics which is beyond us. Or we just stay blinkered in order not to feel emotions we find uncomfortable. This is not mature or fair. Political behaviour begins at home. Responsible, liberated and enjoyable financial behaviour requires that we each of us go through some kind of personal change. In its own small way this will have some knock-on effect, varying in significance, on the interdependent world economy. And because we are bound into this planetary fabric, we need to understand it, to have a basic education.

The interdependence of the world economy is both material and psychological.

Materially, we connect with it at almost every purchase. The food and raw materials we consume come literally from every part of the globe. Changes 10,000 miles away in the cost of labour or commodities can create knock-on effects that may lose us our own jobs, deflate our savings or boost our shareholdings. Equally our own spending habits may decide the future of a rural village or factory whose names we have never heard.

Psychologically, the mass media of our planetary village provide ongoing images of the state and quality of life of our fellows. The Cola-Dallas culture is in everybody's home. At the same time, the images of starvation, death and war are also continually and universally with us. We are stimulated by icons of glamour and plenty. We are also provoked by images of suffering. Psychologically we identify with both the plenty and the scarcity. Our feelings and needs can be profoundly stimulated, and manipulated, by international mass media images. This is happening to all of us, wherever we are. All of this dramatically inflames the whole syndrome of anxiety, identity and relative deprivation which was described in detail in Chapter 2. My sense of relative deprivation led me to steal. Two-thirds of the world's population is bombarded with images that demonstrate not only their deprivation in terms of style, but also their deprivation in terms of substance.

Because of this interdependence, our financial behaviour is *not* a private affair. What we do and what others do influences all of us. There is no insularity.

The History of the World Economy in Two Pages

Although the current economic situation seems very complicated, the general historical pattern is fairly straightforward. There are huge arguments among academics and ideologues about *why* it all happened – what is the driving motor behind the historical process? – but the actual sequence of events is generally agreed and easily understood.

We are already familiar with the origins of money. Objects frequently used for exchange and prestation became generally accepted tokens for exchange. Money began to appear in tribal societies as cattle, beads, etc.

Then, as societies grew bigger and more complex, central authorities, of one kind or another, began to regulate and issue currency. There was the production of the first coinage and the central issue of currency.

A little while later, merchants and traders – separate from government – began to develop their own promissory notes and accounting systems to use among themselves. This was the beginning of the independent banking system.

The political arrangement of territory into nation-states next began to emerge and their governments developed more sophisticated ways of issuing currency, both through wholly owned central banks and through private banks. Independent banks, although dependent upon the central bank for the authoritative issue of currency, flourished.

At the same time that the first nation-states emerged, early capitalism was also developing.

The industrial revolution started getting under way.

As international trade increased, nations began competing and also cooperating. At the same time, the developed states of Europe – particularly Britain, France, Spain, Portugal and Holland – and later the United States and Japan imposed their military dominance, and their political and economic ideas, on the rest of the world. This was the stage of imperialism and colonialism.

Mainly after the two world wars, colonized countries began their independence movements. They freed themselves from external military and political domination, but remained tied into a world economic and political system – a system that was not of their making or choosing.

Two Complications

This history, however, is complicated by two crucial features:

The first is that industrialization and modernization are *still* happening. We are still in the process. Only one-third of the planet's population has been through the industrialization process. The other two-thirds are still waiting to go through it and to become fully active participants. These other two-thirds, although *waiting* for the process and rewards of modernization, are *already* stimulated daily by images of the 'rich' world – a world in which they cannot participate, but which continuously teases them. This leads to immense psychological pressures for economic growth in the developing world and a larger share of the world economic cake. But a larger share of the cake, *if the cake does not grow*, means less for others – which creates other obvious pressures as it threatens the economic well-being of other countries. If the cake does not grow, for instance, the success of Singapore may be to the cost of Germany, and so on.

So there is this huge tension created by the uneven development of the world economy. Some countries are speeding into electronic cyberspace and everyone has cars, telephones and fridges. Others are barely scraping a living producing single commodities, desperately trying to catch up. And in these countries are real people, needing and wanting things. The international system, by its very nature, places nation-states in competition with each other, regardless of humane realities.

The second major feature is the obvious tension and conflict which exists for governments trying to control both their domestic economies and the forces of the international free market. Governments obviously need to control the economic forces that affect their countries, but the open market with international banks, transnational companies and a billion free-playing individuals, has its own life and dynamics. Governments, therefore, attempting to act in the best interests of their people are involved in a perpetual conflict with ever-changing economic forces. The real tension here is that for a government to stay in power, it has to give the appearance of leadership and control. In the rocking ocean of the world economy this is not always possible.

The Nation-state as a Competitive Business

For perspective, it is important to see through the normality of our current way of politically arranging the international world. The very word *international* has within it (*inter-nation*) the idea that the globe is made up of nations and that the global system is made up of relationships between independent nations. Most of us, born in a particular country and possessing a particular nationality, think that this is normal and possibly that this is the way that humanity has always been arranged on the planet.

Look, however, at any country at all, and in the not-so-distant past that area of land was a patchwork of much smaller groupings. Even the old established states such as France or Britain still have internal tensions as minority nationalities, such as the Welsh or the Bretons, seek their own independence. The vast majority of countries that we know did not come into being until the nineteenth century and the vast majority of developing countries did not achieve their current political form until after the various post Second World War independence movements achieved success.

The nation-state as we know it, therefore, is a recent phenomenon and it was created out of the hard-nosed realities of power politics – the power politics of vested interests, high passion, economic conflict and warfare. This *realpolitik* brought nation-states into being and may yet create a different way of arranging peoples. At the time of writing, for example, in the 1990s eastern Europe is redrawing its map, often with blood.

Along with the assumption that nation-states are good and natural things – the German philosopher Hegel thought them the highest and most spiritual way of organizing humans – there is also a second assumption that it is normal for a state to be in competition with all the other states. This is the way to control its own wealth. It is normal, therefore, for there to be international economic competition. The state is thus understood to be a large financial organization which, like any other business, competes in a hostile environment and has to achieve financial growth in order to survive effectively.

If we accept the idea that the nation-state must be a competitive economic creature, then, supported by ideas of nationalism and patriotism, the whole world is turned into a 'them and us' scenario. Indeed we live within this 'accepted' reality, don't we, that the normal and *only* way to arrange the world is as economically competitive nation-states. Accepting this perception of reality, it is only common sense that there will be winners and losers. Indeed it is considered totally normal for there to be winners and losers. The countries that are doing well financially know how to compete well. The countries that are doing badly need to learn how to compete better.

This acceptance of international competition has no appreciation of either historical or contemporary reality.

Imperialism and Continuing Dependence

As a matter of historical fact, most states have tended towards aggression rather than cooperation. The history of international relations is one of warfare and conflict. The nation-state, however, is a western European invention – beginning with England, Holland and France in medieval times (barely six centuries ago) – and it was exported through imperial force to the rest of the world.

There are several interesting theories about what it was that drove the Europeans to explore and dominate the rest of the world. One theory states that the white peoples moved to find religious and political freedom. Another states that it was the natural expansion of strong and militaristic states. A third suggests that God or the World Spirit destined European civilization to expand across the globe bringing its blessings to other peoples. And a fourth theory is that European money, with no room to expand within Europe, reached beyond its shores to seek and create new markets.

Whichever of these theories is true, western Europeans – and then Americans and the Japanese – moved beyond their shores to enter and control foreign territories and peoples, at worst with genocidal cruelty and at best with patronizing manipulation. Sometimes merchants or missionaries preceded the soldiers, but the end result was always a mixture of military dominance and commercial exploitation. The imperialists found raw and useful resources, from slaves to palm oil to gold. With no sense of fair exchange, with no sense of barter, with no sense of humane relationship; with racism, with arrogance, with stupidity, with cruelty, with greed; the imperialists took what they wanted.

These non-European peoples were invaded, over-run and colonized by people from industrialized nations with a more sophisticated technology and more deadly weapons. Without negotiation or choice, their resources, including slaves, were appropriated and exported to sustain and enhance industrial and capital growth back in the mother countries.

In return the imperialists introduced the political and economic ways of the West. All over the world, no matter how people were grouped and arranged – in small tribes or scattered empires – they were forced into the western idea of how the political and economic world should be. The great arrogance of the imperialists – and of many of us still today – is that any arrangement other than a proper country, a proper nation-state, is thought primitive simply because it does not resemble what we are accustomed to.

For decades or centuries peoples were forced to surrender to western culture and western organizational models. When finally they managed to liberate themselves from their invaders, they were not and never could be the same as they had been. Whereas before there had been many tribal groupings or nationalities in a particular territory, the straight lines drawn on the maps created new and unnatural nations. Look at any map and where you can see a border with a dead straight line you can see the result of an invasive imperial history. The reality is that these states were once a kaleidoscope of clans and tribes across vast continents, but the Europeans and Americans and Japanese came and forced a new way of life upon them.

I once heard the African academic Ali Mazrui talking about this situation. He reminded his audience of George Orwell's despairing futuristic novel about fascism and thought control, *1984*. The people of Africa, Mazrui reminded us, did not have to wait until 1984 to experience that form of totalitarianism. They had already experienced it 100 years earlier in 1884 when, at the Conference of Berlin, the European powers divided Africa among themselves – drawing straight lines on maps, ignoring natural and human ecology.

After the Second World War when the European powers no longer had the will or power to hang on to their colonies, when the independence movements were at last gaining full momentum, most states of Africa and Asia gained their independence. They achieved the status of *state sovereignty*, each country with its own government and its own state apparatus. But beneath the appearance of political independence was another economic reality. If these states wanted to join in the game of the international economy, then they had no choice but to play by the already established rules.

So, having finally achieved liberation, what these new states could not be free of was the modern world political and economic system.

In the modernized world we usually behave as if all the nation-states of the developing world *voluntarily and eagerly* opted into the international economic system. We assume that, once within it, these new states warmly embraced the rules and worldview of the West, of the necessity of economic growth. In reality, they had no choice.

At a stroke, these newly liberated nations entered the world as apparently fully-fledged states with governments, rights under international law, embassies, seats in the United Nations and all the other trimmings that go with statehood. Whether they liked it or not, whether it was useful for them or not, they were thrown into the world as apparently complete and mature countries. But, in fact, they never had the time or opportunity to go through a normal self-created and organic process of modernization.

These continents were invaded, dominated, divided and then liberated.

Structural Violence, Frogs' Legs and Peanuts

Just because the countries of the third world were suddenly declared independent did not change the basic economic relationships. If the European country had over many years developed cotton or sugar or coffee, to the exclusion of all other crops or a more balanced production, then that was what the developing nation had to continue to produce. By and large, continent by continent, newly liberated developing countries were economically tied to the strings of their imperial masters. No longer overt colonialism, this new situation was named neo-colonialism or dependency economics.

In order to go through the industrialization and modernization process, these countries also required the skills, expertise and technologies of their past masters. People may remember how, during the period of the Cold War, these developing countries became pawns in the game between the United States and the Soviet Union, as the superpowers offered or compelled alliance.

Economically, these countries were then uncomfortably dependent upon their ex-masters. Their economies were young and frail. Their industries and commercial sections had not been allowed to develop in ways that were natural or appropriate, but had all been geared to supplying their colonial masters with what the home countries and metropolitan cities needed. The reality is that even if they did not adopt the worldview, the internal and external pressures to modernize forced these new countries into relationship with the developed world, into relationships that needed access to cash, cash which only came with the sting of interest in its tail.

As a result, the world economy is certainly made up of some 170 nation-states which, in the theoretical eyes of international law and in our thoughtless assumptions, are decreed 'equal'. But this is not the actual reality. Some forty countries have passed through the classical stage of what the economic historian Rostov called 'economic take-off' into the full status of industrialization and the other 130 are scrambling. Most of these 130 are economic midgets dancing to the tune of the forty powerful giants and the tune of a few mighty transnational organizations. Within their borders they live with the tensions of populations reacting to international images of what a decent lifestyle looks like. Beyond their borders they live in subservient tension with their past masters and other dominant commercial forces.

For any organization or country to develop successfully it must be able to reinvest profits. The money that finances developing countries' economies, though, comes from external sources, from banks and corporations in London, Zurich, New York and Tokyo. One of the most crucial foundations of the developed world is that profits from industry and commerce are ploughed back into the companies and peoples that produce them. In the developing world, however, most of the finance and investment comes from the past masters' countries and any profits are returned to these countries instead of being ploughed back where they are made. In this kind of a situation how can there be growth? The international debt problem, in which the developing world is paying more in interest payments than it actually generates, is a scandalous and well-known farce. Profits go to the metropolitan centres and not back into the developing economies.

The developing economies, so dependent upon these external links, make many economic and manufacturing decisions that are distinctly damaging to the local economy, but bring short-term benefits that meet only the needs of the dominant partners.

This lopsided abuse of economic power would be laughable if it were not so tragic. At the time of writing, in the 1990s, the last decade has seen the general economic condition of the developing countries deteriorate terribly. This neo-colonialism and financial bullying is not necessarily a deliberate policy perpetrated by cunning and sinister merchants. It is built into the system and is what the Norwegian social theorist Johan Galtung so correctly named 'structural violence'; it is unavoidable given the actual structure of the system. There is an ironic story which demonstrates this well:

An Indian merchant, farmer and entrepreneur heard that there was a shortage of frogs in France to supply the French delicacy of frogs' legs. There were many frogs in his area and he employed men and women to crop them. This was a small but lucrative business, bringing employment and cash to local people. The disappearance of the frogs, however, upset the local ecological balance and the insects that were normally eaten by the frogs got out of control. The entrepreneur realized that local farmers now needed insecticide and he imported a very effective brand from abroad, again making a small but useful profit for himself. The insecticide polluted the local area, creating even more problems.

At each stage of this process, his decisions were absolutely logical for an intelligent entrepreneur. As is obvious, apart from some temporary local employment, the results were locally disastrous. The French did all right for frogs' legs. The insecticide manufacturer in Hong Kong did all right. The entrepreneur made some cash. But the local economy was devastated.

These kinds of 'sensible' decisions are being made all the time. For a deal that appears to make sense, local needs are being screwed. This happens small-scale and large-scale. Travelling in the Gambia in 1993 I saw the one national industry, the peanut factory, lying abandoned and idle because the needs of the external market had changed. Whatever some hard-headed free marketeer might say about the Gambia's need to become realistic in the modern world, the reality is that the international system has raped the Gambia. A peaceful and civilized African people were invaded, suppressed and enslaved. They were then given freedom and became victims of the world economy.

The international economy, then, is not simply a group of 170 equals. There are giants and there are vulnerable infants. The irony is that, in the main, these vulnerable economic infants were created by the giants who then threw them defenceless into the harsh global environment. They have all the trappings of independent statehood and we thus refuse to recognize, or we deny, their vulnerability, for which we in the developed world are in the first place responsible. There is a similarity here to the mindless patriarchal culture which might pat a five-year-old on his bottom while sending him off to boarding school saying, 'Behave like a man!' The brave five-year-old represses his whimper. The developing nations also have their pride.

And yet in the midst of all this, in every city of the developing world, there are creative and innovative individuals enjoying the challenges and satisfactions of entrepreneurship. In the West we too had our terrible social problems, slums and infant mortality, while industrialization was unfolding. The clock cannot be turned back. Halting modernization is not possible. Changing our awareness and our strategies, making the process and the transactions more humane, is, however, possible.

Transnational Corporations

Domestically and internationally, most of us are aware of the extraordinary clout which some businesses possess.

Domestically, all businesses are governed by national laws. These laws, in one way or another, legislate economic behaviour so that it runs in an ordered manner and not to the detriment of society in general. On the international scene, however, there is no overarching international government or international legal system to enforce economic regulations. On the world scene, companies are free to do what they like, with no laws to constrain their behaviour.

Transnational corporations, within territorial borders, are bound, like any other organization, by domestic laws. Internationally, however, they can shift and transfer currencies, commodities and futures without let or hindrance. Also, their economic power is so immense that developing countries can simply function like minor departments of these international corporations, subject to their transnational bosses' will. Countries which, for example, are dependent upon one or just a few cash crops are prisoners of transnational corporations.

The standard argument of the developed world bankers, politicians and business people is that the developing countries are going to have to toughen up and become realistic competitors. But this, as I have already suggested, is like sending a baby into the ring with Hulk Hogan. The rattle meets the tank.

The developed states and the transnational banks and corporations treat the developing countries as 'equals', blithely and bullyingly ignoring the inequality of the situation.

You might expect international institutions, such as the World Bank or International Monetary Fund, to have a more mature and holistic attitude, but they do not. These two bodies also apply the same stringent and competitive rules to the developing world with little consideration given either to the history or the vulnerability. Whatever loans these bodies make to developing countries, the repayment of both the capital and the interest is

crippling. As with our private house mortgages, many developing nations are repaying more in interest than the original loan
and this is draining them of any capital that they could use for
their own internal investment and development.

The multinational companies, of course, are simply led by the
profit motive and their financial decision-making is unable to
take into account real local needs or long-term effects. Large
companies have to deliver dividends and profits to their owners
and shareholders. The only industry in an African country –
such as the peanut factory in the Gambia – can be allowed to
collapse by a transnational corporation, but the corporation's
accounting books will show only figures. Shareholders only look
at the bottom line and their dividend.

My description of this economic situation may appear over-
simplified, but over and over again the books and articles of
developmental economists describe this structural bias. The
strong benefit. The weak lose more.

Mindset and Expectations

Why oh why, you might ask, do the leaders and decision-
makers in the developing world accept this state of affairs? Isn't
there a way that they can opt out?

There is first of all the reality of an economic dependence that
simply does not allow room for manoeuvre. Those few countries
who did adopt a more socialist and independent approach were
sooner or later confronted with the reality that people require
freedom from centralized economic control – and that these free
people are attracted to where the money is, which is in the
developed world. States that tried to maintain central control,
independent of the world economy, either changed into more
capitalist systems, collapsed or had to develop greater military
and police control of their people. Central control, free of the
international economy, is not viable.

There is also the psychological reality that the élites and
decision-makers of the developing world are all, more or less,

educated mainly in the West and know no economic culture other than that of the modern world economy. They know only the rules of simple growth, profit and loss.

I particularly remember my graduate students at the London School of Economics who came from all over the world. Before teaching them I was looking forward to the challenge of the seminars and the multicultural mix, but in the event I was disturbed by the cultural similarity of them all. By the time they had become graduates they were all of the same mould, just doing whatever they needed to acquire the right credentials to go into their foreign offices or international merchant banks or law firms or multi-nationals. Once they had been through the western university system, these young men and women from Niger or Thailand now had more in common with their fellows from France and Japan than with their own nationals. Like the Indian entrepreneur who made logical decisions about frogs' legs, all these graduates would make equally logical decisions based on their international mindset.

The decision-makers of the developing world, therefore, tend to play the political, social and economic game according to the guidelines created by the developed nations. These folk make up an *international* group for whom nationality is not a determining characteristic. Despite movements such as *négritude* or *black is beautiful*, African businessmen and politicians are more in tune with their international counterparts than with their compatriots still living in subsistence conditions out in the bush. To be very basic, it is psychologically comfortable to be associated with the powerful international middle class, rather than with their local poor folk.

This international class of bankers, business people, civil servants and politicians accept without questioning the way in which national and international economies are currently organized. It suits them. They make their decisions according to its culture.

The Living Contradictions

In the autumn of 1993 I went with my wife, Sabrina, to the tiny West African country of the Gambia, which lies on the coast between the Tropic of Cancer and the Equator. It is a snake-shaped land, running a few miles either side of the river Gambia which runs 500 miles into central Africa. Here we experienced a strange daily ritual which summed up for me in one situation all the powers and paradoxes of money and the changing world economy.

On its Atlantic coast, the Gambia has beautiful beaches and a warm, soft ocean, which attracts European tourists from the north. Two hours' boat-ride up-river from its capital city of Banjul is the small island of Jamestown. On this island are two dungeons where male and female slaves were held separately captive before being shipped across the Atlantic to the New World of America. On the north side of the river, a mile from this slave compound, is the village of Juffure. This village is made up of shacks and compounds of mud, straw and corrugated iron. It is the home of an international media star who, every day of the year, is visited by groups of tourists. This star featured as a central figure in one of the great literary and media successes of the twentieth century, Alex Haley's *Roots*.

Roots was Haley's story of how he, as a black American, sought to uncover his own historical roots and his identity. Piecing together many bits of a linguistic and geographical jigsaw, he finally traced the village from which his ancestor had been captured and brought to America as a slave. The name of this ancestor was Kunta Kinteh; and Binta Kinteh, a seventy-year-old woman and the last of the Kinteh line, still lives in the village of Juffure.

Tourists visit her and she allows them to take photographs of her, sometimes sitting with one of them. She is a dignified creature, watchful.

At one point Sabrina's eyes met those of Binta Kinteh and they remained looking at each other, with some recognition, for a long ten seconds. Later I asked Sabrina what she had seen in Binta Kinteh's eyes. 'I saw a woman who had seen it all,' she replied. 'A witch with goodwill. No surprises. She understood what was happening around her.'

I could believe this, for every day she experienced this strange circus. The tourists came to the Gambia mainly to escape the European cold and damp, to get a tan and only partly to experience the 'real' Gambia. They flew thousands of miles on holidays that cost what a lucky Gambian might earn in a whole year. The tourists at home had their problems with mortgages, bills, taxes and job security, but here in the Gambia their immediate disposable income was fantastic compared to the dismal earnings in the local economy.

Every day a group of red tourists arrived at Juffure to visit this media star. Having taken photographs, they were then free to give some money. Some of the sums given were meagre; others very generous. All through the village, the visiting Europeans were surrounded by children and young men, asking for sweets, asking for money. One young man, for instance, wanted me to help support his fees as a medical student. He even showed me his compound door which had 'DOCTOR' written on it. I believed him at first, but then it became obvious he was telling a story.

In this one small area was modern madness: disposable income flirting with abject poverty, stories of all kinds being told, confused and hassled tourists, confused and compulsive young people begging with outstretched hands or big eyes or impossible stories.

There was also possibly another great illusion, for Alex Haley had been frequently attacked for having invented the whole of *Roots*'s history. The man, for instance, who had finally confirmed the truth of Haley's research was, in fact, a well-known local playboy and hustler; he might have said anything for a dollar or just to please his visitor. So! Juffure might not, in fact, have been the real village and Binta Kinteh might not have been the real last descendant of the ancestor. If this were the case, then all these tourists were photographing and visiting a complete illusion. Perhaps a different woman played Binta Kinteh every day.

In my pocket, when I visited the village, were notes worth a hundred dollars or so. Here, in the Gambia, this was a fortune. Back home, this amount was what someone on government benefit might receive for a week's support. Or it might be one elegant meal.

Here in this small village, a few miles from what had been a slave centre, were all the powerful paradoxes of the modern economy. Rich people who did not think they were rich. Hollywood images reaching rich and poor alike. Poor folk who saw tourists as walking money, not human beings. Tourists who saw natives as images for their cameras, not people. Tour operators who saw a chance for profit. A government attracting foreign currency.

Yet in the midst of it all were also real people, bemused, amused and touched by the whole strange environment.

Our whole world contains similar confusions and paradoxes created by the uneven evolution of money and economies. Seen at a distance, there is something amusing and exciting about this strange kaleidoscope. Seen more closely, it contains confusion and tragedy.

7

DOMESTIC POLITICAL
ILLUSIONS

Above all things, good policy is to be used that the treasures and monies in a state not be gathered in to few hands. For otherwise a state may have a great stock, and yet starve. And money is like muck, not good except it be spread. (Francis Bacon)

> *Midas, they say, possessed the art of old*
> *Of turning whatsoe'er he touch'd to gold;*
> *This modern statesmen can reverse with ease –*
> *Touch them with gold, they'll turn to what you please.*
>
> (John Wolcot)

Flickering Shadows

This is a hotch-potch of a chapter, in which I need to rant at some of the dynamics running through our domestic economies. We need to see through some major illusions which, at the moment, have great influence. Many readers will be familiar with Plato's description of humanity caught in a cave, frightened by shadows which we take to be real but which are just flickers of another more solid dimension. The particular flickering and bewitching shadows of this chapter are economic growth, the wisdom of our leaders, and the value and issue of money in our pockets. Because they are so much an established part of our environment we take them thoughtlessly for granted and they prevent us from taking a more responsible and confident stance towards personal and political economy.

Stability is Impossible

Most of us reading this book enjoy the economic cake of the modernized world. There are many basic things which we take for granted: a comfortable roof over our heads, running water on tap, power at the flick of a switch, interesting food, clean clothes, the freedom to travel, access to education, telecommunications and so on. We take these for granted, but for two-thirds of our fellow humans all these things are still a hope and a dream. And it is an inevitable dynamic that these two-thirds aspire to the basic living standards which the rest of their fellows have reached. The dynamic, therefore, to modernize cannot be turned back. To reverse the process is practically and psychologically impossible.

Our general expectation is that decade by decade the developing countries and their peoples will come to enjoy and share the economic cake. In the decade in which I write, we can clearly see this happening, for example, in Singapore, Taiwan and China. But for everyone to participate in and enjoy the modernized world economy, the economic cake must grow. If it does not grow but more people eat from it, then everyone's share will get smaller. This is obvious, isn't it? It is the economics of a children's birthday party. There is only so much cake to go around. If more kids turn up, we need to bake a bigger cake. Smaller slices is also a possibility, but then some of the kids will start crying and it will not be an enjoyable party. Providing the resources and technology can handle it, then a bigger cake is more fun for all of us.

But the world economy is not as simple as a birthday cake. It contains a billion interacting factors. One thing is certain, therefore, which is that the world economy may not grow fast enough to accommodate all the new people seeking to share in it. At other times it may grow fast enough. This means something very simple: there are bound to be cycles of growth and recession. They are unavoidable as the peoples of this planet move to share economic wealth.

On a global scale, this general dance between the rate of growth of the economy and the demands of people seeking access to it must lead to periods of depression in certain regions and growth in others, sometimes global depression and sometimes global growth. The nature of this complex and organic beast is such that *an expectation of steady-state growth or a predictable pattern is naïve and unintelligent.* Playing to an audience of shareholders seeking short-term profit, business people might try to pretend that the system is fully understood and under control. Playing to an audience which will elect them, politicians will also pretend to be in control. Playing to an audience that pays their salaries and gives them prestige, economists may rehearse with scientific certainty. But these men and women are simply refusing to see the world as it actually is.

Good sailors do not pretend that the ocean is predictable. Good drivers drive in a state of anticipating the unexpected. To recognize complex unpredictability is not a recipe for anxiety. It is wisdom. People who pretend that the unsafe is safe are neurotic. People who understand and accept reality have a wise attitude and access to more useful and interesting strategies.

Economic planning, therefore, must include the expectation of unpredictable cycles of growth and recession. This is crucial for politicians, business people and ordinary folk managing their personal finances. Total stability is not possible and it is psychologically naïve to aim for stability. Worse still, raising false hopes that stability is possible ensures anxiety when inevitably there is a downturn.

It will only be when the mass human population *feels* satisfied that economic stability will be possible. Long-term care and wisdom could make this possible. Part of this wisdom is truthful communication.

The Marriage of Government and Commerce

It is, it seems, self-evident that a powerful and independent state needs a thriving economy. Minimally one crude reality is that arms and weapons, the means of self-defence, require wealth. But it is not military or political men who create wealth. The reality is that individuals – physical labourers, business people, financiers, merchants and manufacturers, consumers – build and create the economy. A government may want to be wealthy, but that wealth is dependent upon the people who actually create wealth. To put it obviously, if the commercial folk do not create successfully, then a state will not have the wealth to achieve its own goals. Governments are, therefore, economically dependent upon a successful commercial sector.

To survive, governments must adapt to and support the needs of the commercial sector. And, because commerce requires a stable environment commerce itself will support state and government. There is, therefore, an ongoing historical dance between government and the people of commerce. This dance may be very intimate. It is possible to argue, for example, that countries such as the United States were actually governed from the very beginning by political representatives of the specialist commercial class. 'The business of America is business.'

Look beneath surface appearances, suggested Karl Marx, and you will see, in fact, that all governments and states are actually creations of the commercial sector. According to this extreme view, nation-states – all our countries – are simply pragmatic arrangements which suit financiers and merchants. It is a way of creating stability for business. Whether this is true or not, there is a reality here about which we need to be vigilant.

States and governments need money and must, therefore, support wealth generation. There is, however, the potential for evil and stupidity when governments confuse their need for wealth with their general responsibility to the common good. There is a strange haze that comes over the mentality of some governments as they begin to see and gauge their policies purely in terms of economy, cash and wealth. These governments have been hypnotized into knowing no culture other than the commercial and they create long-term domestic distress, fragmenting national community. They are, at best, prisoners of a limited mindset and, at worst, corrupt.

The Culture of Economic Leadership

I keep writing about governments, companies and organizations as entities in themselves. Look more closely, however, and there are of course human beings – human beings with certain motivations, fears and desires – no different from any of us. But are they perhaps different from most of us? I want to make some sweeping generalizations about the psychological make-up and mindset of the people who inhabit the higher echelons of government, business and international financial organizations. As the devil's advocate I am going to paint a caricature.

For a start, these folk are not tribal big men or big women, happy to support communities at their generous distributive breasts. The most successful of them are not distinguished by the poverty of their homes or because they give everything away.

They belong to that slice of the middle class which is 'élite' or at least aspiring to be élite. This élite is caught in the Darwinian notion that everything is a process of growth and evolution through survival of the fittest. They possess a continuous expectation that their responsibilities and salaries will always evolve and grow. The world is a jungle in which the élite succeeds.

They are carefully educated and carefully trained. If they go into banking or multinationals they are carefully taken through a system of education that makes certain they understand the real needs. Linda Davies, who finally dropped out of international banking, described her own merchant bank training in brutal detail:

The training programme was a war of attrition ... 36-hour working stints, exams every fortnight (fail one and you're fired), the removal of all individual characteristics and the pasting-on of a veneer of high seriousness. I was to learn from the training programme not just the mechanics of corporate finance, but how to look, act and survive in the financial world ... Ultimately a useful tool for the City armoury, these were agonizing exercises designed almost to break our spirit and remould us as committed banker clones, motivated by fear. First, we were given four days' work to complete in two . . . I survived and gained confidence. I was extravagantly rewarded, while the unsuccessful were banished with no references and no payoff . . . My introduction to the brutality of the merchant banking world forged feelings of panic, despair and exhausted resignation . . .

The obsessive pursuit of money was boiled down to vicious concentration on the trading floor. It was a bleak 30,000 sq ft battery-farm landscape of grey desks and carpets lit by artificial light and the sickly green pall of the trading screens, and enlivened by the shouts, screams and stomping of the traders. The atmosphere was so aggressively macho that you could practically feel the testosterone pumping around. This was the land of the 'Big Swinging Dick', the self-congratulatory men immortalized by Wall Street legend. The lexicon is overwhelmingly male and sexual: when I started as a salesperson I was told by my new boss that he wanted me 'on the floor immediately' so he could start 'beating up on me'. Clients are 'stuffed' and 'screwed', a good deal is 'the dog's bollocks'. (*Sunday Times Magazine*, 4 July 1993)

This poor woman, although able to manage successfully this macho culture, resigned for more civilized climates. Her story may seem more brutal than an average university economics or business education, but unless you study within a radical department, the commercial worldview and mindset are similar.

At the apex of the great companies and banks are grey-haired distinguished men and women, guiding their great ships of finance through the storms of a dangerous world. These patriarchs have immense experience. They have seen governments come and go, empires rise and fall, countries collapse and disperse, new nations arise. They have experience and wisdom . . . This, of course, is all rubbish. They are not wise. But they get away with it – partly because they want to and partly because we want them to. We need an appearance of wise stability in a world we do not fully understand.

The reality is that all these people are trained solely within the framework of a western economic understanding of the world and they accept the national and international economic situation because in a very *personal* way, it serves them to do so. The way it is gives them status and kudos. Their psychologies have a great deal invested in their cultures. Their identities could be severely threatened by another perspective.

This culture is self-perpetuating. Dedicated hard workers do not have the time to be with any people except those who are relevant to work and business. To succeed there is little choice. For all their lives, the only people who guide their attitudes and actions will be their colleagues. There is also a harsh atmosphere in this culture which many other people may find unpleasant. The tension and speed of financial transaction, the aggression and strategies of selling and competition, are not behavioural forms that we all enjoy. In fact, many of us may be intimidated by it. The dominant warrior mode lives on in this aggressive economic behaviour.

And then we have the politicians. How many seek to serve with wisdom, rather than manipulate or dominate with psychologically reassuring ideology? I have watched with fascination the kind of people who became politicians. Whether of the left or the right, whether introvert or extrovert, whether self-seeking or seeking to serve, they are always people with a thick skin who enjoy, even look for, argument.

The world economy, then, is organized and run by all these people. There are no wise beings who fully understand what is happening. There are a few financiers like George Soros who understand the swings and moods of the market, but this canniness is rarely transformed into a leadership of wisdom. All across the globe there is this international culture which transcends nationality, race and religion. The clothes and the ideas are the same in the banks, multinational organizations and foreign offices of all the continents.

My ranting is, of course, extreme and biased, but if we stop to ask the big macro-economic questions: Why and how did the massive debt crisis build up? Why are poor countries becoming poorer? Why are some countries subject to hyper-inflation? Why can transnational corporations do what they like or why can George Soros make a billion dollars to the cost of our local currency? – then the answer lies in the fact that all the managers and decision-makers share the same mindset about progress and economics.

This is not healthy.

Argument, mental conflict, informed debate and rigorous questioning are healthy.

Unless, for one reason or another, we are concerned activists or have deliberately sought a more well-rounded economic education, then we are innocent and we trust the experts. We trust and believe in them so much that when economies go wrong, we assume that no one listened to them. The reality is that they have been listened to and it has either made no difference or has been actively damaging. For example, in 1993 the *deregulated* British economy, the *regulated* French economy and the *over-regulated* Italian economy all possessed the same rate of unemployment.

What appears to be considered economic planning is usually no more than a particular political ideology confronting the reality of commercial interests and the ever-changing world economy.

Governments and the Issue of Currency

We also need to get some perspective on how money itself is produced. In Chapter 4, on the anthropological background, I wrote that two of the origins of money were the objects habitually given for spiritual and political purposes. These kinds of prestation were made, for example, to pay 'fines' or as sacrifices to the spiritual world. The chiefs or holy people who received these customary gifts were also the people who had the authority to pronounce on what was, or was not, acceptable as a customary or habitual gift. These same people – priests and chiefs – were the same people, as tribal societies became wider and more complex, who later on pronounced on what was or was not acceptable as money. Indeed, one of the roles of contemporary government is to ensure the stability and predictability of whatever is deemed to be money.

In primal or small tribal communities this role of monetary management is always done to the benefit of the tribe as a whole and not for particular personal interests. But in a larger and more complex society, the humane mode can give way to the competitive and selfish mode. In an ideal world, the production of money and issue of currency are acts of public service. But the realities and tensions of power politics and human selfishness are obvious.

In order to stay in power, governments need wealth and this creates a tension between altruistic service to their people and political manipulation. Three thousand years on from the first issue of coinage, we still see the same tensions. Ideally, governments, in their wisdom, issue the appropriate amount of currency to facilitate the smooth flow of trade, innovation and wealth creation. More cynically, however, governments massage the amount of new currency in order to achieve their own political goals.

Because it serves everyone to have a generally accepted currency, societies in general accept the money that their governments give them. It is enough that the government states that a coin or note is worth a particular amount. The British twenty-pound note has written on it, 'I promise to pay the bearer on demand the sum of Twenty Pounds' and is then signed by the Chief Cashier of the Bank of England. American dollar bills simply state, 'This note is legal tender for all debts, public and private.' We need the money, so we accept the promises and affirmations on the banknotes. This acceptance is an informal social contract among all of us.

In situations of social instability and threat, however, there can be severe doubt about the actual value of money, no matter what a government states is its value.

From the beginnings of centrally issued money, therefore, there have been attempts to have money made out of something of 'real' value, like gold or silver. Gold and silver coins, though, were never completely stable because they could be debased, by adding other less precious metals, or having their edges shaved off, thereby producing a lighter coin. A further problem is that if there is an overproduction of the metal, the metal itself loses value because there is too much of it; as a result the money loses value, which is economically and socially destabilizing.

I mention all this because there has always been a strong movement to link the value of money with some object of real value. For many years of the twentieth century the various currencies of the the international financial system were valued against the dollar or pound, which were in turn valued against gold. But the gold standard was finally ditched for not providing a suitable basis for an expanding and fluid world economy.

There are also other contemporary ideas, mainly from green thinkers, about linking money to a bundle of meaningful commodities, such as wheat, rice and copper. These attempts to link money to something materially substantial all seem to make sense, but when we appreciate that money in fact provides opportunity, communication and relationship, then tying it down to a material value no longer applies. It is unrealistic to link the value of money with material objects of value, because the true value of money is in the relationships and opportunities which it provides. In the modern world of information technology and information wealth, this is becoming increasingly evident.

Not linked to a particular commodity such as gold, money is then only worth what the government says it is worth and what people generally accept it to be worth. In times of social and economic unrest, this can have dire results, as people's insecurity and panic becomes externalized into the economic system and money moves into an uncontrollable spiral of inflation. In rampant inflation, people are basically saying: 'We don't believe the money is worth what it says it is – so give me more of it!' Then, given more, they repeat the same disbelief. And so it goes on. The government keeps printing more money because that is what the people want and the government, to stay in power, has to deliver what its people want. Inflation is not the result of bad economic management – too much push or pull. Inflation is the result of people not trusting their governments. No inflation would mean that people had full trust.

We need reliable money, so we allow central bodies to issue authoritative currency. We also need the amount of money in circulation to reflect the current level of wealth creation in our societies. If there is not enough money, it will dampen down creativity. If there is too much, it will inflate the monetary value of what is actually happening. There is a very difficult and complex balance here, which is obviously always changing as societies go around the swings and roundabouts of cycles of growth. It is impossible consistently to provide a level of money that accurately reflects the level of wealth creation. Wise governmental steering is possible, but so is short-term opportunism. Policies which create more money in circulation, for example, raise house prices. This feels temporarily good for the homeowners and may match a political ideology that applauds more private ownership, but in the long term, as it is experienced that the increased money is not equalled by actual increased wealth, the bubble deflates – to everyone's real cost.

National Currency and the Problem of Interest

Because the economic cake is changing size and more people want a taste of it, because the very nature of politics is change, and because of variations between specific regional conditions, there are bound to be continuing fluctuations in the value of currencies. These changing values directly reflect, region by region and country by country, the local state of play in relation to the international game. This natural mobility and flexibility was well symbolized when in the 1980s the system that linked some European currencies was called the European 'snake'.

Domestically, however, governments have a problem because it always seems necessary to have a strong currency. One of the most fundamental symbols of national integrity is national currency. Every state has its coins and notes carrying images of significant national icons. The value of domestic currency, being such a potent and misunderstood national symbol, easily becomes a political football as politicians compete with each other to appear the most robust and nationalistic in relation to currency. When the lira or dollar drops in value, it can be perceived as a lowering of national prestige which in turn adversely affects the authority of the government of the day. Political fighting over national symbols may then take over from sensible and fluidly responsive economic management. Not understanding either the domestic or the international economy, not understanding its natural dance and flux, it *seems* good that the currency be strong and powerful.

But there is another serious problem about the way in which currency is handled and that is the way it actually demands economic growth. This happens because the issue of money includes interest; it includes repayment with a percentage interest.

I find that I am hesitant to write assertively about this issue because it seems to be totally ignored by mainstream economics. It does, however, seem to be blatantly obvious. Most of our contemporary new money is issued by banks or state institutions by means of loans or investments which require repayment with interest. Instead of money being issued as a pure service to facilitate communication, creativity and trade, it has a sting in its tail.

This sting is simple. For $100 that is issued, let us say that $110 needs to be repaid, because there is an interest rate of 10 per cent built into the loan. But where will this extra $10 come from?

If we were setting up this system from absolute scratch, there would simply not be another $10. The government or central bank would itself therefore have to issue that extra $10, just so that the original interest could be repaid. What this means in effect is that the money being issued does not simply go into facilitating human affairs, but has built into it a demand for more money than was issued in the first place. And that extra $10 also carries a 10 per cent charge, which has to be paid . . . and so on.

What this means is that the actual issue of money is done in such a way that it compels growth. In a system with compound interest as a built-in dynamic there is no space to slow down or readjust. The system compels itself in a way that is unmanageable. Any of us who have mortgages understand this. We may borrow $100,000 but over twenty-five years we end up paying nearer $300,000. This compels us into certain expectations and attitudes. At the very least, it means we have to earn that extra $200,000. Napoleon, on first being shown an interest table, said: 'The deadly facts herein revealed lead me to wonder that this monster, *interest*, has not devoured the whole human race. It would have done so long ago if bankruptcy and revolutions had not acted as counter poisons.'

The unjust use of interest has long been recognized but mainly in commercial dealings. Islamic law actually forbids interest completely and is the basis of Islamic banking. Christianity and Judaism also possess injunctions against *usury*, which may best be defined precisely as the unfair use of interest. There are bound to be arguments, of course, about what is and what is not fair. If someone has worked hard to save some money and is now incapacitated from normal labour, it is fair that they gain some return if they lend their money. But the level of return needs to feel good for all parties involved. Too high an interest rate is otherwise just simple greed. Why should anyone make money simply because they already have some?

Historically we have seen more or less continuous economic growth which has been able to accommodate this in-built interest. Nevertheless there has always been a fairly universal suspicion of it, and often only marginalized and disliked social groups have been allowed to practise it. We instinctively recognize the unpleasantness of a loan shark. Most of us grin and bear the interest load on our mortgages (partly because we expect, if not hope, that inflation will remove the main sting).

What we fail to recognize is that the whole monetary system is pressured by exactly the same factors. The most compelling analysis of this problem has been put forward by Jacques Jaikaran in his book *Debt Virus*, which should be required reading for anyone seriously seeking to understand contemporary economics and money flows. His book discusses other models whereby governments could create and dissolve money without resorting to the pressure of built-in interest.

The crucial point which we have to recognize is that the built-in interest in the issue of currency forces growth and actually forbids either a stable-state economy or even an economy which is seeking to contract. Developing and developed states may go through periods of economic stagnation when there is no growth, but the need to pay back interest on the issued currency creates unreasonable tensions. To mention once again the debt crisis of the developing world, these countries are forbidden from moving into recession or even stagnation because of the demands of both the international loans and the issue of their own currency.

When we as individuals unilaterally use our plastic to run up debts which we cannot pay immediately, then we too place ourselves under future pressure. This, of course, in many ways is a voluntary choice, but is not so voluntary if we are hungry and starving.

The horror is that our whole economic system is underpinned by currency issued with interest. We have, therefore, built into our lives a pressure from which there is no escape.

In the penultimate and the closing chapters I shall return more creatively to these issues. My purpose here, though, has just been to point out some features of our political economy that deserve attention. Many readers no doubt already suspected these contradictions and will be relieved simply to have them named. Others will already know about them and be apathetic, antagonistic or supportive. And yet other readers may be genuinely surprised by the actual contradictory nature of these sacred cows.

THE METAPHYSICS

8

THE GOLDEN VORTEX DREAM

The Golden Tornado

When I am working on a particular problem, I often wake in the morning with a solution floating in my consciousness. This happens to me so often that, in fact, I take it for granted. Many of us experience our unconscious working in this way. I was nevertheless stunned by a dream that I had when researching this book.

I woke one morning with a lucid memory whose power and vividness were overwhelming. It was one of those dreams that was not only visually colourful and clear, but that also carried an atmosphere which, awake, I was still experiencing. The atmosphere was vibrant, felt good and life-enhancing.

This dream delivered a vision of how money works, what money is and why money is.

The dream was both complex and simple. The main image was of a swirling golden vortex or tornado, narrow at its base, rising wider and wider. It was made up of particles of energy spinning upwards and outwards on many different paths at many different angles. It was warm and exhilarating. There were other colours mingled with the gold: bright white, other yellows and rose. The whole vortex was radiant. It was also so large that I could hardly gauge its size. Perhaps it was several miles high; perhaps the size of a planet.

The golden particles of the vortex created many different paths, but had a general pattern which reminded me of the double helix of the DNA molecule.

If I looked closely, I could see that each particle was made up of two human beings involved in a money transaction. Every single one of the vortex's particles was, without exception, two human beings in a financial transaction, with money passing between them. The whole vortex was human beings in financial relationship. Particle by particle, through the entire vortex, money was the flowing glowing medium of the radiant system.

In the dream I could actually see some of the particular transactions, such as two Bedouin in the desert drinking tea, exchanging money for goods; or a parent giving pocket money to her son; or one woman's donation to the musician playing in the street.

Many, perhaps all, of these particles were connected with chains of other particles and money transactions. For example, one woman who was passing money in exchange for bread was also connected — through other particles — with the baker, the miller, the shipper, the farmer and so on. Someone buying a car, for instance, was connected through the financial transaction with every human being and element who was involved in the manufacture and distribution of the vehicle. The financial dealer in his electronic office, moving future commodities, was connected in the same way with all the people and natural forces involved in the production, storage and distribution of the wheat or copper. Some of the transactions were so complex that they seemed to spread through the whole vortex.

As I contemplated these images, I wondered what element created the vibrant golden radiance and I focused more carefully on a single transaction. In this particle the two people involved in the transaction were happy and pleased. The deal served them both. The glow came from their satisfaction and pleasure. I moved my focus to study another transaction and again the energetic radiance came from the satisfaction of the two participants. No matter how many particles I studied, they all possessed this same phenomenon. They glowed with healthy, satisfied and creative human energy.

At the base of the vortex, where it was most narrow, it anchored deep into the earth. At this earthy base most of the transactions involved only two people. Higher up the vortex, the chains and networks of connection became more complex and involved. But no matter how complex, there was always creative human relationship. No matter how complex, there were always at the core two people, communicating, sharing, exchanging.

As this was a dream, it had more than three dimensions and people were in many places at the same time. The folk in the highest spirals were also in the lowest. The currency broker, for example, was also buying bread, was also giving money to the street musician, was also on earth.

At one point in the dream the vortex shrank and I could grasp the whole thing at once. At its base was a simple transaction between two people. Going up, more people were involved in chains of relationship. First there was the level of a small tribal or clan community. Another level up and there was a small village. Then a town. A city. A nation. Widening and going up and out into the global economic community.

And then I saw another perspective which, I suppose, can only be described as mystical – and which surprised me. Although I easily understood the dream's message that money is a medium for pleasurable exchange, I was suspicious of the vortex's size. The mystical perspective, however, made my suspicion melt. It also drew me into an altered state of consciousness. I could feel my awareness expanding and a sense of what I might call cosmic connection.

This new perspective showed that the global community of human beings, the planetary village, had been facilitated into existence by money. Money, far from being coincidental in the creation of a self-aware global community, has been creatively instrumental in building it. Money served one-to-one relationships. It served the creation of communities. Money enhanced and expanded the potential for people's creativity, relationships and consciousness.

In this dream, money, in fact, had a creative consciousness

which actively sought to build partnership and community. It would, in fact, be impossible to have a global community if it were not for money. Human beings are evolving from parochial isolation into a global awareness, and this awareness is physically made manifest through the medium of money.

Some great force is running through the evolution and progress of the earth and of humanity. Part of its purpose is to bring humanity into a state of coherent self-awareness as a planetary being, and money is an agent of this great force.

This startled me. Even in my own most romantic moods, I had not considered money to be an evolutionary agent of spiritual intelligence.

Global Flowing

When I woke that morning, I immediately made notes and sketched the vortex. I was exhilarated by this optimistic spiritual vision of money as the vibrant medium of human community.

The dream also reminded me of the idea in some systems theory that humanity as a whole is earth's most sophisticated and elaborate form of consciousness. This consciousness, previously isolated in small or national communities, was now forming into a single web of connections that permeated and covered the whole globe, creating, in Pete Russell's phrase, a *global brain.* Mystics such as Teilhard de Chardin have written about humanity achieving a form of global consciousness, which would be a quantum leap forward in the evolution of the species and the planet as a whole. The theologian Michael Novaks wrote about this idea with a certain charm:

Dostoyevsky once described charity as an invisible filament linking the world in a network of impulses, along which a simple human smile or an aspiration of love could circle the globe in minutes to bring cheer to someone, even a stranger, far away. A person who receives a smile, he noted, often feels impelled to pass it along by smiling to someone else in the next chance encounter, and so with the speed of light the smile circles the globe. The new television and computer images, like impulses bounced off cold and silent satellites in space to touch and vivify every part of earth, may only be metaphors for the nerves and tissues that have always tied together the Mystical Body spoken of by St Paul, but such ligatures seem more visible now. (Novaks, p.16)

The golden vortex clearly suggested that money is an agent for this new consciousness. The charge of this idea is very powerful when placed against the usual spiritual cynicism about money.

Academic Models

In the academic world, people do not talk of dreams, but of *ideal models*, which help people to think more easily and creatively about human affairs. These models are theories which describe how something would be if everything were working perfectly. These models can belong to both the natural and the social sciences. There are ideal models in academic thought to do with the family, with relationship, political democracy and so on.

So the university teacher in me thinks of this glowing creative financial vortex as an ideal model. It is an open structure, a piece of conceptual scaffolding, which describes in the most general way how the perfect money system could work.

These are the notes that I made immediately after the dream, after I had drawn the vortex:

The dream suggests a theory:

• Barter is the reflection of a simple society with elementary production and simple and direct relationships.

Money comes into being to facilitate more complex forms of society, production and relationship. Its invention was miraculous because it provided the means for relationship between people who did not know each other and who did not produce directly for one another. This more complex production and trade, facilitated by money, allowed for a more complex society.

• Through the industrial revolution and through the process of global modernization, the relationships between producers and consumers became international, facilitated by the global economy and the exchangeability of national currencies.

- As production was transcended by pure human relationship and service industries, so money itself became disengaged from physical labour linked to the earth to an unearthed human culture of human purely in relation to human.

- *Insight 1*: This whole flow from dyadic barter to global relationship happens through a series of stages. But instead of seeing them as stages, see them as different points on a double helix spiral, flowing into and out of each other, up and down the spirals.

- *Insight 2*: The different modes of society reflect a movement away from *individual human,* locked in clan, to *universal human* capable of planetary consciousness.

- *Insight 3*: Follow the double helix up higher and we find humans in cosmic relationship and consciousness.

    All through the system, money – barter, notes or electronic information – facilitates humanity in extending its relationships.

    At the base of the double helix, money emerges from the labour of Human + Gaia.

    At the top of the vortex money emerges from the labour of Human + Cosmos (God?).

- *Insight 4*: If the model is dynamic and in flow, then money is a form of fluid and moving relationship. It flows into, from and out of cosmic consciousness. It is mediated by people and it facilitates all human relationship in form.

    (Money is like a musical string, strung taut between earth/Gaia and cosmic consciousness; it vibrates out its own resonances – good through to bad – when played by humanity.)

- *Insight 5*: Healthy money flows because the system is vortical and active, cosmos to earth, earth to cosmos, and radiatory.

9

ARCHETYPES, ABUNDANCE
AND ALCHEMY

Invisible Powers

There is real power in the invisible worlds of the psyche. When
Sigmund Freud began to provide his explanation of the human
unconscious, he was not revealing a previously unknown
domain. The way he drew and explained the map was new, but
through the ages wise folk and students of the psyche have
always been aware of the hidden areas within us all. They were
often, for example, represented as daemons or angels, working
uncontrollably through our attitudes and actions. These daemons
and angels, in psychoanalytic language, are the repressed areas of
our unconscious, the dynamic unconscious material which, un-
acceptable to the conscious mind and therefore repressed, nevertheless affect and sometimes dominate our feelings, moods and
behaviour.

In previous chapters I focused on the more orthodox psychological ideas which explain our attitudes to money and our
financial behaviour. In this chapter, I want to expand these ideas
into other areas of the unconscious and into that invisible region
which is best named the metaphysical. A holistic understanding
of our relationship with money demands that we be open to
these other ways of understanding.

The Herd Instinct and Entrepreneurial Intuition

Most of us are fascinated by flocks of birds, schools of fish and
herds of animals which, in full rapid movement, can suddenly

swerve and change direction as if they were one organism. The extreme speed of the group movement, almost instantaneus, is miraculous if we assume that the movement is signalled and understood simply through body language and eye contact. It is more understandable, however, if we are prepared to play with the idea of a group mind, or a group energy field, which all the creatures in the herd, school or flock *feel* in their nervous systems.

Human beings are also biological creatures with nervous systems similar to those of our fellow creatures. We, for instance, easily notice changes – *invisible* changes – in temperature and we also tangibly notice changes of emotional atmosphere. These vibrations of temperature or mood are felt directly in our nervous systems and communicated to our minds.

Watching one of the stock or money markets in action it is easy to be reminded of the instinctive behaviour of the flock or herd. Anyone who works in one of these markets knows full well how they respond to moods. These moods may be triggered by gossip or real actions, but the moods in themselves have an atmospheric quality to them that is tangible on the market floor and which manifests in actual behaviour. The market may suddenly sense that a share or commodity is on the way up, or on the way down, and there is an electricity that sucks people into action. The herd stampedes and the market collapses or inflates.

The wise traders know how to stay detached, to watch and make more careful decisions. In fact, some of the wise traders have such sensitive noses that they catch the scent of a change days or months before anyone else. Very carefully they sell and move on, creating not a ripple that will draw the rest of the herd. The financial world is full of stories of traders who got out at the right time, before the market collapsed. Watching a market collapse is like watching a herd of deer being prowled by lions. First nervousness, then agitation, then full group anxiety and panic. The communications and feelings of the traders are very primal.

This intense reaction to market 'vibrations' also happens more subtly when business people and financiers intuitively assess potential deals. In reviewing a deal, a business person certainly gives scrupulous attention to the tangibles: the books, records, assets, market, personnel, etc. But attention is also given to how the deal 'smells', and many business people, although attracted by the material prospects, will not move forward if it does not feel good.

The Metaphysical Connections

Mainstream psychology and science provide no coherent full-scale theories that satisfactorily explain the way in which people behave in crowds, nor the way in which people are intuitively sensitive to the 'smell' of a situation.

There are, however, other schools of thought which are quite at home with invisible connections and which provide coherent explanations of how it all works. These schools belong to the mystic, metaphysical and shamanistic traditions of many different historical cultures, are part of new age thinking and also belong to the cutting edge schools of transpersonal psychology and energetic physics. They all talk about and explain this inner world.

This other dimension, although invisible to our usual five senses, is consciously and controllably accessible through altered states of consciousness, using techniques such as meditation, sensory deprivation, trance and psychedelic substances. But whether we consciously access this inner world or not, we live in it and it affects us. Within this invisible world, money has a powerful and influential existence.

Because it is unseen and, therefore, esoteric or occult, because it is accessed through altered states of consciousness, there is often either cynicism or superstition around it, but it is possible to approach it in a way that is practical and pragmatic.

When the cosmos came into being – whether it was a big bang, great breath or divine thought – it came into being at many levels of vibration, energy and consciousness. Modern science speaks of the continuums of space-time and matter-energy-consciousness. The solid three-dimensional forms which we can touch and see are just a material base to far more subtle realities which follow different laws of time, space and consciousness.

This multidimensional world is filled, for example, with energy forms which are made up of thought and feeling. It has floating within it clouds of ideas. If we are looking for an influential patron of this idea we could do no worse than to look back to one of the founders of western civilization, Plato. It is strange how Plato is honoured as a parent of western thinking, yet some of his ideas are dismissed as quirks of his intellect. He was clear that there was an inner world and that in it existed, for example, what he called 'pure forms'. How do we know what beauty is? Because in the inner world there exists this entity which is Beauty. The inner world is full of such forms and we are subconsciously or energetically connected with them. There is, in fact, a particular school of philosophy, Neoplatonism, which explicitly explores and discusses this inner world, its structure and the elements that inhabit it.

The ideas of this Platonic approach are, in fact, the common currency of all mystical traditions and of tribal medicine people and priests. In the esoteric mystical schools of the West and East – Pythagorean, Gnostic Christian, the Qabalah of Judaism, the Sufi teaching of Islam, Esoteric Hinduism, Tao, Zen, Tibetan Buddhism and Tantra – there has always been clear information about this inner world and its denizens. Here exist the great actors of sacred drama: gods and goddesses of mythology, the creatures of the elements such as salamanders and gnomes, the fairies, angels and great archangels; the pure forms of mathematical harmony; archetypal ideals; the presences of the planets, constellations and Zodiac. All these entities possess a form of consciousness and affect human consciousness.

The Swiss psychoanalyst and philosopher Carl Jung was also very aware of this inner world and its profound unconscious effect on his patients and upon humanity in general. Out of Jung's work a whole theory of psychology, archetypal psychology, which explores the power and influence of these great inner world characters, has developed. This, in turn, has been taken further by the transpersonal schools of psychology, particularly the school of psychosynthesis founded by the Italian psychiatrist and mystic Roberto Assagioli.

The Jungian approach accepts that human beings are in continuous relationship with this inner archetypal world. This approach believes that these archetypes have an energetic reality of their own and do not simply live as fabrications of the mind. More than that, archetypal psychology believes that humanity itself creates many of the entities and beings of the inner world. Archetypal patterns and dynamics are actually generated by the experiences, thoughts, feelings and dreams of the mass of people.

Practical mystics have always been interested in precisely the same thing and have worked with deliberate intent to create, change and absorb the energetic forces of the inner world.

This is very intriguing, isn't it? It suggests that when we think or feel something, that feeling or thought continues to exist in its own energetic right. It suggests that the basic laws of physics and energy apply not just in the material world, but also in the immaterial world. The energy that goes into a thought or into a feeling does not just disappear but actually continues to exist. If I feel something, then the energy of that feeling continues to exist on its own. If I feel anger or joy, then a cloud of anger or joy has been created. Or if I think something, then the energy of the thought continues.

This metaphysical approach states that emotional or thought-forms of the same type are attracted together to create huge clouds of the same quality energy. For example, my *Vote Green!* thought joins together with all the other similar thoughts and creates a large *Vote Green!* cloud of thought. There are clouds of thought – political, ideological, fashionable, etc. – and there are clouds of feeling – anger, joy, jealousy, generosity and so on.

The invisible dimensions of our planet, then, are filled with the various energy forms created by humanity over the millennia. The metaphysical approach further suggests that people can become, consciously or unconsciously, connected to these clouds of energy, to these 'thoughtforms', and be influenced by them, like a lightning conductor grounding lightning or like a radio receiver picking up a transmission.

All of this takes us into a completely new dimension in relation to money. This archetypal and esoteric perspective asks us to look at the possibility that money has a life all of its own, as an emotional and mental energy form that exists in this inner world and that unconsciously affects us. The mythic dimensions here are substantial.

Let us toy with the idea that all the angst and hopes ever associated with money throughout human history are floating around in this inner world. Other than sex, romantic love and war, I wonder if there is any other element of human life that has received such powerful feelings and thoughts.

Try and picture what this energy form of money looks and feels like.

The Archetypal World

Jung suggested that our individual human consciousness sits, so to speak, on top of a collective unconscious that belongs to the whole of humanity. He further suggested that this collective unconscious contains a mass of powerful images, forces and mythical stories and beings, which are unconsciously at work through all of us. These archetypal elements form deep historical and psychological patterns. His most dramatic experience of them was in the 1920s when many of his patients began reporting the same dream imagery of ancient German and Norse war gods. Jung recognized here the surfacing, through the collective unconscious of the German people, the archetypes of racial purity and warfare, which finally manifested fully in the Third Reich and the Second World War.

It would be easy to write another whole book on the archetypal patterns and myths around money and wealth, and I hope some archetypal psychologist will perform this service in the future. In these myths we can discover many of the unconscious forces that guide our life with money. There appear to be two recurring themes around money.

- The first is that of achieving immense wealth by chance or from an unexpected source.
- The second is that wealth can itself be macabre and destructive.

Immediately we can see here a dichotomy running at an archetypal level. *We live in the expectation of immense good fortune – but what price will we have to pay for it?*

There are few people, I imagine, who have not, at least once, dreamed of suddenly achieving money and wealth. I do not do it any more, but I remember times when I would disappear into immense daydreams imagining a distant relative suddenly recognizing me as the boy whom they had always wanted to support. *Here you are, my boy. Ten million dollars. Just for being you. Thank you for being you.* I had earlier dreams of being given the financial freedom to take anything I wanted from the largest toyshop in the world. Later, older, I daydreamed of finding hidden stashes of money. My imaginings became very elaborate: new cars, houses, décor, clothing, cocktail parties, buying art, a complete lifestyle.

I entered this dreamworld of unlimited wealth with a thoroughness that always astonished me. As I woke back to reality, I would literally shake my head to bring myself back to here and now. In those moments, realizing that it was all a dream and that I was not rich, I would feel an aching distress. It was a similar distress as when I woke from dreams in which I had been able to fly, but then, awake, found I was earthbound again.

Many people are familiar with the power of these archetypal daydreams about wealth. They have all the force of other primal dreams, which may be erotic or to do with power. These archetypes in the collective unconscious are so powerful that we even dream them while we are awake. Sometimes it seems that they are so powerful they are dreaming themselves, through us.

Even when we are not consciously imagining them, they sit deep within all of us. In my experience, these archetypal myths do not rumble around us like deep earthquakes or the cracking of polar ice. Instead, they have a gentle but consistent murmur, a hum that is continuously singing to us, a lullaby hypnotizing us.

These myths are always humming and dancing their entwinement around and through us. The money dreams permeate our psychic environment. It is so easy to slip into dreaming them. Perhaps, to one degree or another, most of us are caught and bewitched by this enveloping spellbinding dream of sudden wealth. Perhaps our whole culture is caught by it. Perhaps our whole culture is enchanted and drugged and part of the enchantment is that we have the arrogance to think that we are awake.

It is a struggle to wake up.

On top of our biological needs for comfort, on top of our psychological needs for a secure identity, beyond our continual battle with the anxieties of relative deprivation – whether in a developing village or an urban apartment – we are also struggling to wake up in the midst of the overwhelming archetypal dream of unearned and unlimited wealth.

The dream is, of course, shallow.

It is shallow because what we really want is not material wealth, but happiness. We have all had experiences of happiness, even if we have never had experiences of material wealth. Happiness can happen very fast and disappear with equal speed. We want it to last for ever. I want to feel good, now and always. In the dreamworld, my desire to achieve happiness is symbolized by money and unlimited wealth. Money becomes the dream substitute for happiness and for feeling good.

There is a terrible irony, therefore, in these wealth dreams. They distract us from finding true happiness and they also, every time we dream them, increase the power of the fantasy. We are princesses and princes caught in our own sorcery, fuelled by our desire for inner comfort, bamboozled by our images of material comfort.

As a mystic psychologist I would go even further and state that a desire for material wealth is a warped reflection of our need for union with our own souls and inner selves. In many mystical traditions the human soul is pictured as golden, or as a chalice, or as an ever-giving heart. In our daydreams of wealth, we forget the search for the true inner gold and bedazzle ourselves with material glitter. This was always the struggle for the alchemists: were they transmuting material lead into material gold? Or did they understand that the whole al-chemical process was a metaphor for uncovering the inner gold?

The Opposing Myths

It is also hardly surprising, given that the dreams of material wealth are, in fact, about inner happiness, that there are also many myths and dreams that are concerned with disappointment and with being tricked. If we chase happiness through material wealth we are bound to be let down. This aspect of the myths always touches me as a pathetic paradox: we dream of unearned wealth and we also dream of being tricked and failure. At the end of the rainbow is a pot of gold – yet we expect to be disappointed. This is a difficult confusion to integrate.

This paradoxical cauldron of archetypal myth bubbles up into many childhood tales. Here are some of the unearned unlimited wealth myths:

There is a pot of gold buried where the rainbow ends.

By chance, or as part of a bad deal, we acquire a goose. But this is a magic goose and she lays a golden egg – and then another and another. (This is a strange idea, isn't it, gold coming from a goose's bottom?)

In an unexpected place we may find hidden treasure or a chest of wonderful jewels. There is always the quest for hidden treasure.

We may also find an old oil lamp which, when rubbed, provides a genie who meets all our most fantastic needs.

The poor maiden meets the prince in disguise who gives her recognition, love and all the riches in the land.

The goddess or god comes down to earth and marries a mortal, who is then given universal riches.

The young lad saves a maiden's life and does not know that she is the Emperor's daughter. He is rewarded with untold riches by her father.

Poor Cinderella is visited by her fairy godmother who provides her, until midnight, with the possessions of a princess. After midnight her golden carriage becomes a pumpkin and her clothes become rags, but the prince has fallen in love with her. He searches for her and she still becomes the princess.

There is a poor orphan boy or girl, but the unknown multi-billionaire great-great-uncle in Australia has died and left everything to his sole remaining relative.

There are, however, many stings in the tails of these tales:

The goose stops laying the golden eggs.

Jack is stupid and swaps his cow for beans instead of money but the bean grows a stalk high up into the clouds; he climbs and meets the giant who would rather eat than greet him.

Perhaps the most dramatic sour story of money is that of Midas, king of Phrygia, who pleaded with the gods that everything he touched might turn to gold. The gods granted him his request, but everything he touched, including his food and those he loved, turned to gold. He became a man cursed by his ability to create wealth. He, therefore, finally prayed to the gods that they revoke their magic – which, luckily, they did.

This approach to archetypes says that we are dealing with genuine energetic and dynamic forces that play through our psyches. Just a quick look at the myths shows that we are vulnerable to powerful contradictory messages. We are always living in hope for the magical event that gives us great wealth, but who knows what injury it may also carry? There is a powerful opposition here: abundance on one side, a curse on the other.

Nevertheless, even knowing the terrible curse that enchanted Midas, I sense that we are all still tempted by the Midas touch. Everything we touch might turn to gold. What good is gold on its own to us? Our own loved ones turned to inanimate mineral.

Yet we are still tempted. There is some deep and fascinating illusion here, and I am not sure that I understand fully the magnetism of this illusion. Perhaps we are like magpies who are simply attracted to anything that glitters. But this attraction can, for some, become overwhelming and consuming. Folk become lost. Their humanity becomes covered in layers of golden material.

The power of these myths is reinforced by a thousand thousand daily images. The entertainment industry thrives on glamour, unearned wealth and dramatic images of fabulous gain and loss. These are the dramas for which we are suckers.

It is also in the world all around us. In my street, at one end is a public housing estate with run-down jalopies collapsing in the road, and at the other end is a house which owns two of the latest model BMWs. The child at the poor end of the block emerges from his bedroom and from his book of fairy tales or Marvel comics, and goes out into the poverty of his street. He walks barely a hundred metres and enters another glittering world of newly washed BMWs shining their brilliance. Is this mine too? Does it just require a kiss, from a frog, a princess?

We all know people who have married money. We all know people who have made a killing in business or gambling. We all know people who have made huge wealth from sheer hard work. And we know people who have fallen bankrupt and lost everything as the great wheel of fortune turns.

In our biological and psychological insecurity, it is hardly surprising that we should be so attracted by these myths. Here, by the wave of a magic wand, all anxieties melt into abundance. It is a euphoric experience in which all our past pain is healed and we are anaesthetized against any other unpleasant realities.

In general there are two dramatic insights here.

The first is that the power of our feelings towards money does not come simply from within our own psychology. We are often feeling, or are even captive to, the overwhelming atmosphere of the archetype.

When we feel anxious and financially frightened, we are not

simply experiencing our own fear. We are connecting with and feeling the archetypal fear. Equally, when financially happy and feeling abundant, we are also connected to the power of archetypal prosperity and good fortune.

The second is that we ourselves create the power of these archetypes by continuing to feed them with our mental and psychic energy.

The Black Hole of Anxiety and the Golden Flow of Solar Abundance

The inner world contains awesome forces related to money. This world has not been illustrated in map form, but if it were it would be quite bizarre. It might resemble one of those medieval maps – 'Here be daemons, dragons and angelic beings.' In this inner world there exists, as a dynamic energy form around money, the accumulated anxiety, fear, greed and manipulation created by humanity throughout its history. It is easy to visualize this as swirling black and blood-coloured clouds of fear and panic, which form into grotesque figures and beings. The temperature is either burning hot or ice cold. The texture is clinging, sometimes sucking. Movement is like wading through warm mud until we slip into some unknown chasm of total fear, sucking us down into pain and despair.

I call this horrible extreme of the archetypal life of money the 'Black Hole of Anxiety'. It is connected with our deepest primal fears and anxieties. My friend Allen, a financier and transpersonal psychologist, personalizes this black hole and calls it the 'Money Elemental'. Allen noticed many years ago that when he went into financial panic he was connecting with something more powerful than his own inner fears. He was connecting with, experiencing and channelling the Money Elemental. The experience was so forceful and overwhelming that the archetypal energy field seemed to him to have a primitive life of its own, like some massive and shadowy gargoyle.

It is clear that people need to be aware of this energetic reality.

Often when we are dealing with a financial crisis — household accounts or big finance — there is a point when we begin to experience a fear that is more powerful than something that is simply our own. At this exact moment of panic — something bigger than just individual anxiety — we are linked into the collective energy field of the the Black Hole of Anxiety or the Money Elemental. The experience is overwhelming.

Earlier in the book I described the near-death experience of financial entrepreneurs, when people actually feel faint with anxiety. But many others also feel close to the Black Hole, simply by hearing the gentle thud of a brown envelope carrying a bill landing through their doorway.

I have spoken about the Black Hole and its elemental energy many times to different audiences and there is always a gasp of recognition and relief. My accountant, Roxy, who is also a certified masseur (all other accountants, please take note), expects, when sorting out the financial records of a new client, them to enter the Black Hole of Anxiety at least once.

The tactic for disengaging from the panic, the solution to connecting with the Money Elemental, is immediately to identify that the psychological sensation of anxiety is not only caused internally, but is triggered and amplified by this dark external shadow force. Naming the *external* force, beginning the process of detachment, gives freedom. If ever I still feel that sinking financial panic, I stop whatever I am doing, take some calm breaths, and state clearly to myself: 'This feeling is not just mine. Its power comes from the fact that I am connected with the mass financial anxiety of humanity. I guide my breath and disengage from it.' Psychological awareness of the true reality is liberating. It is like a light being switched on in darkness; we can see what we are doing and what is being done to us.

A second strategy is consciously to identify with and align with the direct opposite to the Black Hole of Anxiety, which I call the 'Golden Flow of Solar Abundance'. This other end of the money spectrum also possesses some very tangible feelings. I have found, however, that although nearly everyone has at some stage or another of their lives experienced overwhelming financial anxiety, not everyone has experienced an overwhelming sense of goodwill and generosity.

The archetypal and mythic source of the Golden Flow of Solar Abundance intrudes overtly into our lives every day. The sun provides an endless source of warmth and light without which life as we know it on our planet would not exist. Seen mythically, anthropomorphizing the sun, this great solar being displays an infinite generosity to life on earth. A scientific understanding of the sun – that it is a great orb of flaming gas with internal nuclear explosions – does nothing to detract from the fabulous role it plays in our lives. In a very real sense this is reflected in the life-giving generosity of the mother's breast to her suckling infant.

This archetype of generous abundance occurs in many myths, for example, as the horn of plenty, the overflowing chalice or cornucopia. It is the essence of all gods and goddesses of fertility.

Incidentally, in my money trainings, I ask people to assess – on a scale of one to twenty – where they are on the money spectrum, between the two extremes of the Black Hole and Golden Flow. What is interesting, and follows my argument about the difference between material and spiritual wealth, is that their self-assessment usually bears no relation at all to their actual material wealth. It might be interesting for readers at this point to assess for themselves where they are located.

In the next chapter I discuss how it is possible to build up a greater sense of connection with the Golden Flow. In other times, in other cultures, we might have been involved in great sun-dance rituals, perhaps at Stonehenge, perhaps at the Pyramids. It is, I suppose, unlikely that these fertility rituals dedicated to the sun and prosperity might happen in our city centres, particularly our downtown financial districts. Nevertheless it is useful simply to recognize that, attitudinally, we can make some psychological choices about whether we perceive the world through a lens of anxiety or whether we make a different archetypal connection with attitudes of generosity and trust.

The Magical Approach

On the top of Glastonbury Tor, an ancient site in the west of England, a place legendarily of great spiritual force, I once saw a group of dark-suited businessmen standing in a circle, holding hands and chanting. They were chanting for financial success. A cynical social psychologist might say that these men were, in fact, enjoying some form of bonding ritual and their purpose was unimportant. But these men were deadly serious.

They were using a magical technology to work with real, but invisible, energies for tangible effects. In their chanting they were putting intense emotional and mental energy into the idea of material success. They were deliberately building up a magnetic 'thoughtform' which contained not only the idea of financial success, but also images of money flowing to them and of people cooperating with them to bring success. The more they chanted, the more powerful and magnetized the thoughtform became. They were doing all this on a sacred site, or what is also known as a landscape 'power point', because the natural vortex of energy at such a place is thought to reinforce and amplify the power of desires and thoughts. Mystics throughout history have gone to these places for spiritual enlightenment and to pray for the world for exactly the same reason – the enhanced natural power – but on this occasion the place was being used for selfish means.

The basic laws for this energy work are similar to those of the three-dimensional world: laws of magnetic attraction and conductivity, laws concerning pressure and release, and laws concerning the continuity of energy. Earlier in this chapter I described the basic metaphysical teaching that whatever we think or feel is radiated from our mind-brain-body and continues to exist as an energy cloud in its own right. Moreover, similar feelings or thoughts, sharing a similar resonance or vibration, are attracted to each other and therefore create large clouds of a similar resonance.

People who are sceptical of these realities need to remember their own instinctive connection with close members of their family, or how sometimes they can 'feel' hostile or friendly atmospheres. At the time of writing there is even a research project at Princeton University into how mental attitude can affect both computer hardware and software. The military of the US and especially the now disbanded USSR have put substantial funds into researching this whole area as well.

The group of businessmen holding hands and chanting at a sacred site were creating an energy form of success and financial abundance. Given energy every day, the form would become increasingly magnetized and powerful, attracting the right energies and affecting other people who come close to it.

There are, in fact, many books which deal with this whole business of energetically attracting what you want into your life and I am generally suspicious of them, because they give little awareness either to our inner psychological wounds or to the terrible injustices that exist in the world.

Most of these teachings simply encourage people to get what they want materially, potentially to the cost of their real emotional needs and certainly ignoring the wider community. There are, of course, exceptions. One book, for example, that works carefully with this area is *Creating Money* by Sanaya Roman and Duane Packer. The authors have a caring sense of the context within which this process can take place and are also unusually clear in describing the actual techniques:

Drawing the objects, forms, money and people you want into your life is easier when you work with energy and magnetism before you take action. Creating with energy is done by getting quiet and relaxed, and then bringing images, symbols and pictures of what you want into your mind. Magnetizing what you want requires generating a magnetic force to draw things to you. You work with energy and magnetism all the time, though usually not consciously. You can learn to consciously work with energy and magnetism to amplify the power of your thoughts and create what you are picturing. A few moments of energy work, combined with magnetism and done with a sense of clarity about what you want, can create greater results than hours of hard work. (Roman and Packer, p.37)

Sceptics, very naturally, will wonder whether this all works or whether it is just a load of hocus-pocus. At the very least, even if the energetic realities are illusory, this kind of work is useful for changing attitudes. Disempowered victim consciousness can be lifted into a sense of confidence and hope. Lazy, sloppy and intermittent planning can become a more disciplined and sustained strategy for achieving whatever it is you want.

There is also a politics of magic. Is the magic done selfishly or for the general good? Roman and Packer, for example, are careful to point out the increased magnetism and power which come with thoughts that work not only for the benefit of the individual but for the benefit of the wider community. They suggest, for instance, that if you are creating a magnetized idea of abundance for your particular business, you need actually to expand the magnetism to include a sense of abundance for everyone who is also in your line of business. Wish success and prosperity to your competitors. This is a radical form of invisible cooperation to achieve financial success. Again, even if the energetic reality is illusory, there is at least an attitudinal generosity here.

The Mystical Framework

The essential nature of the cosmos is beneficent, abundant and full of love. Without exception this has been, and is, the experience of all mystics in all cultures and in all ages. When people enter into an altered state of consciousness which peaks in an experience of what is often called cosmic consciousness, the experience and the insights are always the same. The essence of the experience is an overwhelming sense that everything has its life in the same source and that this source – call it God, spirit, All That Is, the Big Bang – is caring, wise and loving. Everything that exists has emerged and is still emerging from it.

This source, this energy-consciousness, for the mystic, is brilliant and incomprehensible, contains everything and is still expressing itself into what we know as the universe. We ourselves are an expression of this source and we are, therefore, in energy and consciousness, connected with everything else in the universe. This source, being everything, is absolutely abundant because it contains everything and there is always more of it continually flooding the universe with its energy, keeping everything in existence. It is an expanding universe.

From a mystical perspective, therefore, one of our obvious pieces of work is to bring our awareness into resonance with this abundant ever-giving reality. If we can connect with this abundant essence, then we become more like it ourselves and we heal the separation between materialistic isolation and cosmic unity. This serves spirit. It also serves our own growth. And it makes us better able to serve our fellows and communities.

True mystics do have this wonderful experience of the nature of the cosmos, and it is so filled with goodwill that the true mystic's sense of abundance flows over into an all-inclusive compassion for suffering and pain. A sense of this spiritual prosperity manifests in an inclusive care for everything, particularly that which is in distress.

Not all of us can be saints, but we can take their attitudes seriously and aspire to resembling them. If we can give some thought to the realities behind appearance, then we can begin to catch that the nature of the universe is emergent and abundant. The paradox is that from our limited psychological perspective of anxiety and insecurity it may not seem or feel that way.

We come from a source of abundance!

How come I don't feel it then?

We live our lives in a world of paradox. The work of an enlightened person, then, is precisely to bridge between the two realities and to resolve the paradox. This is not necessarily a comfortable process.

It is ironic to notice, in the context of this discussion, how many spiritual attitudes there are which do not reflect a mystical perspective which includes money. I am thinking of the monks, nuns and renunciates who will not even physically touch money. Money, to them, is tainted and gross materialism. This peculiar superstition is actually written into the codes of some monastic orders. There is one Buddhist order in which the senior monks are always accompanied by novices who are still allowed to touch money. At first, I was impressed by their detachment from materialism. Later, I began to see their attitude as superstitious posing. Even later, I began to feel that their attitude was positively damaging, feeding people's confusion and adding to the negative thoughts about money. They could only maintain their purity at a hypocritical cost to the other people who would touch it for them. If money were so bad, surely they should be the first to touch it as an act of compassion to their fellow creatures.

Then there are polar opposites of these purist renunciates: the churches and temples which are palaces of coagulated treasure. I dread to think of the harm, for instance, that the Vatican's greed has inflicted upon humanity's general thinking about money and wealth.

Mystics who embrace *all* of life have no trouble with money, recognizing it both as part of the human paradox and as part of the divine flow.

Money as Energy – Flowing and Tithing

One of the clearest metaphysical statements about money is that it is just another form of energy. It represents in symbolic form the energy – human, industrial and natural – that has gone into something. In Sanskrit, the word for the vital energy that flows through the universe and through physical human vitality is *prana*. The Tibetan teacher Djwahl Khul, writing with Alice Bailey, therefore called money *concretized prana*.

Thinking of money as a form of energy, we can recognize that the healthy and natural state of energy is to be in movement, in flow. All through nature, if energy coagulates or is held in one place, a pressure builds up that finally needs to break free. If it does not break free, it begins to stagnate; it becomes unhealthy and putrid. This can be seen most clearly in the natural vitality that surrounds moving water. When water is stagnant, it becomes a stinking mess. Allow it to move again and it can soon return to its healthy state.

Money, as energy concretized through human vitality and exertion, needs to flow and move. Healthy money is flowing money. To phrase it in completely spiritual terms, one of the purposes of this book is to get money dancing for God.

From a metaphysical perspective – if we are to connect with the spiritual dimension of money – we need first to become aware of the natural abundance of the universe. We then need to be aware that healthy money flows and we need to facilitate this flow. We need to do this attitudinally and in actual actions. We need to recognize our own anxious desire to hold on to and accumulate the energy. We need to loosen up this insecure aspect of ourselves. We also need to get our money flowing and circulating. In getting our money to circulate in a healthy manner, we ground our attitude of prosperity and hook more closely into the flowing cosmic rhythm.

Money that is clung to and accumulated is like a congestion in the organic body of human society. Like a congestion in a single physical body, it can cause personal and social cancer. For personal and social health, we have to let it flow freely.

Within a nuclear family or clan, there is usually little hesitation in letting material things flow. It is part of the natural affection of human beings to share material objects and wealth. The family unit is a small social system in which generosity and sharing are normal. The association of monarchs with the Sun or Divinity is not essentially to do with splendour, but is concerned with this role of radiating an abundance that serves the community.

We may not all be parents or monarchs, but we can choose nevertheless to come into harmony with the archetypal principles of generosity and flow. As well as serving our community, this can also work to our own benefit. Indeed, there are schools of thought which are clear that working in harmony with these principles is precisely a strategy for becoming prosperous. As you sow, so shall you reap.

Many people cling to their money, worry about their finances and, thus, create an attitude of poverty-consciousness. This clinging to money, an accumulation of material things, actively distances the individual from the cosmic reality and flow of real abundance. To cling to material objects is to place oneself frigidly outside the universal reality of emergence and flow.

Not letting your money flow can be immediately uncreative. I have seen many people with substantial savings withhold from themselves the comfort they really need. I have seen folk with aching bodies begrudge themselves a rest, a holiday or a massage. I watched a friend with very comfortable savings once torture herself because she desperately wanted a particular vacation but was worried about spending a few hundred pounds. After a long talk in which she realized that childhood anxieties, internalized from her father, had trapped her, she finally gave herself the trip. In releasing the money, she released herself.

There may, of course, appear be a genuine financial risk in letting money flow, but people nevertheless need to let go of their neurotic holding patterns. Anyone who has ever started or managed a business knows the necessity of letting capital flow into areas of risk, so that there can be change and growth. On an individual level, there is also this necessity of letting money flow into those areas of your life that nurture and help you. One of the best contemporary teachers about a healthy attitude to money, Lionel Fifield, recommends, for instance, that everyone regularly buy something special for themselves after they have earned some money. He suggests that in treating ourselves as worthy of care, we initiate an attitudinal healing which spills over into the rest of our lives.

The most well-known technique of allowing our finances to flow in a sharing and generous way is that of *tithing*. Tithing is the habit of regularly giving away some of our income, no matter how small or large that income is. Classic tithing recommends giving away 10 per cent of all income. Other schools, Islamic in particular, suggest 2½ per cent. There is also sometimes an argument about whether we should tithe 10 per cent of our gross or net income. I suggest that it should be 10 per cent of the actual personal income you receive, but if you are sitting on top of investments that recycle themselves, then you will have to consider privately what feels good.

Tithing is considered such a powerful act by some people that they also believe that it is a crucial strategy for achieving financial prosperity. As I researched this whole issue of tithing, I found that there were many stories of extraordinary changes in luck that occur when you take up the discipline. What follows is typical of these stories. It is taken from L.E. Meyer's booklet *As You Tithe So You Prosper*, which Catherine Ponder quotes in *The Prosperity Secrets of the Ages*:

A man who was $10,000 in debt, with his credit gone and a wife and four children for whom he had to provide, took a job as a day laborer in a mill and with his family was compelled to live in a tent. He met two divinity students who convinced him that if he wanted to again prosper, he should tithe. The same week that he began tithing the company offered him one of its houses in which to live. Within a year, he was promoted to foreman. Ten years later, he was free from debt, the owner of a large lumber company, owner of his own home, which was large and beautifully furnished, and owner of a large car, an airplane and other things on a similar scale. He attributes his success to first recognizing his debt to God and faithfully tithing his income.

There are also myths that great millionaires, like the first Rockefeller, based their fortune on giving. In fact, it is reported that throughout his life Rockefeller always carried cash to give away and tithed his money. The philanthropic Rockefeller Foundations are the end result of his general attitude of sharing.

Some people attach a mystic significance to 10 per cent. According to this view, the word tithe actually derives from the word ten. By tithing 10 per cent, a mystical connection is made with God and archetypal abundance. Catherine Ponder is probably the most well-known writer in this field, with many books published, including *The Dynamic Laws of Prosperity* and *The Prosperity Secrets of the Ages*. She claims:

The early Egyptians, Babylonians, Persians, Arabians, Greeks, Romans and Chinese were among those who used this special prosperity method. Even primitive man, through the financial sacrifices he offered his gods, practised this age-old prosperity method.

She goes on to write:

The ancient prosperity law is this: True prosperity has a spiritual basis. God is the Source of your supply. Your mind, body, abilities, talents, education, experience, job or profession are all instruments and channels of your prosperity, but God is the Source. Therefore, you must do something definite and consistent to keep in touch with that rich Source, if you want to be consistently prosperous. Sharing is the beginning of financial increase. Systematic giving opens the way to systematic receiving. (Ponder, 1985, p.175)

Catherine Ponder quotes innumerable biblical texts to back up her basic message, of which one of the most interesting is from Genesis, 28:20–22, where Jacob makes a tithe covenant with God and promises, 'Of all that thou shalt give me, I will surely give the tenth unto thee.' I also like Jesus's injunction in Luke, 6:38, where he says, 'Give and it shall be given unto you.'

In an even more metaphysical mode, Catherine Ponder suggests that:

By consistently giving, you move on universal substance, forming a vacuum which substance then rushes to fill with a new supply. That is the nature of substance: it abhors a vacuum and always rushes to fill it. *Giving in order to make room to receive is a scientific method that always works to prosper those who use it consistently.* (Ponder, 1986, p.173)

The most important thing is to give our tithe to people or organizations beyond our control and with no expectation of thanks or self-gratification. Many people are generous only if they get gratification in some way or another, or if they can sense some form of control over their gift. Tithing needs to be done with a sense of absolute release and detached generosity. It also needs to be given to folk who inspire us in some way and usually the money is gifted with a note of thanks and encouragement. Sometimes it is given personally and sometimes it is given anonymously. It is helpful to communicate appreciation to the recipient. That note can be as simple as, 'Thank you for your wonderful work.' The appreciation that goes with the tithe is reflective of the essential goodwill of the cosmos.

Over the years several people and organizations have tithed to me. I have appreciated receiving the actual money, but I was touched, encouraged and empowered by the accompanying letters which directly expressed appreciation of me.

The warmth and appreciation flowing with the money creates a harmonic resonance with the mystical reality of an abundant source. To give with appreciation does not exclude giving to people who beg on the street When I first began to practise tithing and conscious giving, I became worried about how I should give to beggars. It was hardly appropriate to say to the outstretched hand: 'Thank you for the deeply inspiring work that you do. The kind of human being you are and the way you serve is wonderful.' Contemplating the issue, I realized that beggars on the street touched my heart and evoked my compassion, so I began to give to beggars in a much more careful way. I stopped hurrying. When giving the money, I pause and make some contact with the recipient. I do not want to embarrass them, but I want a certain connection. I pause. I make certain that I am present and that I have goodwill. I give and move on. I am grateful that they touch my compassion and I also know that there, but for the grace of God, go I.

The discipline of tithing, of being in a generous flow, is not easy. When you have only a little money, it seems to be too risky. When you have a lot of money, the tithe seems too great and extravagant. But the precise issue with which we are dealing is to melt that tight sense of selfishness and anxiety, to disengage from the Black Hole of Anxiety, and to get into a Solar Flow of Abundance.

In my own personal and financial life, I tithe between 5 and 10 per cent of everything I earn. I continuously monitor whether or not it feels that I should be giving more. I notice that if I have not given enough an inner tension builds up and I simply do not feel good until I have tithed. Not giving is like holding my breath too long. I have to exhale and come back into a normal breathing rhythm in order to be healthy.

Often I feel resistant to giving away my cash. Usually this resistance coincides with feelings of anxiety about my general economic state. When I finally end the procrastination and release my money, it feels good. I have experienced over and over again that when I feel tight about money, I begin to create an anxiety that totally influences my cash flow. When I release the tension by giving money away, then the cash flow becomes healthy again.

People often ask about their savings. It is, of course, sensible to have savings, but it is unhealthy to have them to an extent that exceeds reasonable needs. People need to decide individually, according to their own lights, what is appropriate.

Two chapters from now we will look at new financial strategies for business, organizations and governments. For the moment, I just want to point out that this need to keep money flowing also applies to economic institutions and systems generally. Where money coagulates, there is an unhealthy overload which does no real good for anyone. In the management of national and world economies, keeping money in flow and circulating is universally recognized as a basic necessity of a healthy market. If people are not circulating their money, then the market stagnates. When the market stagnates, there is depression and crisis. Financial flow, reflecting cosmic flow, is a necessity for health in all areas.

Spiritual Value and God is Money

An interesting question can be posed by the mystic:

'What values absolutely everything?'

'Cosmic consciousness,' comes the answer. 'God, Spirit, the Source – is capable of valuing absolutely everything.'

A second question is then posed:

'Is there nothing else that can give value to absolutely everything?'

'At a material level,' the answer comes, 'the only thing that gives value to absolutely everything is money.'

It therefore follows that money is cosmic consciousness at a material level.

A similar question can be asked about connection. What connects everything? To which we can answer, *consciousness*. We can then ask whether anything else connects everything and we can answer that at a material level, money connects everything. Money is, therefore, like cosmic consciousness.

Cosmic consciousness – the vitality and creativity of the original breath of creation – permeates everything. It is in everything and it values everything. In human culture money exactly reflects this attribute of cosmic consciousness. In the material world of human objects and artefacts, money is the only thing that can flow in and around everything, and give value to everything. Seen from this perspective, money is the most dense form of cosmic consciousness.

Money is the divine breath in material form.

This is a completely metaphysical perspective. It is a philosophical suggestion which, like all good philosophical suggestions, is not important as a truth. It is important as an idea that provokes thought and contemplation, the process of truth.

Transforming the Archetypal World

Modern science is increasingly exploring the continuum between matter and consciousness, how all aspects of life in this cosmos are enfolded in each other; how everything is, in David Bohm's phrase, part of an implicit order of existence.

The wisdom of indigenous peoples and the teachings of the esoteric core of all the world's religions have always taught of this dynamic inner world. To thinkers such as Plato, Einstein, Hegel and Jung this inner world was a real and dynamic source of energy and life. I can only recommend that, like these great thinkers, like the medicine workers and shamans of tribal peoples, like the mystic knowers of the world's great religions, we give this inner worldview an opportunity to play fully in our minds and psyches.

This whole perspective, though, is not simply philosophical and mystical. It could have a profoundly practical side. Its basic contention is that there is a dynamic inner world that affects human behaviour and that money itself has a dynamic inner life which influences everyone. If, therefore, humanity in general is to be free of the gross negativity and greed surrounding money, we need to clean up the energy body of money. The inner dynamic of money needs to be redeemed, transmuted, healed and transformed.

In essence, money is another aspect of the divine breath, but a long human history has polluted it. It is crucial, therefore, that we give consciousness and goodwill to our financial acts and thoughts. The consequences of our thoughts and acts are not only immediate and visible, but also long-term and invisible. In every financial act done with an attitude of goodwill and con- sciousness, we cleanse and revibrate the money archetypes. In every act of financial selflessness, we transform the selfishness and greed. In every act of charity and generosity, we help to get money dancing again for spirit.

In prayer and meditation it is also possible to contem- plate these issues and work directly with the inner causes.

We can seek to connect ourself with the abundance of the cosmos and with the suffering of our fellow creatures. If we can be present to these two realities, then we encompass the paradoxical scope of existence, and achieve a degree of liberation and new compassion. Our consciousness also bridges between and integrates the two realities – cosmic abundance and earthly suffering – and in a mystical way works to the general benefit. Our next step is to hold this consciousness in everyday life and actions.

THE CHANGES

10

PERSONAL HEALING AND A SENSE OF PROSPERITY

It's a sickness I have in the face of which I am helpless. (Ivan Boesky, after his arrest on charges of insider trading, explaining his desire for money)

Money talks through the rich as alcohol swaggers in the drunken, calling softly to itself to unite into the lava flow which petrifies all it touches. (Palinurus [Cyril Connolly])

There are, it seems to me, two different aspects of our money lives which require healing. The first is that of our practical daily relationship with money, the pragmatics of how we handle cash and how we plan and put into practice our financial affairs. The second aspect is our deeper psychological wounds which manifest through our financial feelings and actions.

In this chapter, we look at the strategies for change and healing.

But what would a successful transformation look like? I think the answer is simple: whatever our actual cash situation, we behave with financial goodwill and dignity.

The Unconscious and the Light of Insight

Our deep psychological lives contain the rich and painful dynamics which affect us and create who we feel ourselves to be. These, in turn, play out in our financial attitudes and behaviour. To discuss healing our economic selves is to discuss working on our unconscious nature. In one sense, therefore, all the problems we may have with money are not problems with money, but problems with ourselves. Many psychotherapists recognize clearly that money is a screen on to which clients can project all their inner problems. From this perspective we may never be free of financial worry, until we are free of personal worry.

It would, therefore, be naïve and over-ambitious to pretend that there are quick and easy fixes to our financial distress. The process of psychological change is a long path. Some of us can be slapped in the face over and over again with the same insights. Some of us can be loved, praised and reassured over and over again. Some of us can receive skilled and compassionate help, healing and therapy. Nevertheless we stay stuck in our uncreative patterns.

I am suspicious of the weekend training or help-yourself book which promises immediate financial release and liberty. Even if we are to achieve personal financial comfort, our interdependence with the rest of the human and global community surely makes it impossible for us to relax into being economically content.

But I believe in liberation and I believe in the pursuit of happiness. I have also frequently experienced the freedom that comes from insight and understanding. When I first stumbled, as a confused young man at the age of twenty-two, into my psychoanalyst's consulting room, I had no idea what the process would bring. At one level, there was the healing of simply having an older man listen to me, but I soon discovered a level of help whose simplicity astonished me. I found that if I understood something about myself, then I could so much more easily come to terms with it, change and release it.

Years later, for example, conducting an exercise around why people sabotage their own financial success, I realized that I did not want to take my income above a certain level, because then I would have felt that I ought to support my mother around whom I still had some confused feelings. This insight into myself, a simple recognition, allowed me to be more psychologically realistic. I decided, in the context of my financial life, to ignore my confused feelings, support my mother and increase my income – all of which I did. Recognizing the psychological block I was free to move forward.

I love to understand what is going on beneath the obvious surface appearances. Achieving the understanding may require courage or persistence, but out of it comes a liberating wisdom. This, surely, is the essence of true education. Not knowledge for the sake of knowledge. But knowledge which gives understanding which leads to greater freedom. This, surely, is why we read history, economics, metaphysics or psychology. We want to know the full picture. What are the hidden forces at work?

I have, for example, seen the astonished looks of revelation on many faces when people have suddenly realized that they are treating money in the same way that their parents did. They may well have left home, adopted a completely different lifestyle, have completely rejected their parents' culture, but deep down they maintain the same financial attitudes, whether it is anxious caution or unconscious loose spending. Achieving awareness about the source of their behaviour is a first step in beginning to manage it. We cannot fight or cope with the enemies and influences we cannot see.

Recognizing the Economic Culture

We need to understand the general financial culture in which we have been brought up and educated. Without any education, without any insights, it is only too easy to remain an ignorant puppet of the system, a system that appears solid and confident and wise. This is not an academic issue. When we do not know anything else, then we believe that there is only one way to think and behave. We can believe that there is only one appropriate attitude.

If we believe that macho-economics – competition and accumulation – is the only kind of acceptable economic behaviour, then any of us who want to behave differently with our money may well feel at least marginal, at worst victimized. To be marginal, or a victim, is a genuine psychological challenge which does not feel good and is a recipe for unhappiness.

The realizations, then, that money was originally, and still is essentially, meant to facilitate creative relationship, and that money has been hijacked by macho-economics, should bring a release and liberation. We can behave differently – without being intimidated. Our more generous and sharing instincts about money and materialism are valid, and have powerful anthropological and historical evidence to validate them. To be generous or sharing is not just a matter of morality and ethics. It is normal behaviour temporarily forgotten. The macho-economics players, in both the market and the colleges, have been conning us – and themselves – into believing that their rules were the proper rules. Wrong! It is simply one way of doing it.

The most important thing about the realization that there is another way of understanding money is that it removes a huge cultural burden from our shoulders. Our behaviour no longer has to be restricted. We do not have to feel bad if we do not fit the macho-economics mode. Knowledge brings release.

The information about tribal peoples and the origins of money, for instance, is overwhelming in providing another far more interesting and stimulating perspective about the purpose of money. It undermines so many of our usual assumptions and preconceptions.

Recognizing Anxiety and Relative Deprivation

The information about our primal anxieties and the whole business of relative deprivation is also crucial for our healing. Folk who are hostile to psychology and the culture of personal transformation may look cynically at primal anxiety and relative deprivation. It may seem to be just another piece of evidence for human weakness, but it is evidence that reveals to us just why we become so hooked into, so dependent, so addicted, to our financial ideas and lifestyles. Is there any reader out there – save the one born as an infant saint – who has not suffered envy or anxiety?

The unconscious forces here are very powerful. We are all biologically frightened of famine, cold and dearth. Insomuch as money buys and holds off those realities, no wonder money is entwined with primal fears. We are also social beings, identifying ourselves and finding psychological health in relation to our peers and our communities. If we have little sense of identity, then we may fall into total nervous breakdown. Again, insomuch as money buys those identities, all our concerns about identity and a sense of self are entwined with money.

Knowing all this stuff is healing. Knowing *why* I stole, knowing why I want that new pair of shoes and that bigger car, releases me from compulsive unconscious feelings and behaviour.

Equally, to appreciate the metaphysics, the unconscious and the archetypal life of money is to understand invisible forces that may work through all of us. The Black Hole of Anxiety, the archetypes of plenty, the myths of discovering hidden gold, play through our poor selves. Noticing them, knowing them, gives us control over what we allow to influence us.

And again, understanding the history and sociology of our economic culture frees us from that most awful of ideas: that this is only way it can be. Our economic culture is the result of a specific historical story with specific social forces at work. Within it there is racism, bullying and structural violence, at the cost of cooperation and goodwill. Knowing all this allows us fully to imagine and then actually to create other economic models and ways of life.

Understanding brings freedom. It is like noticing that a tree is about to fall on you. Noticing is enough to make you move.

Change First, Therapy Second

We may have financial attitudes that emerge from substantial inner wounds, but often it is best and easiest to change the attitude before dealing with the wound itself.

There are other areas of our lives where this is obvious. If I see someone bullying a child or being racist or sexist, it has to be stopped immediately. I know full well that the abusive behaviour comes from some inner wound, but, in the moment of bullying or abuse, the most important thing is simply to make it stop. Later we can get the therapy for the underlying cause. It is often a fatal mistake to wait for healing before putting a clear boundary around pathological behaviour.

Many of our financial attitudes are abusive, to ourselves and to our friends, relatives and colleagues, and to our ecological communities. We simply have to stop financial abuse. The self-imposed boundary is the first step in a more profound self-healing.

If we have understood the real nature of money, if we understand the social history of our economic system, if we understand the dynamics of anxiety and relative deprivation, if we understand the metaphysical dynamics, then I believe we ought to make a clear choice to behave with financial goodwill and dignity whatever our actual cash situation. Throw off the anxieties and addictions – they are not worth the emotional cost – and behave with a new degree of financial maturity.

Resistance to Change and Motivation

One of the strangest characteristics of being human is how we sabotage ourselves with self-destructive attitudes. Even after we have recognized and understood these negative patterns, we may nevertheless continue to act them out. The momentum of habit and the psychological safety that come from familiarity are often stronger than our instinct to change. It is often easier to remain dysfunctional than to make the painful effort of change. Self-honesty, discipline, goodwill cost too much. Some schools of psychology refer to our ingrained resistance and negativity as the human 'shadow', and this shadow is an obstinate destroyer of healthy growth. The shadow is fascinated by death and meaningless destruction. It sucks all energy to itself and is primally selfish.

In practical terms the shadow resists healing and the psychotherapeutic process. This resistance can manifest in simple laziness and inertia, or a thousand different excuses and rationalizations. We just keep on spending. We just keep on borrowing. We never give. We never wisely monitor our consumerism. We do not look carefully at bank statements. We do not open invoices. We delay paying. We do not care if our purchases are socially or ecologically damaging.

Psychotherapists and self-reflective Buddhist meditators recognize that the awakening and healing process itself is not painless. In fact, there is one courageous Buddhist prayer which grasps the pain of change by the horns, gloriously asking, 'Lord Buddha, give me enough suffering that I may achieve enlightenment.'

But the enlightening knowledge that we are shackled by the chains of financial illusion may not be enough to release us. We have to deliberately throw off these chains, take control of our financial lives, become money-mature.

To change our financial behaviour, to heal our financial attitudes, therefore, requires more than therapeutic insight. It requires a *willingness* to change, determination and motivation. We need to uncover what motivates us and to draw on its energy. Let us list the possible motivators.

First, there is the very personal sense of integrity and of feeling good. This can seem a selfish motivation, but it is good to be realistic. The reality is that as long as we live with these unpleasant unconscious forces controlling how we feel and act, there is no sense of real personal ease, no integrity, no happiness. The worms of sour financial feelings are horrible. These worms motivate us to change because we will feel better when we are financially wise, assertive and generous – rather than financially stupid, victimized and selfish. This is a very personal carrot. Through financial wisdom and generosity comes self-respect and a different form of satisfaction. There is also the satisfaction and integrity which comes with growing awareness.

All of this personal motivation derives from our basic instinct to fulfil our potential, in the language of humanistic psychology, to self-actualize. The one drive which runs through all our lives is the drive to manifest and experience who we truly are. The chains and illusions that surround money have to be recognized, healed and transformed, before we can fulfil ourselves. Remember again the multimillionaires who are still anxious and infantile. Money itself cures nothing.

There is also a moral element that must guide our actions. There are certain things that we simply do not do because we know that they are wrong. Philosophers may want to argue about the relativity of morals – one person's morality is another's poison. But that is an argument not worth having here. We know not to kill, not to abuse, not to bully, not to restrict freedom. Our problem is not in deciding what is or is not moral. Our problem is in giving it awareness. Professor Money could not bear to have his freedom to shop restricted, but he had simply not expanded his consciousness to include the possibilities of child slavery or the structural economic violence that might be involved in his purchases.

We belong to a human family. We have solidarity with all life.

We have a natural sense of morality to which we need to give awareness. Morality's power comes from our hearts and we need courage (French: *coeur-rage* = rage of the heart). We need to let our hearts rage in our financial affairs.

We also have a natural sense of community that derives from our shared humanity and experience of family. There is an instinctive communal morality which demonstrates easily in blood ties, but becomes more relaxed and forgotten as we meet people who are socially more distant.

But today there is no avoiding our involvement in the whole human community, and that contemporary interdependence means we all affect each other. The morality inherent in the primal family expands now to include the whole human race.

When I write about expanding our moral awareness, it might be better be phrased as taking a psychic sledge-hammer to our thick and stupid brains. I don't know how many children have to die, how many cities have to riot or how many communities have to die, before we wake up to what is appropriate behaviour. I have this image that, just before we all brush our teeth in the morning, a friendly tentacle comes at us out of nowhere and slaps us across the face saying, wake up. Be aware.

If we have awareness, this usually fires a passionate sense of outrage at the gross social injustices and victims of greed and mindless economic growth. Our contemporary attitude to and understanding of money are directly responsible for this pain and suffering. What choice do we have but to take a clear stance, aligned with our outrage, against greed and thoughtless accumulation? This is a moral imperative. It does not have to manifest in externalized political activism, but it does need to begin in the private politics of our own awareness. Most of all, this awareness needs to be constantly with us and not just when it suits us or when we are overwhelmed.

And then, finally, there is the motivation that all life is sacred and that we are spiritually interwoven with the growth and fulfilment of all beings and life forms. Some people claim to have no experience of this sacred magic, but I have never met anyone who has not at some time or another been speechless, touched or transported by the beauty of nature or the night sky or human touch or great art or music or movement or a baby . . . That experience of the deep meaningfulness and beauty of existence is a constant underlying reality, not a temporary warp in our usually selfish and cynical feelings. If we believe in the beautiful or the sacred, how can we justify selfish or victimized money behaviour? It hurts too many people. It abuses life. Aligned with beauty, we can find a comforting, supportive and inspiring motivation for transforming our financial lives.

Changing Attitudes Fast

The most common financial wound and fantasy that people carry is a sense that if only they had more money, everything would be all right. There is an interesting and provocative psychological exercise for exploring this idea. I use it frequently in trainings and on myself. The exercise is very straightforward.

You take some paper and jot down over five to ten minutes what your perfect life would look like. You then approximate how much money is needed easily to sustain this lifestyle well into the future. Because you will need to live off interest, the figure is not usually less than a million dollars. You then go into a relaxation exercise in the usual format: relax your toes, your ankles, your calves, your knees, your thighs and so on up the body. Perhaps there is some relaxing music in the background. You make sure your breathing is calm and rythmic. Then you are led into a visualization process.

In this process you subtly build, in your mind's eye, a picture and sense of your new fulfilled lifestyle. You have your houses and vacations. You have the relationships and the freedoms you desire. You have the money, investments and possessions. You construct a very clear psychological sense of what it would be like to have that complete financial success and everything that goes with it.

Led carefully, as people work with the imagery, they begin to feel very good, safe and prosperous.

You are now asked to monitor how your body feels as you enjoy prosperity: its degree of relaxation, where it feels particularly good, how your breathing moves. Then you look at your emotional feelings and identify what feels good about them. Then you monitor how your mind-brain feels. You are led into a full awareness of all the positive feelings that arise from this imagery.

Very gently, you are then brought out of the whole exercise and given time to make any notes you need. If done in a group, this is followed by some time to share your experience with one of your fellows. Finally, you are brought back to normal focus. In a group, the ensuing dialogue would look like this:

The facilitator asks, 'How do you all feel?'

There is a general murmur that everything's okay.

'Did everyone catch an experience of what it would *feel* like to achieve that financial success?'

People nod. (In all the times that I have led it, I have not yet encountered anyone who did not, to some degree, enter the experience.)

'So, you are clear how it feels?'

'Yes.'

'And you are feeling it now? Right now?'

'Yes.'

The facilitator takes a pregnant pause.

'I would like you to notice something,' the facilitator continues. 'During the exercise you felt the comfort and fulfilment that will come when you have financial prosperity in the future. But, in fact, you felt it *now*, before you have all that money. You know, from the experience you have just had, what it would feel like to have that level of wealth.'

The group is then presented with the following:

'Now, do you really want that feeling and sensation of prosperity – or do you want the money? You may not get the money for five years, ten years, ever. Your financial plans may always be thwarted. Not everyone can be a millionaire. What do you really want? If you want the feelings and sensation that go with wealth, then please notice that in the last hour you have already had those feelings. *You had those feelings as the result of a change in your psychology, not as a result of a change in your actual circumstances.*'

The facilitator then states the obvious:

'You will notice, therefore, that what you want, what you really want, can be achieved psychologically – and not through material means. As you have already experienced what you really want, you know that you can achieve that feeling. It is already in you. So, if you really want it, why not simply feel it all right now? Just because you want to, feel it now.'

To say the least, this might not be the best exercise if you are facing famine and your family is starving, but for those of us living relatively supported lives this exercise has a certain useful bite and sting. It brings us out of the dream-world of future expectations and the reliance on external factors for our happiness. It brings us into the here and now reality of our own psychologies. It dissolves the naïve spell that travelling the rainbow path we shall finally reach the material pot of gold. Being realistic, we will definitely not all achieve our financial desires. But we can re-create our psychological modelling, so that we feel what we want to feel and it is not dependent on any external factors.

For people who have never considered such ideas, this exercise can be inspiring because it brings us immediately into what we really want in the first place, to feel comfortable and fulfilled. It also builds confidence actually to go for what we really want.

What it means to each of us to fulfil our potential is an *inner* idea. It is an inner image and sense of ourselves. We know when we are fulfilling our potential because of how it feels: we no longer feel frustrated, disempowered, anxious, fearful, ambitious. We feel the opposite. It is a peak experience of feel-good. In the kind of exercise described above people are led into that feeling simply by working with inner images.

Certainly, as many of us grow older and lose the raw energy of young confusion, we also come more easily into that sense of ourselves. There are also calm and graceful people who seem easily and naturally to carry a sense of themselves. In fact, there are many people who are, by nature, good and decent folk.

In the image work, in a growing maturity, in a graceful and calm sense of who we are, there is one fatal mistake that we no longer make. This fatal mistake is to judge who we are and whether we are fulfilling our potential by comparing our financial standing with that of other people. Keeping up with the Joneses is a recipe for pain and unhappiness.

Whatever goals we have, whatever our sense of potential is, these are really psychological needs and expectations. The sensation of fulfilling our potential is, therefore, by no means necessarily related to their actual physical fulfilment. Unfortunately we live most of our lives in psychological frameworks which we project out on to the outside world – and we need the outside world to fit our expectations in order to feel OK. But as it is all, in fact, a psychological reality, we can if we want work directly on our own inner experience and liberate ourselves from the need to make the outside world fit our expectations.

Many of us, however, find it difficult to achieve such an attitude. We are caught in the psychological layers of wounding, confusion and disempowerment, and we do not have the motivation or inner power to cut through to another attitude. We continue to judge ourselves in relation to our material context.

Identifying That We Have a Money Problem

Professor Money did not think he had a problem with money. A warm extrovert woman friend proudly wearing her *Born to Shop* badge thinks that she does not have a problem. Perhaps they don't have problems. Often, influenced by the negative resistance of our shadows, we simply cannot see or admit our challenges. Self-honesty, self-reflection and psychological self-appraisal often require courage.

In this section, I want to put forward some ideas that can help stimulate our self-awareness. We could start with the simple question: do I behave with financial dignity and generosity whatever my cash situation?

There are many indications that we have money challenges. Some of the section headings in Donna Boundy's *When Money is the Drug* are very useful and stimulating. Here are some from her chapter 'Money to Burn':

Compulsive Spending – A Penny Earned is a Penny Spent.
The Need to Buy *Some*thing.
Inability to Tolerate Frustration and Accept Limits.
Vagueness.

Spends Most When She Has Least.
Satisfaction Short-Lived.
Often Spends More than Planned.
Pays Down Debts in Order to Spend Again.
Saves Only to Spend.
Angry if Confronted about Spending.
Image Spending.
Bulimic Spending.
Compulsive Shopping.

Then, from her chapter 'Fear of Spending':

Spends with Difficulty.
Finds Gift Giving Especially Painful.
Evaluates Everything by How Much it Costs.
Fears Being a Sucker.
Always Says 'I Can't Afford It.'
Fascinated with Money Itself.
Pays Bills with Compulsive Promptness.
Fears Being Able to Generate More.
Covers up Feelings of Dependency.

Mark Bryan and Julia Cameron, having both worked with people recovering from addictions, have a clear sense of a general pattern or cycle of many people with money problems: 'tension, spending, relief, remorse, a period of abstinence, or control, and then the cycle begins again' (Bryan and Cameron, p.8). For those who might not recognize this cycle for themselves, Bryan and Cameron also pose some questions so that people can determine whether or not they are 'money drunk', which means that we behave in a drunken way with money, from meanness through to wild abandon. The authors suggest that if we answer yes to two of the questions, we may have grown up money drunk; if we answer yes to three, we probably are money drunk; and if we answer yes to four or more, we can safely say that we are money drunk. These are the questions they pose:

1. Did your family believe that the rich got what they have:

By screwing over someone? By cheating someone? Because
their family had money? Because they are lucky? Because
they are morally bankrupt?

2. Did your family believe that money was evil?
3. Did your family feel that poverty was morally superior?
5. Have you ever traded sex for financial security?
6. Have you ever decided not to ask someone out because of
   your financial status?
7. Did your parents fail to teach you useful tools for managing money?
8. Did your parents physically fight over money?
9. Was money a taboo subject in your family?
10. Was money a family secret?

I, incidentally, answer yes to 7, 9 and 10.

Unless we are angels, it is probably safest just to sigh and
admit that we have a problem with money.

The Basic Strategy of Counting

Financial counsellors have a basic first strategy for dealing with
clients who have trouble organizing their financial lives. This
strategy is to give meticulous attention to every detail of their
money transactions. For money, this means only one thing:
counting. Mark Bryan and Julia Cameron begin their programme
in *The Money Drunk – 90 Days to Financial Freedom* with a four-
week section called 'Awareness'. 'Counting is the most basic tool
for gaining clarity. When we spend, we count the amount. And
when we make money we count that too. Money in – money
out. Counting. The exercise is just that. We're just looking,
thank you. No need to fix anything, no need to be cross, no
need to beat ourselves up about it That's not the plan. We just
want to see where it goes. Easy. Simple.'

Joe Dominguez and Vicki Robin begin their New Road Map
Foundation programme by asking clients to count.

a. Find out how much money you have earned in your lifetime – the sum total of your *gross* income, from the first penny you ever earned to your most recent paycheck. b. Find out your net worth by creating a personal balance sheet of assets and liabilities.

They also provide a helpful checklist to facilitate discovering the sums involved:

1. Statement of earnings from Social Security.
2. Income-tax returns.
3. Cheque book records.
4. Old and current bank books.
5. Gifts.
6. Winnings.
7. Loans.
8. Capital gains.
9. Illegal sources.
10. Contract labour not declared to the tax people (tips, baby-sitting, errands).

In both these plans, the counting is meticulous. The counsellors want every penny and cent put down on paper. At last, therefore, sitting on paper in front of us is the information that has never previously been accumulated. The history and the events of the transactions were always there, but we had never added them up. This is true psychotherapy, as a previously unknown and unconscious part of our life is brought into the light of day. The results of these sums can be startling. Someone who feels herself to be a pauper will suddenly find that since childhood hundreds of thousands of dollars have passed through her hands. Others, unknowingly, have conduited a million. (For example: $30,000 per year multiplied by 30 years = $900,000.)

The figures in themselves are meaningless. What is meaningful is that people who do an exercise like this come into psychological relationship with an unrecognized but major dynamic in their lives. We may think we have hardly any relationship with money, but when we look at its historical flow through our lives, it forces a different perspective.

This first exercise of counting is also applied to an exact daily, weekly and yearly budget on income and outgoings. In particular people are forced to look meticulously at their spending habits. Folk sometimes do this with the greatest reluctance. It can be embarrassing as the money spent on alcohol, casual comfort food, hobbies, cars, clothes begins to build up. Poor people who always claim to be broke suddenly notice that they spend $5,000 a year on alcohol, cigarettes and casual food. Rich people who always claim to be broke find that their casual hobbies, clubs and cars can amount to $40,000 a year. People's sense of skating over thin ice, always holding panic at bay, suddenly appears fully justified as they realize that their lack of consciousness over what they spend is indeed jeopardizing their financial health.

I was surprised at one of my trainings to find eight people who were already keeping exact accounts. Each carried a small notebook and wrote down every single transaction in it. There was a single parent on state benefit who did this. There was also a successful businessman.

This careful tabulation wakes up the consciousness to daily financial reality. Nothing slips by any more. It is a way of taking control and knowing exactly what is happening in our cash lives. It is the beginning of knowing exactly what is in the brown envelope containing the bill or what your bank statement amounts to. Again and again, I have been surprised by the number of people who have no idea what they have in their bank accounts and who deliberately avoid looking at any correspondence from the bank. No wonder they are at a disempowered loss when it come to their relationship with an inquiring bank manager. Someone may have the best communication skills in the world, have done the most effective assertiveness training, but if they do not monitor the basic facts about their financial transactions, then they are quivering melting jellies.

This coming to terms with everyday financial reality is similar to getting over any phobia. Familiarity with the beast that frightens us – dog, snake, height, bank, cash exactness – allows us to befriend it and work cooperatively with it.

There are now several books and programmes that offer

detailed plans for practical financial healing and control. Having brought the client or reader to a realistic awareness of their cash lives, they are then introduced to further strategies to give them ongoing financial health. Some headings from the programme of *When Money is the Drug* provide an indication of the kinds of strategy that are suggested:

- Pay First Things First.
- Open Your Eyes.
- Take Back Responsibility – and Your Power.
- Learn to Receive.
- Expand Your Definitions of Wealth and Security.

I also particularly like Dominguez and Robin's book, *Your Money or Your Life – Transforming Your Relationship with Money and Achieving Financial Independence*.

Deeper Therapy

I have been associated for many years with the therapeutic world. My father was a psychiatrist. I went into analysis myself for three years when I was twenty-two and I worked professionally for ten years with adults and adolescents with special needs. I am only too painfully aware, then, of the length of time and consistent delicacy that the therapeutic process requires.

I was very touched by a story told by Donna Boundy in *When Money is the Drug*.

In a culture that judges self-worth by net worth, children growing up in poverty often cannot help but incorporate a deep-seated sense of shame, shame that later shapes their own relationship with money. Sandra's parents fought a lot about money, her father having gone bankrupt twice. She remembers people coming to the door to repossess things and hearing that they were going to lose the house, lose the car. For a while, she says, the corner store had a collection box for her family, and at Thanksgiving, they got a box of food from the town . . . One incident still haunts her: 'I remember one day watching my

mother scrounging the bottom of her purse for the last pennies she
needed to buy me a stuffed animal for Christmas. That dog became
a symbol of shame to me. I could never even play with it. I hated it.
It seemed so pathetic to me, the way I felt we were, the way I felt I
was.'

In the opening pages of this book I mentioned a woman
whose asthma suddenly disappeared as she began to realize the
financial traumas she had internalized off her mother. What I
did not mention was that this woman was herself a psychotherapist, but even with her own initial therapy, then training
and supervision, this particular money wound had remained
uncovered.

We cannot be glib about the deep psychological healing that
some people need. There are so many ways in which we
have been hurt and abused, so many hidden wounds that affect
how we are and how we act.

In general, in one way or another, all of us have been
emotionally deprived. Who had perfect parents or perfect schooling? Who was brought up in a safe, loving and perfect society?
Unless we were taught the skills of dealing with our emotional
distress, or unless graceful life circumstances naturally healed us
from the distress, we tend to repress awareness of the pain.

Our emotional poverty may lead us into an over-identification
with the overt victims of this world – starving children, destroyed forests – and we may then express our anger against
the abusers. We displace our anger about our own deprivation
and project it into another situation, a safe distance away. We
may also, in our emotional deprivation, over-identify with the
victims of poverty and get caught in poverty-consciousness,
comfortable only with rags and hostile to riches.

Yet again, unable to accept in full awareness our own deprived
child, we may find it impossible to look at or give sympathy to
poverty. To give attention to the poverty around us would
mean touching something that echoes and reverberates in our
own wounds and vulnerability. To focus, therefore, on a starving
child places us in touch with our own starving child. This

may be unbearable. We therefore stay attached to images and artefacts of luxury and glamour, like a child clinging to its comfort.

The range of human denial is impressive. To one degree or another, we are all unable fully to look at and be open to the tragedies around us, because of what it would trigger within ourselves. Our own vulnerability and anxiety are too raw. In many cases the strength with which wealthy people accumulate and defend their wealth is the same strength with which they defend themselves from acknowledging their own anxious inner child. Those of us who cannot be present to suffering and poverty fear the power of our own wounds.

I keep saying that no book, let alone a single chapter or just a few pages, can deliver psychological healing. The therapeutic process is rarely a simple business with a clean and 100 per cent happy outcome. Change and transformation take a while. The important thing is to get things psychologically moving – like great icebergs slowly breaking up, groaning, shifting and moving. So if you do have deep problems which manifest in your financial life, I encourage you to take these problems seriously, and give yourself the time and energy to work with them. There are counsellors, therapists and support groups, some of them especially for financial problems, such as Debtors Anonymous. Although I am cautious about quick-fix books, there are those which have already been mentioned in this chapter and which I recommend in the Appendix. There are also support groups now for rich people, especially those with inherited wealth, which work to disentangle their core identities from the personalities created by the wealth. One of the features of these groups, for example, is that they learn together how to give away some of their money.

Family and Social Background

Without the help of counsellor or programme we can anyway start to recognize, and in the recognition begin to liberate ourselves from, the family and social backgrounds that have helped create our money attitudes.

What we absorb off our family and culture does not affect us casually. In Chapter 2 I described the psychological dynamics of internalization and identification, which is the process whereby an infant, or an adult, absorbs into their psychology the attitudes and actions of other people, of significant others. Once internalized, these attitudes are now experienced as being our own attitudes and identity. These feelings and behaviour patterns about money, about life in general, do not sit lightly upon us but govern and dominate us. Many of us, as we get older, arrange our lives differently from our parents' or childhood culture, but just below the surface we are often still our parents' children.

My father gave an appearance of dignified calm and financial security, but the truth was otherwise. He was mean and at the same time careless about money. He carefully kept his accounts and was mean with presents and allowances, but went gambling five nights a week. He never talked with me about money or what he earned. I was frightened to ask him. There was no open discussion about money and accounts. There was no family process whereby financial decisions were made. Money flowed out to us in dribs and drabs from the great provider, who never seemed entirely comfortable with his position. Yet at the same time he always had this fat wadge in his wallet and always gambled.

It is not difficult to uncover what I internalized off him. To distil it down to a few key words, I can say that I internalized anxiety and abundant carelessness all done with an air of calm. If I put those words into an 'I' statement, in which I take full responsibility for my own attitudes, then I find myself saying uncomfortably: my attitude to money is that I appear calm, but I am, in fact, a mixture of anxiety, carelessness and abundance.

I know other people who, after reviewing what they took on from their parents, say: I am meticulously careful with money, yet deeply frightened of financial disaster. Or: despite an appearance of nervous poverty, I am actually very comfortable with money and always have a nice stash put safely away.

It is worth taking a while to contemplate our parents and their money attitudes.

It is also worth noticing the more general culture of our backgrounds, which is often like a Russian doll, with layers of different and conflicting attitudes. There is, for example, the culture that belongs to the class system. Put in a very simplistic manner, it could be provocatively generalized 1. A person with a working-class background may have little expectation of rising income and upwardly mobile financial circumstances. 2. A middle-class individual expects more money and better financial prospects. 3. The upper-class (inherited wealth) nob expects, almost without working, to stay rich.

We are also affected by the general milieu in which we are educated and raised. Those of us brought up with a Protestant work ethic – endless hard work will get us to heaven and money is not to be enjoyed – will have a different attitude from those of us brought up in a Muslim Sufi home – money is a gift of God, like fragrant wine, to be enjoyed and shared in a way that is honourable.

Being brought up in a farming community may lead to very different money attitudes from those we absorb brought up in the commercial centre of a city.

If you are interested in exploring these issues, it is easy enough to draw up your own self-audit sheet and check it with the help of a good friend; or do the programmes in the books I have already mentioned.

But brought up in our contemporary global culture, in which the spirit of international consumerism affects everyone and everywhere, there are general money attitudes which we are all absorbing all the time. In the sections about relative deprivation and the nature of the global economy, I have described the features of global commercialism. We are all, whether first world city-dweller or third world villager, subject to the same images and, therefore, the same aspirations. It is clear that within the glamorous images of middle-class comfort, there is also ongoing stress involved in achieving and maintaining that style of life. We live, most of us, with a passive acceptance of the stress that comes from just keeping our financial heads above water.

The consumerism we internalize is very intense. It has a frantic and obsessive quality, similar to a hungry child seeking immediate gratification. The badges *Born to Shop, Shop Till I Drop* and *When the Going Gets Tough, the Tough Go Shopping* are realistic icons, clarion calls to the warfare of consumerism.

Born to shop! What a message! Woman was born to shop, but everywhere she is in debt.

This is a dangerous culture to internalize, for it wounds us and it wounds our communities. It wounds us because in our own eyes we become less than human, we lose our sense of worth, if we cannot meet our expectation to consume. It wounds our communities because we thoughtlessly use resources, with no sense of the effects.

Sometimes it seems almost impossible, unless we are spiritual or social renunciates, to avoid this addictive consumerism.

All of this is not meant as a moralistic judgement. It is just meant to reveal what is really going on and make it *understandable*. My need for new shoes or my friend's need for five St-Laurent suits is understandable. Imelda Marcos's 500 pairs of shoes; the Queen of England's castles and paintings; the compulsive credit card spending; the anxious denial of bills and debts; theft and corruption; hoarding; selfishness – all these behaviours, placed within their social framework and psychological history, are understandable.

Self-hypnosis, Affirmations and Cosmic Help

I had known for many years about the use of self-hypnosis and affirmations as forms of therapy, but avoided them like the plague. There was, it seemed to me, something vulgar and slick about them. I was suspicious because my own background contained a considerable investment in 'serious' psychology, my three years of psychonalysis, the years to get my doctorate, the years working with special needs, the years of daily meditative self-reflection . . . And, of course, the years of taking psychological problems very seriously – specially my own. Small wonder, then, that I avoided the apparently shallow techniques of self-hypnosis and suggestion.

I am, however, a diligent researcher and I could not avoid the fact that the use of affirmations is strongly recommended by many sources as a cure for financial problems. So I tried them out.

Affirmations are listed in many self-help books. An affirmation is a statement about yourself or about the nature of the world which, having placed yourself into a relaxed state of mind, you repeat over and over again to yourself until it feels authentic. Even if you do not believe the affirmation, you state it *as if* you believed it. The *as if* is the clue. Like a good actor, you 'psych' yourself into the part until you believe you are the part, thereby giving it authenticity.

So you sit or lie down, take yourself through a relaxation procedure, calming the breath and emotions, and then you mentally state the affirmation *as if*, you believed it. At some point, having repeated it enough times *as if*, you then find yourself actually stating it with real belief. From one perspective you have simply hypnotized yourself into the belief.

The most frequently used kind of affirmation is one like: 'I am a good and lovable human being.' Most of us do not feel good and lovable, so just play-acting the affirmation may be good for us as it can give us a taste of the actual feeling and this is supposed to be the key to affirmations. The temporary experience of believing 'I am a good and lovable human being' may be a psychological trick, but even a temporary experience of it is better than having no experience of it at all. At the very least you have a starting point for changing a basic belief about yourself. So, yes, the self-suggesting affirmation works at a shallow level of the psychology – but it also gives us a taste of what we may never have previously ever experienced. Here is a sample of money affirmations drawn from various sources:

A lot more money is flowing into my life. I deserve it and will use it for my good and that of others.

I deserve to be prosperous and wealthy.

I deserve to be paid for enjoying myself.

I have an unlimited number of valuable ideas in my consciousness.

My personal connection to infinite being and infinite intelligence is adequate to yield me a large personal fortune.

I love what I do, and that love brings me all the money I want.

Money is my friend.

Every pound I circulate enriches the economy and comes back to me multiplied.

I have plenty of money.

Every dollar I deposit is accumulated wealth for my personal pleasure.

I am at one with the power that is materializing my desires.

No matter what I do, my financial worth increases every day.

My presence alone produces valuable results.

All my investments are profitable, either in money or valuable experience.

My financial life is easy.

It is OK for me to exceed my goals.

Beauty, power and harmony abound in my mind.

I now allow others to support my financial success.

My well-being has nothing to do with my financial success.

I forgive myself for using money to control people.

I forgive myself for wasting money.

I feel safe whether I am rich or poor.

I feel prosperous whether I am rich or poor.

It is a blessing for the world that I am wealthy.

I am the source of my abundance.

I focus on what I love and thus draw it to me.

My choices and possibilities are expanding every day.

I am unlimited being. I can create anything I want.

I picture abundance for myself and others.

My financial dreams come true.

I live in an abundant universe. I always have everything I need.

I radiate self-esteem, inner peace, love, well-being and happiness.

I create money and abundance through joy, aliveness and self-love.

Everything I do brings me aliveness and growth.

I honour my integrity in all that I do.

I am a success. I allow myself to feel successful.

I forgive myself, knowing that I did the best that I could at the time.

I give myself permission to have what I want.

I love getting there as much as being there.

When I started experimenting with affirmations I began with the simple, 'I am abundant and prosperous' and also the extraordinary 'My personal connection to infinite intelligence and cosmic creativity allows infinite abundance to radiate through me, drawing to me absolute prosperity.' Both statements seriously challenged my credulity. But following the spirit of the exercise and as a diligent researcher I persisted in using them. I affirmed them twice a day for one minute, usually in the middle of my normal meditation.

In using these financial affirmations, I experienced a strange sequence of total resistance to the whole process. First there was intellectual snobbery. Then there was the sheer inertia against anything new that might change me. There was also shame and worthlessness. Who was I to make such grandiose statements? Even if I were not a feeble creature, in the face of terrible world poverty and human suffering, how could I dare to make such statements? And there was also the detached and observing psychotherapist in me who was worried that such confident self-assertion would smother and repress genuine emotional distress that needed, in fact, to surface in order to be healed.

After a couple of weeks, the resistances began to subside and I began to be able to state the affirmations mentally as if they were true. I remember my surprise at the experience. Instead of experiencing something that was purely mental or conceptual, I felt a flood of warmth and confidence running through my whole body. It seemed that in re-programming some basic assumptions, I was also allowing myself to have access to some deeper psychological stability and health. In stating clearly to myself 'I am abundant and prosperous' I sounded out a very private and personal note of self-affirmation and confidence. All the other voices of disempowerment and poverty-consciousness were forced into the background as I put persistent psychological power behind this idea of being abundant and prosperous. Why shouldn't I believe that I am abundant? Why should I stay wounded by my own insecurities and the scars of rearing and schooling? Why should I be a victim of poverty-consciousness just because the world as a whole was economically unjust? Why should I not flow with the experience simply because I was an educated snob?

In authentically experiencing the assertion that I feel abundant, my worst crime was to express confidence in myself. In nurturing my own sense of prosperity, it in no way separated me from the realities of my life or the communal life of the planet as a whole. In fact, it did the opposite, for it gave me added strength and less anxiety to confront the real issues.

The repetition of the affirmations and the authentic inner experience of their truth re-created my whole paradigm for perceiving and experiencing both prosperity and poverty. It also made me feel dramatically different.

To deepen the process, however, and to check my naïveté, I began also to work deliberately with financial images that caused me anxiety, such as an uncontrollable overdraft, a threatened mortgage, unopened invoices, loss of all income. In the midst of these unpleasant images, I experimented with my affirmations.

First, I would conjure up images of personal financial disaster and destitution, and let myself experience my emotional reaction. In fact, I created the worst scenario possible: we could no longer pay the mortgage; we had a young child; we were made bankrupt; we were put into a single room in state subsidized accommodation. I pushed the scenario further. I was now alone, destitute, having lost my family, and living on the street, and also in bad physical pain.

Into the centre of these imagined nightmares, I took my affirmations of abundance. It took me another few weeks of peristent use before I could authentically experience the affirmations as true in the midst of the conjured nightmares. But, after those weeks of practice, I had an authentic experience of prosperity in the midst of all the terrible images. I could envisage myself in physical pain, lying in the gutter, yet feeling prosperous and psychologically comfortable with the situation. I grant you fully that the situation was only in my mind and not in physical reality, but all through this book we have been discussing the power of psychological reality. At the very least, I was psychologically able to integrate images of destitution with a sense of personal abundance.

This was a very powerful personal healing for me. When I teach meditation, I suggest to my students that they always keep one part of their mind switched on and watchful. I suggest that they have an inner radar scanner sweeping back and forth, always ready to pick up bullshit. My own bullshit scanner was kept on full alert during all this work with affirmations. This was partly what was so healing, that even with watchful cynicism I was still feeling a sense of abundance through my mind, my psyche and my body.

I then took the affirmation procedure one step further. Alongside images of my own personal nightmares, I began to work with images of the suffering and pain that exist generally across the globe. I included, for instance, the image of the child slave that sits above my desk. I deliberately opened myself to a connection with these painful realities and included them in the practice.

I also tried carefully to make sure that my sense of prosperity was neither competitive nor purely egoistic. I put alongside the affirmations a wish, or a prayer, that everyone else also enjoy prosperity. I particularly wished prosperity to my competitors and people with whom I was in conflict.

The sustained use of this whole practice was very effective. It was also deeper than I had expected. The inclusion of my worst fears, of the general suffering and poverty, and also my competitors and enemies, integrated the whole technique into a practice that avoided selfishness and embraced holism. I managed to catch the resonance and feeling of prosperity and abundance without separating from the wider and struggling community.

And it was in the midst of all this that I also experienced a gentle miracle that is still with me. When I found myself able authentically to feel the affirmations, even in the midst of nightmare images and all the other connections, I realized that I was connecting with something far bigger and more powerful than myself. I use the word 'powerful' in a way that is meant to evoke the sense of a gentle, persistent and irresistible power, like that of an ocean. This ocean felt like warm waves of energy and consciousness running through me. I was genuinely experiencing the sensation of an abundant universe.

This was no intellectual insight and I challenge cynics to get out of their heads and into their hearts before they criticize me for naïveté.

Because we work as a partnership in our family, my wife Sabrina began to do the prosperity meditations as well. It took her longer to be able to experience the affirmations authentically – about six months of daily practice – and now we are in a pleasant and supportive groove together. We feel abundant. We have what we need, and more. We tithe and support others. We remain politically and socially active. We give awareness to all our financial transactions. It might be interesting for readers to hear Sabrina's experience of the process:

When William first encouraged me to say daily prosperity affirmations I felt complete resistance. I have never enjoyed doing anything regularly and the thought of having to do them daily seemed like drudgery. Secondly I didn't believe that they would work. However, my finances, self-esteem and sense of abundance have always been irregular and on contemplating the idea it seemed worth a try. I also appreciated William wanting a sense of partnership, and this was particularly important as I was about to have my first child and become financially dependent upon William as I stopped earning.

I began by spending a couple of minutes at the end of my morning meditations on 'I am prosperous and abundant.' At first I just rattled it off in the same manner as I may have rushed through my homework as a child, just to get it over and done with. Simply saying the words had no effect and I began to sense that if they were going to work I needed to invest some energy into them.

With this in mind, I began to say them while still in a meditative state and not as an afterthought. I began to imagine what abundance would feel like and to envision things that meant prosperity to me and times when I have felt prosperous in the past. In short, I put myself in resonance with the quality or energy field of prosperity itself. Slowly I began to allow this external sense to permeate my mind, emotions and body. I began to think thoughts like, I have all the air I need, all the water that I want to drink, I have many rich experiences in my life, etc. I began to feel very prosperous – first for seconds, then minutes and longer.

Funnily enough, being prosperous had less to do with money and more to do with the attitude with which I viewed myself and life. I recognized that the key to an abundant lifestyle was to maintain that sense of prosperity which would also magnetize to me the things that I needed as well as making me feel secure enough to pass on those things that I did not.

Were this process speeded up, it would appear to be magic: a few simple words and presto! an abundant lifestyle. In actual fact it is a very careful, almost scientific process of daily discipline and focus. I am still engaged in this process and my lifestyle has changed dramatically. I now feel like the biblical cup filled to overflowing and I am part of a chain of good deeds and wealth.

What I hope you can see from this whole story is that even if we did not do deep psychotherapeutic work on ourselves, we managed to move our alignment away from the archetype of anxiety into that of abundance. We did so without repressing our own psychological problems, nor did we ignore the greater social problems of our community. Moreover the shift in basic attitude also allowed us to be more confident in our generosity and giving.

Smugness and Depression

There is one down-side to the use of affirmations which I have experienced. This is an unrealistic euphoria in which one gets so carried away by the experience of abundance that one loses track of the real world.

This happened to me when I was feeling really good about the financial changes that I had been through. I felt connected to the universe. Money was pouring in. I warmly welcomed invoices and I made out my cheques with affection.

But then I began to feel differently. As I did my accounting properly, I realized that I owed more than I had thought. As I did all the sums, I realized that at the end of that period, instead of being £15,000 up, I might be only £5,000 up – and there was still a tax bill to come. I instantly became reluctant to write out those cheques and I could feel the affection turning into self-pitying resentment. It was a particularly strange change of mood because my general cash situation was very healthy. In fact, I was jammy.

But I felt sorry for myself because I did not have *all* the money that I had been dreaming about. What was also strange was that I knew full well, from my planning, what the outcome of that period would actually be, but I had managed to slip off into a financial dream-world. The mythical world of the hidden treasure, the kiss that would turn me into a royal billionaire, had caught me again.

Although I was fully aware of all the psychological dynamics that had taken me into this dream-world, my insight was not enough to lift me out of the stupor. I was particularly shocked when I monitored back over my mood when all the money was coming in and I realized that perhaps, instead of experiencing a sense of cosmic abundance, I had simply been enjoying a private gloat. Mr Clever-Dick-Money-Bags-Financial-Know-All-Great-Manifester-of-Abundance had been pleased with himself.

I moved from euphoric gloating into depression and then gradually brought myself back to stability.

Getting Rich

Well, I have to put in a section on getting rich, don't I? It is unavoidable. No matter how much people understand the difference between material and spiritual wealth, they still want to get rich. Well, it is very simple. If you are not born rich and you are not prepared to steal, there are only two methods.

The first is to be brushed by good fortune. This happens. I have a friend, for example, who was part of a company that was being sold by its parent company. There was a management buy-out and he then became part-owner of his own company. A few months later, an even larger company bought his company and his share of the profit was 10 million dollars. Other people win the sweepstakes. It happens.

Most of us do not get blessed by fortune in this way and there is only one basic strategy if we want to become very rich. We need a clear vision and a plan for achieving the vision. We need to employ intelligent tactics. We need to be adaptable and we need to be persistent in the pursuit of our vision for as long as is needed. This requires hard consistent effort for years. And we have to really want it. If we have the desire, the vision, the motivation and the intelligent persistence, we will achieve financial wealth.

Without exception, the people I have met who complain about not being wealthy have never worked hard to achieve it.

That is all I have to say about how to get rich. I am more interested in other forms of wealth. But as Voltaire wryly noted in the *Philosophical Dictionary*: 'It is more easy to write on money than to obtain it; and those who gain it, jest much at those who only know how to write about it.'

Possible Ways Forward

At the end of my trainings on the inner dynamics of money, I make certain that participants ground their insights and new information by planning their immediate next steps. These next steps are practical acts that they can do the very next day. They might perhaps be the beginning of a much grander strategy, but most of us need to approach change carefully and realistically. It is best to start with a simple action that is easy to fulfil.

Before actually planning these first steps, I share a simple map to clarify their purpose. This map is based on the assumption that people want to move from poverty to wealth, but first people have to recognize whether their challenge is to move from psychological poverty to psychological wealth, or whether they want to move from material poverty to material wealth. Or both.

By the time they do this exercise they recognize that material wealth will not bring psychological happiness; and they also realize that a personal sense of prosperity will not in itself bring material prosperity.

Obviously different types of strategy are needed for the psycho-spiritual problems compared to those needed for the material challenges. In general, I suggest that in moving from material poverty to material wealth, people need to move from being:

Material Poverty		Material Wealth
Naïve	to	Intelligent
Visionless		Inspired
Purposeless		Purposeful
Lazy		Persistent and consistent
Ungrounded		Grounded
Romantic		Realistic and strategic
Stuck		Adaptable

To move from psycho-spiritual poverty to psycho-spiritual wealth, in general people need shift from being:

Spiritual Poverty		Psychological Wealth
Wounded	to	Healing
Disempowered		Assertive
Victimized		Confident
Unconnected		Connected
Agnostic		Believing
Limp		Strong

What now follows are some of the next steps that people chose to implement. They might stimulate some ideas for your own life.

'Tomorrow I will, for the first time, thank my husband for supporting me so generously over the last two decades. I will tell him that I need to be more involved in our financial planning and I will start the process of working out a weekly budget.'

'Tomorrow I will buy a golden notebook, not a little black one, and I shall begin to keep track of every penny I spend and receive.'

'Tomorrow I will give $5 to beggars in the street and when I give it I will be centred and aware of them as complete human beings. I will give away some money every day.'

'Tomorrow I will go into my garden and I will sit down and focus on one flower for five minutes. During this time and with the help of the flower I will become aware of the abundance and creativity of nature and the cosmos. I promise to do this every day for the next two weeks.'

'Tomorrow I will spend five minutes, for the first time, talking with my cleaner before I give her her wages. I will begin a relationship with her and find out her situation and whether the money I am giving to her is fair.'

'Tomorrow I will take some money out of my nest egg, which I have not touched for fifteen years, and I will buy myself an aromatherapy massage. I will do this every week for the next six months and also give myself a holiday.'

'Tomorrow I will brainstorm for ten minutes the skills and strategies available to me for making money. I will repeat this brainstorm every day for a week. Tomorrow I will also do some research and find a small businesses adviser and book an appointment for some business counselling.'

'Tomorrow I will look at my bank statements for the last six months and match them against my cheque book stubs.'

'Tomorrow I will look for a Debtors Anonymous group.'

'Tomorrow I shall start research to find a therapist who can help me deal with the financial neuroses I have inherited from my family.'

'Tomorrow I will work out my income from the capital I have invested and I shall give away 20 per cent of that income.'

'Tomorrow I shall begin to tithe 10 per cent of everything I earn.'

'Tomorrow I shall begin a daily practice of abundance affirmations. I will start at 11 am tomorrow morning and do it for three minutes.'

'Tomorrow I shall ask my accountant out for a meal.'

'Tomorrow I shall visit my mother and begin the process of evaluating her financial position and seeing what I can do to help.'

'Tomorrow I shall begin a daily practice of opening my heart to the suffering and economic injustice in the world. I shall pray for healing and prosperity for everyone and all life.'

'Tomorrow I will walk slowly around my business and begin to get to know my employees. I will put faces to names and I will then look at the salary roll and know what they each earn. I shall meditate for a few minutes every day on this whole area and see where it leads me.'

'Tomorrow I shall begin the practice of never buying anything without acknowledging first the human being with whom I am in transaction.'

'Tomorrow I shall begin to monitor what I buy and attempt never to buy anything that is ecologically or socially destructive.'

'Tomorrow I shall ask the executors of my trust fund to give me a detailed account of my investments. I will then begin the process of turning them into ethical investments. If the trustees protest I will not be frightened of them, but will persistently insist. I will, therefore, also research and go on an assertiveness training course.'

'Tomorrow I will give my son his weekly allowance with a warm smile and affection. I shall share with my wife some of my confused feelings about money, ask for her understanding and forgiveness and begin a dialogue. If I do not have the skills to maintain this dialogue, I will look for counselling help and perhaps seek a couples counsellor.'

'Tomorrow I shall begin a daily practice of giving thanks for everything I have and for the universe's abundance. I shall also begin to give regularly to famine relief.'

'Tomorrow I shall organize a monthly banker's order to contribute to my two favourite charities.'

'Tomorrow I will ask my company lawyer to begin the process of setting up a charitable foundation and I will consult with my board of directors about a suitable sum or percentage of turnover to place regularly in this foundation for granting.'

11

THEORY, ORGANIZATION AND GOVERNMENT

Only when the last tree has died and the last river been poisoned and the last fish been caught will we realize that we cannot eat money. (North American Cree)

The Miracles of Historical Change

If it is tough for us as individuals to change our financial attitudes, how much tougher is it for us as organizations and political societies? Not only are we dealing with the combined attitudes of all the individuals involved, we are also confronting the inertia and fixed patterns of organizational culture.

Many people, I know, are overwhelmed by pessimism and inertia. The great machine of commerce, the world economy, has, they feel, a monumental life of its own, fuelled by too many vested interests, and nothing can stop it, turn it around or transform it. For the pessimists the only real hope lies in a disastrous world crisis – out of which, phoenix-like, would arise a new beginning. This crisis would be caused by the terrible internal contradictions of the world economy, in particular the conflict between those who have and those who do not have. It would also be fed by the wild and inflated prices of the world markets, supported only by the greed and frenzy of the traders. This crisis would entail the total collapse of the international monetary system and all the world's stock markets. It would also include ecological disaster.

These prophecies need to be taken seriously, but I do not accept their fatalism. An often quoted fact about the Chinese language is that there is no word for 'crisis', but there is a word for 'an appropriate moment to make a decision and take action'. This is our situation. We are already in an ecological and economic crisis. Global warming, third world debt, the depletion of the ozone layer, the danger in western inner cities, global infant mortality – all of this is obvious economic crisis.

I believe that the great mass of people, most of us, are sick and tired of a meaningless materialism and brutal economic system. I believe that, even if we repress the information in our subconscious, we are all acutely aware of the terrible cost that the present system exacts from all of us. And I am certain that our mass need for a change will actually manifest in real change.

We need to remember the miracles of history. Do we remember the fearful monolith of the Soviet Union? We need to appreciate that Mikhail Gorbachev succeeded in dismantling Soviet totalitarianism because the mass of the Soviet people wanted it to collapse. The bureaucrats and politicians may have wanted to hang on, but they could not. The situation was unhealthy, uncreative and deadening to the spirit.

We need to remember all of the historical miracles brought about because finally the situation was unbearable to the mass of people. After centuries of conflict, climaxing in the Second World War and the Holocaust, European peoples could no longer tolerate the savagery, and now the European nations are cooperative partners in a community of common interest. Jews and Arabs now embrace. The Berlin Wall fell. Nelson Mandela became President of South Africa.

These great changes did not happen by chance, but were driven by mass human need. The great leaders appear to make incisive decisions, but their real power lies in the fact that they are on the crest of a wave of need, a mass need that demands and forces change.

When we confront, therefore, the apparently insurmountable momentum of the global economy and the human drives behind it, it may seem impervious to change. But there is a mass human need that it change and the world economy, the spirit of money, will not be able to resist.

It's Getting Bigger and Smaller

The world economy is now so complex that it would seem absolutely impossible to plan or initiate overall transformational strategies. But here, in fact, lies a great hope. Its complexity actually demands new understanding and its complexity actually encourages individual initiative.

Economics is now so complex that formal or classical theory is incapable of understanding it. Maths and equations and statistics can no longer be used as a basis for general theory. The number of decentralized major actors, each making optimal decisions, is too great, too eccentric and too scattered for centralized strategies or regimes. The central pillar of orthodox economics – that of competitive general equilibrium (i.e. that demand and supply, economic push and pull, always even out) – is flawed beyond repair. As Roy Radner wrote, the model of competitive equilibrium 'is strained to the limit by the problem of choice of information. It breaks down completely in the face of the limits on the ability of agents to compute optimal strategies.' There are just too many actors. The amount of money and the number of transactions in the international system are growing at an explosive, incalculable rate. Money itself is rapidly becoming completely electronic. The nation-state as the most important unit of accounting is giving way to the thousands of other actors on the electronic networks. The classic debate, for example, about whether national currencies should merge or stay separate – such as a single European or African currency – is becoming irrelevant as electronic transactions invisibly take account of differing local exchange rates. Whether national governments like it or not, power is devolving to all these other actors.

You and I are part of this new economic environment scene. With our plastic electronic credit cards we can create money unilaterally. We can decide to go into debt without consulting anyone! This is a huge shift in power. Remember interviews with bank managers for a small loan!

The mammoth transnational corporations are also affected by

these same dynamics. The technological world is changing too fast and there is too much new information coming in daily for large centralized organizations to function successfully. Monolithic organizations cannot respond to change fast enough to meet new market demands. Large corporations, therefore, are having voluntarily to break down into smaller units so that the information and technological changes can be integrated. This requires devolution of responsibility, and many more independent units and independent managers.

There is, as you can see, a huge paradox here. As the world economy gets bigger and more interdependent, the players are becoming smaller. A large economic organization with centralized control – state or corporation – is like an ocean liner trying to run white water rapids. It has no steering mechanism that is fast or flexible enough. It keeps crashing. Its future is uncertain. It needs to break up to run the rapids of the growing and changing economy. John Naisbitt, in *Global Paradox*, put it succinctly: 'As the world integrates economically, the component parts are becoming more numerous and smaller and more important. At once, the global economy is growing while the size of the parts are shrinking' (p. 16). In commercial terms he forecasts clearly that 'the bigger and more open the world economy becomes, the more small and middle-sized companies will dominate'.

Is this a horrible or a wonderful prospect – that there are now hundreds of thousands of influential economic actors?

The answer to this is that it depends on the mindset of the people who are playing the money game. Their general financial attitude – *our* general attitude – can continue to be based in anxiety, in a complacent acceptance of competitive cash economics and in the delusion that short-term gratification feels good. With this worldview we dig our grave deeper quicker into ecological disaster and into such a fury of resentment from the world's poor that the two world wars and the Cold War may look like casual beach parties. Imagine that the current division between the world's rich and poor continues to grow. Imagine the growing resentment of two-thirds of the global population.

Imagine their governments not able to meet their people's demands. Imagine the military regimes, the dictatorships, the corruption. Imagine this spilling over into global terrorism and a third world war. Imagine a new holocaust caused by this fundamental economic imbalance. This future war is possible for our grandchildren. In a sense we are already experiencing it in our uncontrollable inner city violence.

Or, as the intelligent human species that we are, responding to what we really need, we shall adapt our ideas and our behaviour.

As the organizations of the world economy decentralize, this increasingly places power in more hands. It increasingly means that decisions can be made without going through months or years of bureaucratic process. It means that each of us can take more meaningful action and be more influential. The size and complexity of the market makes each of us a meaningful player.

In the complex world economy, unlike the old monolithic economy, we have more influence to change things. This has to start with our individual economic behaviour. We have to give full awareness to our money transactions and we have to play a part in making sure that money circulates – with dignity and generosity. We have also, each in our own way, through example and through ordinary communication, to persuade other people to consider making the same changes. It starts with raising our own awareness and then communicating about it with our family, friends and colleagues.

There is no institution or organization in the world that is not made up of family, friends and colleagues.

New Economic Theory

The purpose of any theory is to help us understand what we are studying and to guide our actions. Contemporary mainstream economic theory does not satisfactorily meet either of those purposes and, therefore, desperately needs to change. Economic theory that is relevant to the twenty-first century has to appreciate the dynamics of complexity and the need for humane awareness.

The current purely 'scientific' quantifying methodology simply cannot work. A new humane methodology would not exclude the maths and modelling, any more than any business organization can afford to ignore its balance sheet, but its core basis must be humane.

In *Future Wealth* James Robertson is crystal clear about the general direction in which a new economics should go. He states:

- It should be systematically enabling for people.
- It should be systematically conserving of resources and environment.
- It should treat the world's economy as a multi-level one-world system with autonomous but interdependent parts at all levels.
- It should be supported by up-to-date economic ideas. (Robertson, p.1)

In *Alternative Economic Indicators* Victor Anderson suggests that the three major areas which have been marginalized in contemporary economic science are:

1. 'Human economics' – the economy seen as grounded in the lives of human beings, in our roles as producers, consumers, members of families, citizens, etc.;
2. 'Natural economics' – the economy seen as grounded in natural resources and the biological and physical processes of the natural world; and
3. The economy seen as something for which moral evaluation is relevant.

He goes on to write that in an enlarged economics – or a renewed political economy – there would be three parallel ways of describing economic processes:

1. The economy considered from a monetary or *financial* point of view (which is the one emphasized by present-day economics);
2. The economy considered as consisting of *human* beings organized together in particular ways; and
3. The economy considered as a set of arrangements for mediating the relationship between human beings and the *natural* world. (Anderson, pp.45–6)

This necessary change in economic thinking is similar, for instance, to the change currently happening in medical theory and practice. The purely scientific and mechanical approach is having to be incorporated into a holistic framework which takes account of the whole system, including its human eccentricities, unpredictability and chaotic creativity.

There is already a group of economists who have aligned themselves with a wider vision of their purpose and who are working on new economic theories applicable to the contemporary world. These economists are the women and men whose academic background is in ecology and developmental economics.

Ecologically inspired economists are tackling the very immediate business of integrating into classical economic models, costs and factors that are directly related to what the economy is taking out of the environment and putting back into it. Up until now, businesses' accounting books have shown many different cash factors, but have never costed in environmental depletion or damage. A business, for example, can make perfectly sensible cash cost-effective decisions that work towards a profit, but if we look at the effects of that business on its local community, in terms of using up non-renewable natural assets or pollution, then the community as a whole may be making a terrible loss. Pollution needs to be cleared up. This costs money. Environmental disease costs money in terms of health care. Who pays for this? Not the originating business. The community, therefore, may be subsidizing a profitable local company.

At the time of writing there is great corporate resistance to legally enforced tax penalties on companies that act detrimentally to the environment. But why should communities pay the price for these companies? It is not fair. The short-termism and self-interest of these companies are understandable. It is understandable that business should fight its corner to protect its cash interests. But businesses are run by human beings and mindless short-termism will end because the workers and managers will not be able to face their own consciences. It simply is not right that businesses 'externalize' their hidden environmental and humane costs – thereby ducking their own responsibilities – when these costs should be 'internalized' and taken into account in their own budgeting. This ignorance and selfishness is self-destructive stupidity when costed against the future of their own grandchildren.

Developmental economists are also fully aware of the human costs of the western economic way of thinking. Specializing in the process and progress of third world developing economies, most developmental economists have spent time or actually live in the locations which they study. They have full, first-hand experience of the terrible human costs of thoughtless economics: the breakdown of community, the increase in social injustice and the lessening of welfare.

A financial deal to do with a cash crop such as coffee or a mineral commodity such as copper can make perfect economic sense to the company initiating the transaction. Looked at more closely, however, the deal may have disastrous effects both for the local community and for the general balance of payments situation of the state. Remember the apocryphal tale of the Indian entrepreneur cropping frogs for the French market and creating a local ecological disaster. There is a terrible lack of awareness of the true implications of what appears to be simple and healthy profit-chasing business.

This form of financial behaviour – beneficial to the metropolitan business, detrimental to the local economy and people – emerges directly out of accepted economic theory which focuses purely on money flows with no awareness of other factors. Organizations, therefore, like individuals, need to assess a wider set of factors than immediate cash information.

These other factors are not easily quantified and put into measurable units, but there is a growing body of research trying to solve this problem. Working on a very provisional approach, Wolf-Dieter Grossman of Leipzig's Centre for Environmental Research and I have come up with what we call True Value Units. We are attempting to create a simple model which can quantify environmental and humane values in parallel with the usual units of cash value. This is part of a wide endeavour among developmental economists to incorporate other definitions of wealth. There is already an early clarity about what these classifications need to be like.

Victor Anderson suggests the following classifications as possible indicators of humane value. These are very realistic:

1. Net primary school enrolment ratio for girls.
2. Net primary school enrolment ratio for boys.
3. Female illiteracy rate.
4. Male illiteracy rate.
5. The rate of unemployment.
6. Average calorie supply as a percentage of requirements.
7. Percentage of the population with access to safe drinking water.
8. Telephones per thousand people.
9. Household income received by the top 20 per cent of households, divided by that received by the bottom 20 per cent.
10. Infant mortality rate.
11. Under-five mortality rate. (p.64)

Later, he suggests clear indicators for environmental factors.

12. Deforestation in square kilometres per year.
13. Carbon dioxide emissions from fossil fuel use, in millions of metric tons per year.
14. Average annual percentage rate of increase in population.
15. Number of operable nuclear reactors.
16. Energy consumption (in tons of oil equivalent) per million dollars of GDP. (p.74)

These kinds of classification have also filtered through into mainstream financial institutions as they attempt to respond to ecological and humane pressures. The economist and futurist Hazel Henderson noted that even the World Bank was beginning to expand its understanding of economic growth. She quoted from its 1991 World Development Report:

The weakness of income growth as an indicator is that it may mask the real changes in welfare for large parts of the poor population. Improvements in meeting the basic needs for food, education, health care, equality of opportunity, civil liberties, and environmental protection are not captured by statistics on income growth.

Hazel then went on to ask whether the World Bank, in redefining economic indicators, had done anything to change the ways it pulls together its statistics in a way that has a wider perspective than cash values. 'It has not!' she exclaimed.

Neither has it retrained its staff of economists and statisticians, nor, significantly, has it made any changes in GNP, GDP accounting or even incorporated the changes advocated by its own staff, such as valuing infrastructure and human capital and environmental assets . . . (Henderson, p.161)

The World Bank may be resistant to initiating change in its philosophy of auditing, but I celebrate that even in this bastion of orthodox financial thinking there is clear awareness of true values rather than cash values.

It is understandable that as institutions change the way they think, there will be glaring inconsistencies between their statements and their procedures. There is bound to be hypocrisy, but, as Oscar Wilde wryly noted, 'hypocrisy is vice acknowledging virtue'. Acknowledging virtue is better than ignoring it completely.

It is stimulating to look at other suggestions concerning the guidelines that can be used for alternative indicators of economic growth or Real Value Units. Len Doyal and Ian Gough have suggested a model which has a range of opposing values.

Regress ⟷ Progress
Limitation of Capability ⟷ Optimization of Satisfaction of Needs
Reduction of Choice ⟷ Humanization of Choice
Human Constraint ⟷ Human Liberation

(Doyal and Gough in Paul Ekins (ed.), p.77)

Ian Miles also suggests four dimensions of welfare which he presents as oppositions:

Health ⟷ Disease
Survival ⟷ Vulnerability
Autonomy ⟷ Constraint
Identity ⟷ Alienation

(Miles in Ekins and Max-Neef (eds.), p.293)

Manfred Max-Neef has also produced a scheme that fully grasps the complexity of human psychology and needs. His indicators range across various states of human activity: Being, Having, Doing and Interacting. Within these human states, he identifies nine sets of needs: Subsistence, Protection, Affection, Understanding, Participation, Leisure, Creation, Identity and Freedom (Ekins and Max-Neef (eds.), pp.206–7).

All this pioneering groundwork by 'new' economists will sooner or later have to be integrated into mainstream economic teaching. I can foresee a day not too far away when the machinery of every economics department in every college and university in the world will be focused on understanding and meeting these problems as a normal part of their core curriculum.

To summarize then: a new economic theory needs to incorporate the emerging realities of size, scale, complexity and decentralization; auditing real costs and wealth other than simple cash values; and a change in the general framework of understanding away from savage competition for scarce resources to a more realistic appreciation of natural cooperation. The most basic supposition of mainstream economics – that we are savage beings competing for scarce resources, and that demand and supply reach equilibrium – will be replaced by other more creative and cooperative assumptions.

We need an economics that, as well as encouraging creativity, initiative and wealth creation, also asks questions about shelter and food, physical and psychological safety and the fulfilment of potential.

Conservative Opposition and Humane Realities

Conservative economists, such as Nobel prizewinner Friedrich Hayek and Milton Friedman, will no doubt continue to argue rigorously that the business of business is only business. They will argue that the free market, in the end, is the only mechanism that ensures genuine human liberty and the best chances for economic growth. In this philosophy money is the medium of communication in a culture that is purely competitive.

This is a very attractive argument because of its simplicity and because of its clear opposition to a nannying or totalitarian state. It is particularly attractive to macho business people, who do not want to be bothered with caring because it goes against their competitive adrenalin. It is also attractive to insecure and wounded folk who cannot bear the notion of caring because it resonates too painfully with their own wounds.

It is also attractive because it contains a powerful grain of truth. The market does function best left to its own devices as individual entrepreneurs and businesses compete.

It collapses as a useful theory, however, because it ignores the wider human context concerning the purpose of money and the market. The context for human life is not the market. The market and money actually exist within the wider context of the whole human community. This means, whether the free market-eers like it or not, that there must be compromise between the dynamics of the free market and more general humane and environmental needs. Not even Adam Smith, the father of free market theory and originator of the notion of an 'invisible hand' that guided market behaviour to the best possible outcome for all, believed that the market should be left free of moral guidelines.

In its most elementary form, for example, the market could not exist successfully without certain fundamental rules. One of these is the simple law that contracts be honoured, that a deal agreed is a deal that is kept to. Without it the market collapses. Simple-minded macho free marketeers take for granted the social devices – such as law of contract, laws against theft and corruption – that serve them, but wish to ignore the reciprocal responsibilities and awarenesses. The market only exists in the first place because of a cooperative agreement among the traders. It is the human context that allows and supports the market. It is not as such *free* of rules and guidelines.

The real problem is that getting a business off the ground and then sustaining its profitability is hard and difficult work. It requires a persistent competitive spirit. The threat of contraction or closure is always there. Successful business requires that people work with an edge. It is tough and it seems that there is no space to worry about ecological or humane concerns.

Life, however, is never simple. The aggressive spirit of business has no choice but to work with the reality of its actual environment. Like any other aspect of human life, there are compromises and deals to be made.

A business nowadays has to recognize that it is as much a humane organism as it is a pure commercial venture. How each business integrates this reality will vary from situation to situation. Equally, there needs to be a relationship of give and take between the two realities of commerce and caring. When profits are low and there is a situation of financial threat, then obviously there are less resources to support humane values. The problem, then, is in selecting clear boundaries concerning humane values.

When Ben Cohen, one of the pioneers in the United States of 'socially aware business', resigned as chief executive of Ben & Jerry's ice cream organization, he recognized the necessity of sacrificing certain principles because of a declining share price on Wall Street. To attract a strong successor, the company abandoned its policy that no executive be paid more than seven times the salary of the lowest-paid employee. This particular stretching of a rule about wage differentials does not seem earth-shattering, but which humane rules should we not break or stretch?

There are some rules which are enshrined in national and international law. One of these rules, for example, concerns child labour. National and international law forbids child labour. A purely free market, however, with no humane morality, employs children if it can get away with such low-cost labour. There are also laws concerning health and safety. Which of these should be sacrificed when financial survival is threatened? Should children still be sent up chimneys? Should men and women work twelve-hour days seven days a week in below-zero or sweatshop conditions because it is profitable? In the United Kingdom recently, the financial rationalization of the coal industry led directly to less safe mining methods and the loss of life. Can the financial imperatives of the free market ever justify loss of life? We have to keep our eyes open to these realities. We have to practise vigilance.

Step-by-step Change and Adapting Existing Procedures

Many organizations shy away from new attitudes because they are frightened of the cost of change. A change in attitude exacts a psychological cost and a change in organization may be prohibitively expensive in pure cash terms. Change, therefore, has to be managed.

That change requires management is accepted wisdom. This wisdom needs also to be applied to changing money values.

A strange paranoia sometimes comes over business people when you talk to them about ethics or the environment. They cannot see how to include these factors in their business without going out of business. When introduced to step-by-step strategies for change, however, they can begin to feel comfortable and accepting.

I watched this happening, for example, at a training day for managers in charge of purchasing in large organizations. These managers came from large commercial and municipal corporations, and they were working with budgets in the multimillions and with up to 20,000 different suppliers. The purpose of the day was to help them devise strategies that were more environmentally and ethically responsible. They all faced similar problems, the major one of which was to deliver efficiency and economy. There was little room for increasing green and ethical awareness if it were at a financial cost.

They came into the seminar realistic about how their organizations were *now*, but unclear and unrealistic about what their new policies might be. They were all thinking in terms of making one huge leap into a new strategy.

A presentation was made by the Scotts paper company which was inspiring and intelligent. Their chief purchaser, who also sat on their board, had been faced with the same problem of wanting to go green and ethical, but without hurting profits. He developed a strategy in which he sent a questionnaire to all his suppliers to discover how they rated ecologically. He then ranked his suppliers and simply excluded *the worst 10 per cent* from any tenders for a contract. He could still do business with the other 90 per cent. Moreover, he communicated to the excluded 10 per cent exactly why they had been put out of the game, thereby giving them the chance to clean up their act and get back into the action. In this way, he did not risk profits and also encouraged all suppliers to move in a cleaner direction.

He used imagination, time, intelligence and persistence to transform the situation. Asked about what motivated him, there were several answers. Market forces were bearing down on him as consumers demanded cleaner products. Governments also were introducing more stringent pollution controls, as a result of pressure from public opinion and pressure groups. There was also his own innate desire to be a good guy, and pressure from his own children who asked the right questions about the trees that were making the paper he produced.

The Body Shop organization, for example, demonstrates clearly that it is possible to hold to ethical and communal ideals and make a profit in the international market. They precisely monitor the effects and implications of their business on suppliers, staff and consumers.

Most organizations, in fact, already possess intelligence and strategic thinking teams which can be turned towards devising cost-acceptable tactics for including values other than cash in financial decision-making. When a large company, for instance, is about to participate in a substantial transaction, it puts into action the services of what is called its 'due diligence' department. The object of the due diligence unit is to examine the hidden aspects of a deal, to be duly diligent to the real factors and risks involved. Due diligence is an intelligence unit that deliberately sets out to uncover the full financial background and implications of a deal. Normally its remit is concerned with the pure cash viability of the transaction, but the remit of the due diligence unit could easily be expanded to include hidden ecological and humane costs.

Also many companies employ risk assessors whose purpose is specifically to search out and advise on risks that might hurt the company. These units are particularly aware of hazards in the health and safety arenas, and also look for any other conditions that might contravene local or national government regulations, or increase insurance costs. As governments legislate new health and safety or ecological regulations, so the risk assessors look around their companies advising on appropriate action. Again, the responsibility of these intelligence units can expand to include ethical factors.

Companies have to choose whether they will simply stay within the legal limits imposed by legislation and insurance restrictions, or whether they will take a more initiatory role in being humane and ecologically responsible. Many companies recognize that a more proactive policy pays off in better employee relations, healthier community relations and a generally enhanced sense of feel-good. This feel-good cannot be quantified as cash value, but is a public relations asset that can bear real cash returns.

Pressure on companies to take a wider perspective can also come from investors who only want their money involved in companies that are ethically responsible. For many decades there was a powerful movement that steered away from investing in companies with a large stake in the South Africa of apartheid or in companies involved in armaments manufacturing. Today that form of ethical investment monitoring has expanded to exclude companies whose policies are anti-environmental and many other humane factors, for example, the company's attitude to its employees and its local community.

In most countries today there are investment brokers who specialize in ethical and green investments, and their share of the market has substantially increased over the last decade. Their performance is also respectable. Spurred on by this increasing interest of ethically minded investors, companies have another motivation for taking a wider view than that of simple cash profit. Stronger influence could be exerted if the substantial funds of pension funds, religious institutions and philanthropic foundations were invested with integrity and awareness.

A small company or one-person business might say that it does not have the resources to be able to give attention to all this ethical stuff, but the request here is not for a sudden and complete company transformation. It starts with simple first steps of giving a new awareness to purchasing and environment; for example using recycled paper or making sure that your staff do not suffer because of cheap lighting. It also starts with the purely personal activity of making sure that we recognize that everyone with whom we have financial transactions – customers, clients, suppliers, deliverers, cleaners, bankers – is a human being. We do not have to go to bed with them. We do not even have to like them. But we do need to give them some awareness as complete human beings, and not simply as some relevant cog to the machinery of our business. At a very practical level, every business with a cash-flow problem knows the benefit of good personal relationships with its debtors and creditors. When money is owed or an order is late, it is the personal relationship which reassures and which stretches the time limits.

We may not have the time or the trust to sit like Bedouin in the desert exchanging sweet coffee and feeling our way towards a mutually rewarding financial settlement, but perhaps we need to create a bit more time and trust. It is like taking a moment's reflection before eating. It is like stopping before beauty, not rushing past, but stopping and acknowledging the wonder in that moment and that space. It is a matter of giving awareness. Touching money, writing cheques, sliding magnetic bars, reading bar codes, pressing the TRANSACT key, can be signals for a greater humane awareness.

This is like creating excellence in an organization. Or ensuring efficiency or good communications. It has always to begin in our own units. It all starts with us. This is similar to ecological campaigning. It begins with our own actions at home and work. And, as always, it is particularly important that role models – chief executives, directors, managers, parents – take a lead, encourage and empower.

Each of us needs to attempt new ways of working within our organizations and managing our finances. It will serve our own deeper needs as well as the communities in which we live. It is amazing how our individual behaviour can reverberate through our whole financial, social and cultural systems. When one unit in the great economic machine begins to display novel, eccentric or intelligently self-adjusting behaviour, the other elements of the economic machine are receptive and respond to its influence.

Economic Efficiency Versus Caring

The commercial economic culture and the humane economic culture are distinct and in conflict. They possess very different values and very different operating procedures. The commercial culture contains the adrenalin and excitement of innovation, pioneering and creative conflict. Money is the fluid medium of communication which keeps the whole operation moving. The focus in successful commerce must be on cash values and cash flows, and everything that affects them. Information, technology, markets, products and human resources are all equal factors which the commercial operator watches and assesses.

In the humane culture, however, the important factor is the quality of life, the freedom of human beings and of other life forms to fulfil their potential. This requires cooperation, generosity, friendship, connection, warmth, support and nurture. The purpose of money is to enable the circulation of these qualities in a complex community.

It is crucial to recognize the difference between the two cultures and to notice a very practical psychological dimension of this clash. People function effectively and successfully in an environment which meets their sense of who they are. For psychological happiness we need our workplace to meet our sense of ourselves.

This has very dramatic implications for the efficient running of an organization. Across the world over this century the experiment of centrally directed economies has failed terribly. The market does indeed only work efficiently when people are left free to pursue their own interests. All across the Soviet Union, for example, the agricultural yield on tiny private small-holdings was up to twenty times larger than the yield on centrally organized collective farms. The smallholder, the entrepreneur and the business person need a high level of freedom to release their creative energies. When the overarching culture – such as in a centrally directed economy – interferes with this freedom there is a great clash between the individual's sense of self and external reality. The individual, in this psychological clash, does not deliver full involvement and efficiency.

In exactly the same way, if social services such as education or health are run according to market principles, there is again a profound clash between the workers' sense of who they are and what they want to be doing, and the culture in which they work. Over and over again we can see the drive for economic efficiency and the application of free market principles to social services, resulting in a miserable workforce and huge losses in efficiency.

For efficient government and management, we desperately need to recognize and understand the two money cultures: one that is free and competitive; the other which is caring and personal. It is the role of wise management and government to recognize these two separate dynamics – not to force one on a situation which is inappropriate – and to merge them carefully when possible. Is such a merging possible? Yes, but it takes time, energy and awareness.

The most ugly example of the cash culture clashing inappropriately with the humane culture is the sealed bid situation, when people tender for a servicing contract and when the sole criterion for accepting the bid is that it is the most economic in cash terms. Without any negotiation or awareness of the other folk involved, money alone is talking. When I hear of sealed bids being tendered for hospital cleaning contracts or for prison services, my heart drops. I find it hard to believe that the worship of efficient budgeting has reached this level of inhumanity. Cleaners are an integral part of a hospital community, in many ways enhancing the culture of care. The idea that prison services can be run well by the most economically efficient outside contractor is also a recipe for social disaster. I am bemused by the level of stupidity in governments who think that a cheap and severe penal system is an economic choice.

Certainly the idea of cheapness and severity appeals to the shallow authoritarian personalities who vote for narrow-minded politicians, but the real economy is strained even further by social decay. Short-term uncaring and purely cash budgeting are sowing an expensive crop for the future. They are the enemies of a decent and humane world. In the long term, say ten years or so, they carry terrible cash and humane costs. Over and over again we can see that organizations that feel themselves to be part of the community service sector – such as health, education, public transport – collapse into demoralized inefficiency, at terrible economic and human cost, when forced into operating according to market standards and a market culture.

Government

I have several times pointed out the symbolic and real parallels between the fertility and furies of nature and weather, and the expansions, growth and collapses of the world and national economies.

In the same way, therefore, that tribal societies are vulnerable in the face of ecological realities and natural disasters, so modern countries are also vulnerable in the complex interdependent uncontrollable economic world. Cycles of growth and depression, expansion and contraction, are inevitable. As technology changes and as developing countries enter the modern economy, local and out-of-date industries are bound to collapse. Whole economic and industrial cultures decay and have to transform. There is no safe predictability. All that can be safely predicted is the reality of ongoing change. No government can alter these realities.

Nevertheless we still romantically expect our governments to be in full control and the people in government love to pretend that they are in control. This is a political romance which politicians, electors and economists are accustomed to acting and believing. In fact, the best that any modern government can do is to manage change and to help set and maintain priorities. Human beings, however, like simplicity and they also like drama. In the face of a generally unpredictable economy, political economy has fallen into two conflicting camps: the commercial folk and the caring folk. The right wing is for business and the left wing is for caring. This is an important conflict, but all across the democratic world we can see political parties of both sides recognizing that this argument is no longer relevant, that they have to support both business and caring. When I listen to politicians nowadays I am scanning for those who understand that they are part of an inclusive human community. The laissez-faire capitalists exclude that huge section of the community that has neither the skills nor the interest to join in the capitalist game. And the socialist democrats equally tend to exclude that huge section of the community who are the creative individuals and entrepreneurs who make change and wealth and economic growth.

Let me return to the basic tenets of this book which are very relevant again in this political context. In Chapter 5 I listed the nine factors that had drawn us away from humane economic behaviour. When we begin to contemplate the role of government it is helpful to bear these factors in mind. My hope is that government can become an active agent in reversing these tendencies.

First, we are bewitched and hypnotized by the glitter and power of the new economy.

Second, it has all happened so fast that we are in a state of shock.

Third, as population grew and societies became more complex, people from alien cultures met, felt threatened and reacted aggressively. We can write this as an equation:

Primal community = Solidarity and Trust = Sharing and Generosity.

Larger Community = External Threats and Internal Strangers = Anxiety and Accumulation.

Fourth, sharing stopped and accumulation began, triggering a social fragmentation based on possessions rather than who we are as actual people.

Fifth, as societies grew, we could no longer keep a family eye on everyone and unrestrained rogue elements could surface.

Sixth, we created a group of money and trade specialists, separated from the values of their primal communities and creating their own money values.

Seventh, informal and fluid loans and arrangements become legalized and contractualized.

Eighth, as more and more money enters circulation it becomes separated from its association with natural life and relationship.

Ninth, the centralized and authoritative issue of currency can easily become a tool of power political games more interested in domination than community.

As a response to these nine factors, I keep coming back to the same few attitudes which we need to adopt. If we are to return to some kind of sanity and communal decency in our financial lives, we need to give true awareness to our financial transactions. This awareness is made up of three parts and again it is interesting to relate them to government.

First, we need to give awareness to the human beings involved in any financial transaction and we need to make this humane contact as the transaction happens. No transaction is in itself more important than the human relationship of which it is a part.

Second, we need to give intelligent and informed awareness to the implications of the transaction, to be aware of all the other people, processes and natural commodities that are involved. Are the resources circulating in a just way?

Third, we need to give further awareness to whether the transaction *feels* good – for us, for our partners and for all the other living elements involved.

The more important contemporary argument, therefore, is about whether government is stuck in old economic thought, conflictual and ideological, or whether it is realistically open to the contemporary situation. It is clear that modern governments have four orthodox major responsibilities which impinge on the economy. Let's phrase these in orthodox concepts:

1. To legislate and maintain a generally agreed level of expenditure on social goods such as health, social security, health and safety, and so on, regardless of the ups and downs of the economic cycle.
2. To maintain a free market which is fair and not open to abusive bullying and leverage.
3. To encourage, especially in times of slump, the entrepreneurial spirit which is the real dynamo of future growth.
4. To manage and fine tune, using macro-economic strategies such as interest rates and levels of taxation, the nation's economy as it rides the global trends.

Fixation on either free market or socialist ideology is not relevant to these responsibilities. What is relevant is that government has a holistic understanding of economic issues and of the modern realities of an overwhelmingly complex economic system.

A New Framework for Political Decision-making

When I look at the economic policies of political parties I am looking for signs that they understand these issues of complexity and true values. The major problem in the first place is to change the way, as citizens and political decision-makers, we think about money and politics. If we can engage in a new way of thinking, then the whole framework by which political and economic policy is worked out has changed. In a complex world, actual strategies will vary from situation to situation, but if we are not thinking about them in the right way in the first place, then we are lost.

Following the argument of this book, a consistent framework can be easily suggested.

1. Economic policy is understood to be a servant of the people, of the whole community, and not simply a servant of the market and commerce.
2. Economic policy is concerned with ensuring financial and social justice.
3. Economic policy monitors and prevents financial bullying and manipulation.
4. Economic policy stimulates creativity, innovation and the entrepreneurial activity that adds cash and humane value.
5. Economic policy understands that the minting, printing or issuing of money is a service intended to facilitate creative relationship and community. The central issue of money is not a political tool to sustain governments or the vested interests of one particular commercial segment.
6. Economic policy understands that in a healthy community –

local and global – money flows and does not coagulate in specific areas. Economic policy stimulates this real circulation.

7. Economic policy understands the reality of the new financial complexity.
8. Economic policy recognizes the inevitable rhythm of growth and recession due to the nature of the growing world economy.
9. Economic policy recognizes the difference between the commercial and the caring culture.

This can be distilled to three distinct strategies.

A. The need for decentralized flows of information and more humane monitoring.
B. Clearly agreed economic support for social goods regardless of economic cycles.
C. Clearly agreed economic support for wealth creating industries regardless of economic cycles.

A. INFORMATION AND MONITORING. The good parent or chief knows what is going on in the family and tribe, and monitors that there is fair distribution and no bullying. In a complex society, government has to devise ways of monitoring what is happening beyond its immediate vision. This, of course, has always been the purpose of local government, of breaking down the centralized state into counties, regions, boroughs and so on. Wherever possible, government needs to decentralize monitoring and economic decision-making to the smallest local level. There is no other way of ensuring responsible economic awareness. This principle of devolving monitoring and responsibility to the most local level possible is called subsidiarization in the European Community. It is a strategy that is relevant not only to big government but also to small local government. We do not need self-important local bureaucrats and they, in turn, need to hand over monitoring to the people on the spot. Localizing awareness and decision-making has to be operated at all levels and sizes.

Within a small parish there can be clear awareness of what

services need providing to whom. There can be good awareness of how local revenues can be fairly circulated to create a healthy community. This is also the job of national government but on a larger scale, to monitor the whole national community, both geographically and in cultural ways – such as race, gender, religion and class – and make certain that resources are fairly and healthily circulated.

The ongoing figures that demonstrate time and time again that a small proportion of the population owns the vast majority of resources should trigger serious questioning about whether a healthy community can sustain such unbalanced coagulations of wealth – whether the community is local, national or global.

The challenge here is to create information feedback systems which people take seriously and which stimulate ongoing debate and changing strategies. The economic situation is ever changing and requires continuous adaptability.

B. SOCIAL GOODS. The explosive and complex nature of the emergent world economy means that there are bound to be long cycles of growth and recession which cannot be effectively managed. Economic policies need, therefore, to support shared values and goals, rather than being uselessly aimed at a single goal of economic growth, which cannot anyway be controlled.

In times of. growth and economic boom, government and business should, therefore, plan for the next inevitable period of depression.

In times of depression, government and business should support agreed cultural values, accepting the cost (already planned for in the time of boom), and at the same time encouraging conditions which stimulate and protect new business.

It is obvious, therefore, that societies need to agree certain minimum levels of public welfare and social goods, and not go below those minimum levels whether the economy is in depression or boom. We are all generally agreed that child slave labour is not allowable under any circumstances. Our communities also need to decide on other base-line priorities and decide that, regardless of the economic situation, they will be supported at a certain minimal level: for example, education, health care, military security, public communications, policing, the arts. In times of depression, then, when it appears to be more difficult to allocate sufficient financial resources, there will already exist a consensus on priorities and efficiency. Schools and hospitals are not allowed to run down. Local arts do not disappear. The police or armed forces do not get depleted to a level of insecurity.

But in order to continue to support priorities in a depression, the community will have to allocate a greater proportion of its wealth. The major arguments, then, will not be about whether there can be cut-backs in the prioritized areas, but will be about how to pay to maintain the agreed level of service. This means an informed discussion about how and where we tax. In good communities, the adults tighten their belts when living through a time of crisis. The fat cats do not continue to eat their cream teas while the children, for example, lose their educational chances.

C. SUPPORTING ENTREPRENEURIAL CREATIVITY. The primary economic drive is *not* an ability to play with or massage figures. The primary economic drive comes from our instinctive creativity and sense of experimentation and adventure. We know, therefore, that a healthy economy and society encourages individual initiative. We know for certain that societies which limit this freedom create catastrophic economic and human results.

In times of economic depression it is precisely these innovative types who will reinvent the wheel, cut corners, devise new modes of production and new products – all of which will take a community forward into its next phase of expansion and growth. In times of depression, therefore, while belts are being tightened to support agreed communal values, another form of care must be given to that part of the community which is innovative.

That care and support for new enterprise has to be led by government, because the commercial sector will be too self-involved and under-capitalized in periods of recession. When the economy is booming, banks and lenders tend to overextend themselves. Inevitably the boom ends, businesses fail and banks find themselves constricting. In these situations there has to be political leadership – local, regional and national – in supporting and generating new enterprise. From where else can it or should it come?

Communication and Education

In the same way that a true understanding of the humane dynamic of money was hijacked by the commercial classes, so the whole discussion around what is good economics has been hijacked by people who like political argument. This, of course, is to take the lid off a real can of worms. It is a wild generalization – but how wild? – that politicians are more concerned with power than with caring for their communities. In tribal societies many of our respected political figures would be laughed out of the village as pompous, time-wasting buffoons.

Public economic argument, then, is often shouting about undeliverable promises. Who will create the most cash for everyone? Who will deliver us from recession?

As I wrote above, we are all guilty of supporting simplistic economic arguments. We want to believe that government, like the Great Parent in the sky, can fix everything – and that we are not vulnerable to environmental and world economic forces. This is naïve and we have to grow into a more mature economic outlook. The issues are not simple, but very complex. What really interests me is a new model of political communication which is not concerned with short-term economic fixes or with manipulating the sentiments of its citizens. We need a new kind of political culture, a culture in which the major discussion is not about economics as a means of increasing cash wealth, but is about economics as a means of increasing the chances of all life to fulfil its potential.

We need a maturity where political economic argument stops being competitions about who promises the most cash growth and becomes an enlightening debate about how to manage a complex economy for humane values. This requires an education and awareness that will need to permeate the whole of our societies. This education could begin in our schools with some basic life skills training in money awareness and management. Did any of us, as children, get a single lesson in how to think about and deal with money? This education needs to include a truthful history on the origins of money and a truthful history about the development of the modern world economy. Children also need to be introduced to the realities of how other people live, to get a full understanding of both dire and fatal poverty, as well as the creative nurture of wealth.

World Economy

The world economy is a huge natural organism, growing and pulsating as two-thirds of humanity still seeks to proceed through the industrialization process and as the already industrialized world goes through its next stage of electronic change. The problem here is not simply the functional one of technological modernization, but also includes the whole package of dangerous psychological dynamics that arise when so many have-nots are confronted continuously with images of the haves.

There is a terrible dreamworld here of glamorous bewitchment as the banking and managerial classes impose a single vision of economics and development on native peoples. This narrow-minded viewpoint is directly fuelled by a simplistic understanding of money and cash economics. Third world decision-makers are following already set European industrial patterns, rather than relying on internal and local initiative. As I write, the IMF, the World Bank and major international banks are still dancing along ignoring the structural stupidity and malevolence of the situation, rejuggling their debts, pretending that they are still in a normal banking situation. In the 1970s, 80s and 90s the living standards of most developing countries deteriorated terribly.

In our domestic economies we clearly recognize the evil of loan sharks, preying on the financially vulnerable, victimizing those who are already victims. The structural bullying that exists between the developed and developing world has to end. In the long run everyone will pay for these blatantly stupid policies.

It is obvious that the international arena – like the local arena – contains strong and weak players. Provision has to be made so that the weak are not repeatedly abused. The developed countries themselves cannot afford to be complacent, because on the swings and roundabouts of international finance who knows when it will be their turn to be weak and disadvantaged? The British are still smarting from their experience of the IMF in the seventies when they were forced cap-in-hand to accept a loan with restrictions that were socially destructive and humbling to the sense of national community.

Understanding that there are strong and weak brings with it a parallel understanding that the weak need protecting with appropriate policies. It is only the strongest economies who can afford a free trade world with no barriers of any kind – and even they will squeak to erect tariff barriers when their own domestic markets are threatened. The great bastions of free trade, at their will, erect tariffs when and how it pleases them, but forbid smaller and more vulnerable countries to do the same.

There is, therefore, a place for appropriate protectionism. If ever the IMF or GATT became wise, it would actually encourage certain forms of protectionism to help vulnerable nations in times of difficult transition. The ideology that the free market is the best way to sort out these problems is factually, pragmatically and morally bankrupt. The only people to whom it makes sense are those still taking home comfortable wage packets and those still hypnotized by a self-serving ideology that is as shallow as it is harsh.

At the same time, as with domestic economies, the free flow of the world market needs to be encouraged, but once again we hit a disturbing challenge. Domestic national economies and markets are governed by the laws of their countries. The world economy and market has no laws. This is why huge companies and banks which could not even begin to think of abusing their home economies can act freely in the world economy. There are also huge areas of electronic trading which have no humane guidelines at all. Earlier in this book I wrote about the electronic trading in currencies where computer programmes detect minute fluctuations in currency values and can buy and sell within the space of seconds. This is only one example of the international market where people are making money trading money. There is a whole field of the financial industry devoted purely to 'products' derived from other forms of trading. There are also the futures and commodity markets.

According to the people who support these areas, it is just business being business. But it is business that is completely separated from communal and humane life. These substantial transactions are motivated only by the pursuit of cash profit, but their knock-on effects can be huge. When a currency falls or rises because of currency trading, there is a direct effect on government, on industry and ordinary women and men.

I complained to a financial trader once that he worked in an environment that was completely unaware of the implications and effects of what it did. He answered that if governments held their currencies at inflated or deflated values, then I should be grateful that the market put it all right. The financial market, he claimed, made currencies move at their true values. And that, of course, is true. But the value about which he is talking is purely cash value. Trading in commodities, currency, futures, derivatives, has direct knock-on effects. The demand and the prices settled in these markets ripple through to affect millions of women and men who work with their hands. Countries which are dependent for foreign currency on one cash crop, such as coffee or sugar, or one metal such as copper, can have their whole economy devastated by the workings of these markets.

'Inefficient' businesses are knocked out. 'Inefficient' communities are rendered workless. 'Inefficient' lands are laid to waste. We are back in a culture that lacks morality, that would have children as slaves. Do we really want the international market to have this unboundaried power? The word inefficient needs to be reconstrued. It is meaningless to call a child's smile inefficient – or efficient. What has efficiency got to do with love, community, fun, adventure, inspiration?

Over and over again, we see on television and in the press the grinning or grimacing images of frenzied young international traders, gibbering monkeys in the cages of the adrenalized markets, succeeding or failing in their swift and intense deals. I do not mind rich young men and women, but when their frenzied trading directly affects the lives of ordinary families who have not the slightest say or influence in the trade, this is simply not fair. At least when people are involved in explicit violence we can name and condemn it But the violence here is implicit in the system as it destroys communities, cultures and families. The young traders, immersed in their yuppie culture, do not know any better, receiving no guidance from the elders of their own communities.

These international markets have no concern for the human beings involved in the trading. They have no concern with either the short-term or long-term implications of their trading. They have no sense of any values other than cash.

Perhaps these markets are creative and beneficial insomuch as they facilitate the complex new world economy. But they are beyond the boundaries of common sense and common decency.

It is obvious that some overarching economic order has to be introduced. This would be no different from the order that already exists in our national economies. We cannot tolerate internationally what we do not allow at home.

There must be a return to the understanding that the purpose of money is to facilitate humane relationship and creativity. Money cannot remain a servant of short-sighted materialism that damages so much and so many.

CYBERSPACE, CASH AND COMPASSION

A man who dies rich dies disgraced. (Andrew Carnegie)

Wealth unused might as well not exist. (Aesop)

Heart or Corruption?

There is an image which fascinates me. I am told that if we take a soccer ball and spray it with paint, the thin coating of paint is proportionately a thousand times thicker than the effect of human beings upon the planet. Then beyond us there is the universe.

We are a microscopic layer of life in the greater scheme of things.

Both earth and the universe have a certain grace and beauty. Certainly, throughout the ages and cultures, mystics – and ordinary people – have tended to swoon when connected with them. One rarely meets people who, on contemplating a mountain or a river or the night sky, say, 'Yeuch.'

So in this picture we are surrounded by heaven: nature and the cosmos. We have, however, in our tiny human film of life around the earth managed to create a form of hell. It seems that we cannot handle the tension, the awful paradox, of being both biological animal and creature of imaginative consciousness. We are caught in the unbearable tensions of biology, creativity and consciousness. Each is a beautiful element on its own, but experienced simultaneously they create the weird bubbling cauldron of psychology, culture and society. In this cauldron bubbles money.

*

This is the most shocking story of abusive money behaviour that I know: it is happening as I write this passage in 1995. In China there are many thousands of men and women awaiting execution in prison. Some of these people are there for political crimes or crimes not considered a capital offence in other countries. The timing of their execution is frequently in response to the market forces calling for fresh organs for transplant. The corruption of the political system is such that Communist Party officials or rich Chinese in Hong Kong, requiring a fresh organ to heal their illness, can pay/bribe the penal authorities for an execution. A medical team attends the execution, immediately taking the required organ and transporting it to where it has been ordered.

Money is about relationship.

This is an extreme and grotesque example of corruption and abusive financial behaviour. We share our humanity with these people – there but for the grace of God go we – and we know clearly that the corruption should end. It is part of the hell we have created between earth and heaven.

I tell this story, hoping that its stark obscenity will startle us into further questioning our own actions. There are many other obvious obscenities, for example, organized crime, prostitution and slavery. But in what ways, symbolic or real, are we ourselves corrupted or prostituted? In what ways, simply by turning away, do we support obscenities we choose not to see?

These are not nice thoughts. But they are not nice realities in which we may be participating. Because money facilitates relationship, large amounts of money can create a chain of relationship, a huge solidarity, a bribed and corrupt culture, that overwhelms and subjects those without the money.

I once watched a millionaire ethical activist trying to set up a centre. She bought one property which she decided a few months later was not suitable. She did precisely the same thing with a second property. On both occasions she lost large amounts of money and, as one of the advisers on the project, I shared with her that I did not think that this was a good way to husband resources dedicated to a philanthropic end. She giggled and dismissed the idea.

I am not happy with people giggling and looking away from reality.

The Possible Beauty of the Emergent Electronic Economy

Human life, caught between earth and heaven, contains many things of beauty. Recently we have been surprised by computer-generated fractals. The images of chaos, although apparently random, display charm and harmonic form. There is an interesting discord and ambivalence in fractals.

How is it that images of chaos should arrange themselves harmonically and pleasurably to the human eye? We are learning that this is a natural property of complex systems which are emerging. At a certain point, the random elements self-organize, self-catalyse into structure and form. This is the basic quality of *emergence* and we are taught in new science that this is the way of nature and the cosmos in general. We can see it in fractals, or in a seed becoming a plant, or in the Big Bang that expresses itself as this universe forming harmonic galactic spirals. Emergent complex systems self-organize into harmonic form.

We can also see this principle at work in the original emergence of money and complex economies. With no overall planning or central organization, the national and world economies should be completely chaotic. They are not. With very little central organization and certainly with no planned strategy, a pattern of highly complex and innumerable money relationships came into being in a form that is coherent, structured and dependable. Despite the millions of independent actors and the shocking speed of its manifestation, the economic systems function coherently.

The new electronic forms of money, rapidly bursting into our reality, may also emerge into a surprising harmonic form.

Cybermoney and Humane Connection

I have argued that for a general revolution in our money world we have to begin to reclaim the humaneness of our financial transactions. It may seem, therefore, that the world of computer-based money – *e-cash* – is yet another step away from flesh and blood reality. But electronic cash is generated by real people and the women and men sitting at computer terminals are not themselves computers.

In 1994 an amazing thing happened. As the first e-cash was being placed within the framework of the Internet, the organizers realized that to bring people into this new electronic community they needed to give away money. One million dollars' worth of e-cash tokens were offered up freely in order to attract people into playing in this new arena.

Electronic cash in cyberspace, far from creating emotionless zombies, actually creates new communities of human beings seeking relationship through shared creativity and shared interests. This happens because our real geographical communities are now so big and complex that it is very difficult, as we all know, for people to meet and connect. A computer-based bulletin board, however, accessed through a home computer and telephone line, positively helps folk to connect with like-minded others. They can then communicate, relatively inexpensively, with each other through this medium and, when they want, choose also to meet in real life.

This is crucially relevant to the future of money because there is a possibility that in a few decades the vast majority of money transactions will be done electronically. There is, therefore, an ongoing opportunity here to humanize the economic system.

Today, when I go to buy anything, it is difficult to get all the information on where the source materials come from, who exported it, what the working conditions are, where it is manufactured and so on. This kind of information is generally inaccessible.

It is, however, very easy to post this information on an

electronic bulletin board so that anyone can, in a minute or so, call up the background information on the product or service that they are thinking of buying. It is also possible to communicate directly with the individual or sub-group in a large organization in order to get specialist information.

Product inquiries nowadays are met, if at all, by public relations people rather than by the people who have hands-on experience. It is easily conceivable that the mammoth bureaucratic hassles now involved in getting clear information will simply dissolve in a new communications culture of open information systems. This would be a true economic democracy.

In fact, the new electronic cash, hand-in-hand with open access information – instead of blocking humane economic transactions – can actually encourage and facilitate increased awareness about the effects of any money transaction.

This, then, is the totally optimistic picture of the future of money. Weaving through the complex world economy, electronic money coupled to open information systems allows real connections to be made between the people involved in any transaction along with increased awareness of the ramifications. This kind of connection and monitoring is hardly possible with the old communications systems and hierarchical closed-information cultures.

The hardware and software are becoming increasingly less expensive and more user-friendly. New generations are now coming through for whom this electronic world is simple everyday reality.

The idea of a planetary village is becoming more vivid as the ability to communicate globally, to groups and individuals, day by day becomes more accessible.

Taken to its extreme, it would be possible for me to buy a rug and scan its barcode. Immediately on screen I might see a picture of the people who wove it. Click here and I could learn of their working conditions. Click there and I discover the exporter – and his cash mark-up. Another click could take me into a variety of information: the source of the yarn, the transporter, the import tax, the dyeing process . . . I could do the same with a car or a computer or a cola. There could be open information about products and services.

This is an open information economy. And it is being developed right now. It might seem unrealistic or romantic, but the technology is overtaking us and our decent human need for a creative life with meaningful human relationships provides the drive to create this new culture.

Organizations clothed in opaque corporate images will have to transform their images, become transparent and display the people and systems that actually make up their total structure. An interesting question is whether, in a few years from now, people will want to do business with an organization that does not provide open information about itself. Cyberspace, cyber-money and open access information are creating an environment in which we can re-create our financial culture, so that we can know all we want to know about the people with whom we are in money relationship.

In the great ocean of the world economy, however, as fortunes rise and subside, there is going to have to be ongoing governmental monitoring – global, continental, national, regional and local – to ensure that human dignity and ecological well-being suffer as little as possible due to changing economic circumstances. This is a challenge that is not beyond our organizational skills. It does mean, though, that folk who want to surf the information world with no sniff of Big Brother will have to surrender to the need for governmental intervention – taxes, levies, trade barriers, enhancements, regimes – which ensures the support of human dignity and a healthy ecology.

This, of course, will lead to interesting, heated and continuous political debate. This debate, I imagine, will continue for ever and it needs to. It is the essence of meaningful politics: the protection of human rights and freedoms, the allocation of resources, setting priorities, preventing abuse.

Resistance and Creative Aggression

People, of course, will also resist – already are resisting – open information because information is power.

To bring in a new money culture requires a diminishment, the gradual disappearance, of the macho style of aggressive economic competition. This means that the men – and women – who like the adrenalin rush of success and aggression need to re-imagine and re-frame how they express their dynamic energy. Their dynamic energy needs to be harnessed to visions of the common good.

In the new world of information and electronic money courage will be displayed in who is the most transparent, not in who wears the most powerful armour. The ignobility of faceless competition, of brute power, gives way to a more personal form of creative conflict.

Global and Local Community

Cyberspace, e-cash and the planetary village do not, despite appearances, work to create a culture of further alienation and increased distance between people.

Transcontinental connection is fun, but geographical proximity is also important because it indicates the possibility of other shared interests, such as children at the same school or use of the same sports facilities or relaxing in the same bar. Geographical proximity means a tendency towards shared cultural and political interests.

In fact, the increased awareness of the enjoyment of human contact may also completely alter the money relationship, sometimes make it disappear completely. Sprouting up all over the world, for instance, are local exchange trading systems (LETS) in which people swap skills, time and resources. No cash is involved and small independent local economies are created. I am a member of a LETS scheme and when one of the people running it telephones me, she is encouraging me to participate in an economy where the chief pay-off is human contact. She does not encourage me to spend money, but to use services and meet local people.

My whole house, in fact, was decorated by a wonderful man, Jan, and for his services I exchanged some money, free entry to my workshops and some copywriting for his business. When we wanted the house decorated we had three firms come in and quote for us. My wife and I chose Jan, not because of his price, but because we liked him and wanted to work with him. Where profit is not the main incentive, then we can choose with whom we do business not purely on the basis of financial costs, but on the basis of other human and more enjoyable considerations.

Urban Fear

Born into riches or born into poverty we are imprisoned by our lack of experience. We do not know the whole picture. And even if we do know the whole picture, it is often more comfortable to forget it. Holding our awareness open to general realities – not just our own – is crucial.

At this time of writing I have a one-year-old daughter, Sophia, who is the apple of my eye. I adore her. As she grows older I want her to have the freedom to walk the streets of this city, London, without fear, but there are young men and women without money – without the means to purchase the images that will give them identity and respect – and they may threaten my beautiful girl. These frightening street kids are also just children. They have been brought up in a culture that does not care for them with wise love. There is the rude and harsh lack of money.

Where some people have money and others do not, those who are without it receive little respect. We treat our poor badly. We have moved so far from the instinctive glue of community that poverty is considered some kind of failure, a crime – be poor, feel guilty.

The innovative Bangladeshi banker Mohammed Yunus looked

at the directors of the World Bank and IMF at one meeting, and asked, 'Who decreed that only those who have, shall receive our loans? We did. Human beings did. We can change that.'

George Bernard Shaw had a clear understanding of money. He wrote in his introduction to *Man and Superman*:

The universal regard for money is the one hopeful fact in our civilization, the one sound spot in our social conscience. Money is the most important thing in the world. It represents health, strength, honour and generosity, and beauty as conspicuously as the want of it represents illness, weakness, disgrace, meanness, and ugliness.

These words are a wonderful and unusual attitude for a socialist. For Shaw, money is wonderful because it provides the means for society to right the social wrongs, it provides the means for a beautiful and aesthetic existence. He stands full opposite the radicals of the left who see money only as the tool of manipulative commerce. He also stands full opposite the mean-spirited who see money only as a tool for ego gratification.

How do some of us get to be mean-spirited and others filled with the spirit of sharing and generosity? The book of life answers that question by speaking directly through our hearts. I know, though, that it takes courage and effort to move from an attitude of meanness to one of generosity.

There is a fact that I have heard many times, yet every time I hear it I am shocked. According to the information of opinion polls and academic research, the rich give far less proportionately to charity and distress than do the poor. To put this information another way, the poor are more generous than the rich. This is a terrible shaft of insight into the contemporary human condition that shames us all. Somehow or other, as people become clothed in the insulating layers of 'civilization' that are bought by money, they lose their connection.

We shall have no civilized future until people understand the full dangers of a culture dominated by the dynamics of relative deprivation. We shall have no civilized future until those who are wealthy, relatively wealthy, understand the need to be as generous as those who are poor – and experience the creative release of gifting and sharing.

The very moment that I write this, I recognize that I too must give away more of my money – and I feel resistant. I notice that I am caught again in the anxiety that there is not enough.

Scarcity, Evil and the Anima Mundi

This psychological sense of scarcity seems reflected in ecological realities. In *Unlimited Wealth*, however, Paul Zane Pilzer states provocatively that the source of material wealth is not the natural resources of the earth, but that the real source is human ingenuity and technology. He quotes the wonderful example of sand. It is human technology that turns sand into glass. Without human ingenuity the sand is only sand. Once people looked at black sticky stuff bubbling in the earth and thought it ugly and useless. Who ever imagined that gas, locked in pockets under the oceans, could be used by us? Recently astronomers discovered a huge cloud of natural alcohol floating in space 10,000 light years away. Who knows how that might be harnessed? The problem is not with scarce resources, but simply with the technology. Anything can be turned into anything with the right technology.

Pilzer is right that the challenge lies in the technology, but more importantly it lies in the human management of the technology. If that management is brain-dead to implications beyond the cash bottom line, if that management is brain-dead to communal and ecological effects, then that technology will take us only into deeper alienating crisis.

Holding on to money, the inability or unwillingness to let it flow, approaches – through the gateway of psychological terror, selfishness and anxiety – the domain of evil. Our prisons are filled mainly with men who have sought more money. The danger on our city streets comes from a similar source. The origin of so many bloody relationships has been the inability to share resources, wealth and money. Coagulated in personal or collective stashes, its effect is toxic. We have to release. Release. Release.

In contrast, there is the creative warmth of money. The poet Ezra Pound, in his *Cantos*, suggested that money is the *anima mundi*. Money is the spirit that communicates between all things material and, as such, is the soul of the world. What a provocative thought from which to begin a contemplation or appreciation of money.

We rarely appreciate the beauty of money's work. The idea seems absurd, to appreciate money as we might appreciate nature, but look at the extraordinary service money does to facilitate our world and our communities.

The soul or essence of the material world – the *anima mundi* – sits in our pockets, wallets, banks, credit cards, in many different vessels. When we use the smallest coin or make a huge electronic transfer, we are acting in more than one reality. We are in the obvious and existential reality of the numerical transaction. Units of cash are flowing in one direction. There is a debit and a credit. Goods or services are transferred. There is also the human reality of the people involved in the transaction. Emotionally, psychologically, what does the money represent? It may be influence and power, both gained and lost; or it may be affection and love; or security; or anxiety. In every transaction there are feelings and connections or alienations. In every transaction – from the purchase of a small bag of peanuts through to a new home – there are implications.

We express who we are through how we use our money.

Eskimos and Medicis

So my mind is continually drawn back to the Eskimo hunter-warrior whose sole indication of being the greatest hunter in the clan was the poverty of his own home – for his duty was to share and to support the weak. I also think often of the clan elders, always watching, preventing injustice, encouraging the relationships of sharing and communality. I want these qualities to manifest among our bankers, our politicians, our entrepreneurs and our business people in general. I want these qualities to belong to all of us. 'I'm banking on you' means that I am putting my trust in you and that I value you.

When success and wealth on a large scale have allied themselves with goodwill and the common good, the results can be spectacular. The rise of the gothic cathedrals and first European universities was directly linked to wealth and the emerging banking system. The relationship of the Medicis with the Renaissance still glows in Venice and Florence. There is the flowering of Arabic culture when the great Islamic traders and bankers harnessed their wealth to the high ideals of Islam. All of this is more than philanthropy. It is an inspiration to understand that the purpose of good banking and wealth creation is the enhancement of life, respect for the sacred and all living things.

Although as individuals we may not build public monuments, we nevertheless always have the opportunity to act with financial goodwill and dignity. If these actions come from a psychological base of security and confidence, then we have a genuine inner wealth.

Behaving with financial dignity, awareness and goodwill benefits us. It benefits the communities in which we live – from the community of our nuclear families through to the planetary village. We need to put this behaviour into action in our personal, business, social and political lives. And we need to demand the same of others, educating, persuading and inspiring.

All across the world people are struggling to make sense of money. The simplistic view that money represents only cash value carries no real satisfaction. As our children grow up and enter adult society, as the people newly liberated from communism re-create their cultures, as two-thirds of the world passes through development into modernization, we desperately need an approach to money which satisfies heart and mind.

We *can* re-create money as a servant of true wealth, creativity and relationship.

The Crisis and Solution

The Tibetan abbot and teacher Djwahl Kuhl stated with great clarity, 'Our period is simply one in which human selfishness has come to its climax and must either destroy humanity or be brought intelligently to an end' (Bailey).

This climactic selfishness is explicit and obvious. There is a simple and obscene reality which many of us seem able to gloss over, throwing token concern in its direction, which is that every day 30,000 children die through malnutrition.

At the same time, men and women are choking on their anxiety to maintain their mortgage payments, hold on to their homes, build their careers, sustain their self image – sustained by alcohol, crippled by stress, slain by heart attacks.

We recognize these sicknesses of our culture and society, and we may look to government and to leaders to create a new model for our collective life. But looking to others for leadership can be a terrible naïveté, for they too are caught by the *spirit* of our times. They, like us, are bewitched by the spell.

In this spell the greatest illusion is the idea that we are, by nature, nasty, selfish, anxious brutes. Part of this illusion is the macabre but casually accepted notion that it is the nobility of the state, of government, of the captains of commerce and industry which organizes us into a semblance of civilization. This is rubbish. It is similar to the idea that war is the result of an instinct for mass aggression, when the truth is that for centuries it has been the leaders, monarchs, emperors, war cabinets which have declared, mobilized for and sustained war.

The mass of people also has little interest in or liking for greed and social injustice. Robin Hood and Jesus and Buddha sit in our hearts, models of generosity.

We are not as a species greedy selfish brutal creatures fighting for dominance. Some of us are, and occasionally all of us may feel that way, but that is not our dominant attitude. It is a political idea, serving particular interests, that we are brutes, not a truthful psychological insight into human nature. There is the overwhelming anthropological evidence of the generous instinctive behaviour of human beings in tribal communities and families. There is also the experiential and very personal evidence. What do we really want from ourselves and from others? We want cooperation, sharing and generosity: a manifestation of our basic instinct to love.

Most of us, though, are frozen in the ice spell of false consciousness, of seductive consumerism, of a worldview that says savage competition is normal. It is an overwhelming, frightening and sexy spell.

We seem to be waiting for some supernatural occurrence to shake us free. The Messiah, the Avatar, will appear. The Revolution will finally come. The Market will work so miraculously that everyone will be trickled down to and nurtured. There will be ecological Apocalypse out of which will rise a new socially just, humbled and green consciousness.

We have tried on all these ideas, and each one takes away our personal power and leaves us like a fish on the shore, dying futilely waiting for the tide to turn.

If we want cooperation, sharing and generosity, then we have to put it into practice ourselves. Day by day we need to review our personal and business lives and assess whether we have supported a culture of sharing; or whether we have been enslaved by or are enslaving others in a worldview and experience of meanness. Collectively, our personal decisions create the change and create the leaders and ideologies we need.

Expansion, Transformation and the Re-creation of Community

We are living through a historical period of huge change, equal to the time when the first hunter-gathers settled as pastoralists in the river basins, or the industrial revolution. The major features are information technology and the ability to experience the planet and humanity as a whole. The very real effect of being in a global village, cliché though that may seem, is that we genuinely receive the images and communications; we can now experience the totality of our community.

It has been a strange evolution of collective consciousness.

Once we were all in the safety of primal and tribal communities. These communities grew, became more complex, met and frightened each other. Separated from primal community, we then became naturally lost in a period of alienation. Now in a wonderful monument of historical paradox, the global village gives us back our community. Once only in relationship with our kith and kin, now we are explicitly in relationship with everyone and everything. We now rediscover our family and our tribe – and this tribe is everyone everywhere.

This re-creation of community – it requires only an expanded imagination – is hand-in-hand with other great social changes. The centralized thrust of economic growth and industry has lost its organic coherence. Monoliths are fragmenting into humane units. Communication is becoming patterned and losing its authority-led linearity. We are regaining power and responsibility.

We can, therefore, no longer remain cold in our financial transactions. This frigidity is only appropriate when we are dealing with strangers and today we are no longer strangers to each other. We may wish, fearful of intimacy and responsibility, to be strangers but this is no longer realistic. No living thing is now excluded from the community of our awareness. Financial acts can carry once again the charisma of meaning and of relationship.

This new world questions not only the awareness with which we handle our actual money, but the whole way in which we engage with the world to earn our living. Profound questions of right livelihood are posed to each of us to be answered in the privacy of our conscience. Responsibility is thrown back at us.

The new world emerging supports this responsible individuality. Individualism - alienated personal fulfilment – gives way to self-aware collective sensitivity. The rugged individuals, echoing the conscience and natural generosity of the tribal hunter, now find their self-respect only when knowing and acting towards their communal connections. This is not a romantic ideal. It is anchoring even into the basic structures of industrial production and work patterns. There are no longer jobs for life or vocational skills that will guarantee ongoing employment. The one fundamental skill now required for successfully navigating the emerging economic world is the ability to learn anew, to know how to change and adapt. Multidimensional awareness, the ability to flow and transform, are the features of the new work world. The pursuit of excellence in any company now requires the multidimensional awareness of its workforce.

Once the perceived enemies of humane progress, industry and commerce now encourage, they actually need, flexible humans with collective awareness. Technological progress once again can mean progress for everyone.

The crisis of collective selfishness demands our new personal awareness. The dynamic of technological change and the new economic realities demand precisely the same.

The global village seduces, cajoles and shocks us with consciousness of our interdependence.

New Worldview, New World Order

Simultaneously, as we experience this new world, a new worldview, a new understanding of life, is also surfacing. Quantum physics through to chaos and complexity, science is reframing the world from a cold harmonic mechanism into an emergent juicy creature of chaotic beauty, in which the essence of life is neither particle nor wave, neither here nor there, always appearing, emergent, organizing, subsiding.

In this new scientific vision, the world retains certain patterns of predictability and at the same time becomes a far more artistic expression of unpredictability – all of this demanding that we retain our attitude of logic and consistent focus, yet also that we expand our consciousness into a more intuitive and multidimensional awareness.

The social sciences of politics and economics will have trouble following these new models. The new models are not psychologically safe. They do not support centralized power or know authority structures.

Managers of financial wealth will also have trouble in understanding these new realities, for in understanding them they must begin to disintegrate, releasing their wealth into the complex flow of relationship which is the norm for a global village. In tribal communities the accumulation of wealth was considered a laughable piece of dangerous buffoonery and we too can now see accumulated wealth for what it is: a cancerous anomaly clogging the system, feeding false and life-destructive addictions, relieved only by the sometime innocence and naïveté of its possessors. Responsible and successful management can be seen in sharing, flow, and true responsibility for and love of the collective.

The resistance in the transnational structure of the world economy will be huge. Public opinion must force the governments of the world and the United Nations to organize the system so that the world's natural resources are shared. Just as in our domestic economies we cannot allow our citizens on the margins to perish in body or mind, so we must organize as a planetary collective to redress the most basic stupidities of a market that follows the old and frigid laws of money.

History teaches us the fabulous impermanence of our most cherished notions. The passage of time is in its very nature iconoclastic, punctuated by short-term faiths, beliefs and structures. It is not safe or intelligent to adhere to accepted ways of thought, accepted modes of interpretation. Yet it is possible to find some sort of essence in all human life.

One such essence, seemingly permanent, is our need and love of connection and relationship. This is partly a sexual and biological imperative. It is also a psychological drive. We are also conscious and creative beings. If we then cut through the layers of accepted thought, of complacent habit, we reveal money as a servant of connection, relationship and creativity.

Strip away the changing ideas and forms, perceive the essence of human and humane connection, and money is part of that essence. As we pass through our time of historical change, gloomy poverty-consciousness is no answer and certainly no fun. Equally, the blind pursuit of material success and financial wealth is only a recipe for temporary euphoria and long-term distress. Nor is a flabby middle-of-the-road attitude appropriate, for it is based in a cowardice which as a collective phenomenon passively supports economic injustice.

We have little choice, then, but to trust our essence and to have the courage to act in new and generous ways. It starts with tiny but regular acts of giving and of financial awareness. It starts with smiling at the bills and statements. It starts with recognizing the interdependence of all life.

The purpose of this book is to support a process through which we change the way that we think and feel about money. Human freedom, social justice, ecological sanity, for example, are also issues which we approach with both the heart and the mind. They require a consistent and passionate concern without which we may create cruelty and the imprisonment of the human spirit.

There are moments in history when we are called to engage in collective events and when we cannot stand aside. This is not a comfortable process. It needs us to sacrifice some of our habitual behaviour. In terms of money and our global economic culture we are precisely in a time when we have to participate in collective action. This particular action, however, does not require us to take to the streets or risk our lives. It simply requires that we live our financial lives in a decent, creative and humane way. The fact that it is not a mass political movement in which we have to stand up and be counted may, of course, make it easier for us to avoid doing the right thing – but our natural instinct for love, our integrity, our self-respect, our compassion, our ability to perceive the results and consequences, can guide us.

Every action involving money is an opportunity for life-supporting awareness. This awareness then enlightens our own psychological shadows, enhances the individual transaction and, through the web of interdependence, works to transform the collective money world. The spirit of money is liberated.

Money no longer alienates and separates, but is a gesture of our hearts.

APPENDIX

Further Action

If you are interested in putting into practice some of the ideas in this book – e.g. local exchange schemes, ethical investment, tithing or granting – and are not sure where to go next, two organizations are providing up-to-date resource material.

In the US a Resource list is available for $15 (cheques made payable to The Impact Project). Write to:
Alden Hancock,
More Than Money,
2244 Alder Street,
Eugene OR 97405 (Tel: (503) 343 5023)

In the UK a Resource list is available for £5 (cheques made payable to New Economics Foundation). Write to:
New Economics Foundation (Money Project),
Vine Court,
112 Whitechapel Road,
London E1 1JE

Workshops, Trainings and Cassettes

If readers are interested in William Bloom's workshops, trainings and cassettes, please write to:

Alternatives (Money),
St James's Church,
197 Piccadilly,
London W I V 0LL

Further Reading

To reframe your understanding of money completely or for the anthropological perspective, Marshall Sahlins's *Stone Age Economics*. Academics have no choice but to look at Paul Einzig's *Primitive Money*.

There are many books in the field of new economics. I particularly recommend Lutz and Lux's *Humanistic Economics*. People educated in economics might like to look at Paul Ormerod's *The Death of Economics*.

For the metaphysically create-your-own-reality folk, I particularly recommend Roman and Packer's *Creating Money*.

For reorganizing your personal finances, the best programme in my opinion is Dominguez and Robin's *Your Money or Your Life*.

General Bibliography

This general bibliography lists the books mentioned in the text and also others that have interested or influenced me recently.

Albert-Poissant, Charles, *How to Think Like a Millionaire*, Thorsons, 1989.

Albery, Nicholas (ed.), *The Book of Visions*, Virgin, 1990.

Anderson, Victor, *Alternative Economic Indicators*, Routledge, 1991.

Bailey, Alice, *The Externalisation of the Hierarchy*, Lucis Press, 1980.

Berger, Peter, *The Sacred Canopy*, Anchor Press, 1988.

Bloom, William, *Personal Identity, National Identity and International Relations*, Cambridge University Press, 1990.

The Book of Sufi Chivalry, East West Publications, 1983.

Borneman, Ernest, *The Psychoanalysis of Money*, Urizen Books, New York, 1976.

Boundy, Donna, *When Money is the Drug*, HarperCollins, 1993.

Breton, Denise and Largent, Christopher, *The Soul of Economics – Spiritual Evolution Goes to the Marketplace*, Idea House/Green Print, 1991.

Bryan, Mark, and Cameron, Julia, *The Money Drunk – 90 Days to Financial Freedom*, Ballantine Books, 1992.

Budd, Christopher, *Of Wheat and Gold*, New Economy, 1988.

Carlisle, John A., and Parker, Robert C., *Beyond Negotiation – Redeeming Customer / Supplier Relationships*, John Wiley, 1990

Chopra, Deepak, *Creating Affluence*, New World Library, California, 1993.

Crump, Thomas, *The Phenomenon of Money*, Routledge & Kegan Paul, 1981.

Dauncey, Guy, *After the Crash – The Emergence of the Rainbow Economy*, Green Print/Merlin Press, 1989.

Dominguez, Joe, and Robin, Vicki, *Your Money or Your Life*, Penguin, 1993.

Einzig, Paul, *Primitive Money*, Pergamon, 1966.

Eisler, Raine, *The Chalice and the Blade*, HarperCollins, 1990.

Ekins, Paul (ed.), *The Living Economy*, Routledge, 1991.

Ekins, Paul, and Max-Neef, Manfred, (eds.), *Real-Life Economics*, Routledge, 1992.

Ekins, Paul, et al., *Wealth Beyond Measure*, Gaia Books, 1992.

Elgin, Duane, *Voluntary Simplicity*, Morrow, 1981.

Evans-Pritchard, E. E., *The Nuer – A Description of the Mode of Livelihood and Political Institutions of a Nilotic People*, Oxford University Press, 1940.

Fisher, Mark, *The Instant Millionaire*, Sidgwick & Jackson, 1988.

Francis, Susan, and Crofts, Andrew, *Nowhere to Hide – A Mother's Ordeal in the Killing Fields of Iraq and Kurdistan*, Weidenfeld, 1993.

Frazer, James, *The Golden Bough*, Macmillan, many editions.

Freud, Sigmund, *Group Psychology and the Analysis of the Ego*, Vol. XIV of Standard Works, Hogarth Press, 1921.

Gillies, Jerry, *MoneyLove*, Warner Books, New York, 1981.

Hamilton, Clive, *The Mystic Economist*, Willow Park Press, 1994.

Hawken, Paul, *The Next Economy*, Holt Rinehart, 1983.

Hayek, F. A., *The Denationalisation of Money*, Institute of Economic Affairs, 1978.

Healey, Joseph G., *A Fifth Gospel – In Search of Black Christian Values*, SCM Press/Orbis Books, 1981.

Henderson, Hazel, *Paradigms in Progress*, Berret-Koehler, 1995.

Henderson, Hazel, *Building a Win-Win World*, Berret-Koehler, 1996.

Hoogendijk, Willem, *The Economic Revolution*, Green Print, 1991.

Hwoschinsky, Paul, *True Wealth*, Ten Speed Press, Berkeley, 1990.

Hyde, Lewis, *The Gift*, Random House, 1983.

Jackson, Kevin (ed.), *The Oxford Book of Money*, Oxford, 1995.

Jaikaran, Jacques S., *Debt Virus*, Glenbridge Publishing, Colorado, 1992.

Jevons, W. Stanley, *Money and the Mechanism of Exchange*, London, 1975.

Kennedy, Margrit, *Interest and Inflation Free Money*, Permaculture Institute Publications, Steyerberg, Germany, 1988.

Keynes, J. M., *The General Theory of Employment, Interest and Money*, 1936.

Kurtzman, Joel, *The Death of Money*, Simon & Schuster, 1993.

Laut, Phil, *Money Is My Friend*, Trinity Publications, California, 1985.

Lévi-Strauss, Claude, *The Elementary Structures of Kinship*, Eyre & Spottiswoode, 1969.

Lieberg, James E., *Merchants of Vision*, Berrett-Koehler/World Business Academy, 1994.

Lutz, Mark and Lux, Kenneth, *Humanistic Economics*, Bootstrap Press, 1988.

McBurney, Stuart, *Ecology into Economics Won't Go*, Green Books, 1990.

Macpherson, C. B., *The Rise and Fall of Economic Justice*, Oxford University Press, 1985.

Malinowski, Bronislaw, *Argonauts of the Western Pacific*, Routledge, 1950.

Mauss, Marcel, *The Gift*, Norton, 1967.

Max-Neef, Manfred, *Human Scale Development*, Apex Press, 1991.

Mead, George Herbert, *Mind, Self and Society*, Chicago University Press, 1934.

Mill, John Stuart, *Principles of Political Economy*, London, 1878.

Mogil, Christopher, and Slepian, Anne, *We Gave Away a Fortune*, New Society Publishers, 1992.

Naisbitt, John, *Global Paradox*, Nicholas Brealey Publishing, 1994.

Needleman, Jacob, *Money and the Meaning of Life*, Currency/Doubleday, 1991.

Novaks, Michael, 'Eight Arguments about the Morality of the Marketplace' in Jon Davies (ed.), *God and the Marketplace*, Institute of Economics Affairs, 1993.

Oliver, Douglas, *A Solomon Island Society*, Harvard University Press, 1955.

Ormerod, Paul, *The Death of Economics*, Faber, 1994.

Packard, Vance, *The Ultra Rich – How Much Is Too Much?* Little Brown, 1989.

PAID (People Against Interest Debt), *Usury: The Root Cause of the Injustice of Our Time*, 1987.

Peck, M. Scott, *A World Waiting to be Born*, Random House/Rider, 1983.

Phillips, Michael, *The Seven Laws of Money*, Word Wheel/Random House, 1974.

Phipps, John-Francis, *The Politics of Inner Experience*, Green Print/Merlin Press, 1990.

Pilzer, Paul Zane, *Unlimited Wealth*, Crown, 1990.

Poissant, Charles-Albert, *How to Think Like a Millionaire*, Thorsons, 1989.

Ponder, Catherine, *Pray and Grow Rich*, Parker, 1977.

Ponder, Catherine, *Dynamic Laws of Prosperity*, DeVorss, 1985.

Ponder, Catherine, *The Prosperity Secrets of the Ages*, DeVorss, 1986.

Price, John Randolph, *The Abundance Book*, Quartus, 1987.

Radner, Roy, 'Competitive Equilibrium under Uncertainty', *Econometrica*, Vol. 36, 1968, quoted in Ormerod, p. 90.

Rawls, John, *A Theory of Justice*, Oxford University Press, 1972.

Reay, Marie, *The Kuma*, Melbourne University Press, 1959.

Robertson, James, *Future Wealth – A New Economics for the 21st Century*, Cassell, 1990.

Roman, Sanaya, and Packer, Duane, *Creating Money*, H. J. Kramer, California, 1988.

Russell, Peter, *The White Hole in Time*, HarperCollins, 1992.

Sahlins, Marshall, *Stone Age Economics*, Routledge, 1988 (wonderful introduction to the anthropological perspective).

Saltzman, Amy, *Downshifting: Reinventing Success on a Slower Track*, HarperCollins, 1991.

Sampson, Anthony, *The Money Lenders*, Hodder & Stoughton, 1981.

Sampson, Anthony, *The Midas Touch – Money, People and Power from West to East*, BBC/Hodder, 1989.

Sardello, Robert J., and Severson, Randolph, *Money and the Soul of the World*, Pegasus Foundation, Dallas, 1983.

Simmel, Georg, *The Philosophy of Money*, Routledge, 1990.

Sinetar, Marsha, *Do What You Love, The Money Will Follow*, Bantam Dell, 1987.

Slater, Philip, *Wealth Addiction*, Dutton, 1983.

Smith, Adam, *Paper Money*, Macdonald, 1981.

Spencer, Robert F., *The North Alaskan Eskimo: A Study in Ecology and Society*, Smithsonian Institution Bureau of American Ethnology Bulletin 171, 1959.

Steiner, Rudolf, *World Economy*, Rudolf Steiner Press, 1977.

Taylor, F. M., *Chapters of Money*, Michigan, 1906.

Thomas, Elizabeth Marshall, *The Harmless People*, Knopf, 1959.

Vadillo, Umar, *The End of Economics – An Islamic Critique of Economics*, Madinah Press, Granada, 1991.

Vadillo, Umar, *Fatwa on Paper-Money*, Madinah Press, Granada, 1991.

Vilar, Pierre, *A History of Gold and Money 1450–1920*, Verso, 1984.

Waldrop, M. Mitchell, *Complexity – The Emerging Science of Order and Chaos*, Simon & Schuster, 1992.

Ward, Sue, *Socially Responsible Investment*, Directory of Social Change, 1986.

Wilde, Stuart, *The Trick to Money is Having Some!*, White Dove, 1989.

World Bank, *World Development Report 1991*, Oxford University Press, 1991.

INDEX

identity and, 36
and prosperity-conscious-
ness, 47, 50–55

tariffs, 248
Taylor, F. M., 70
technology
changes in, 239
and human management,
260
and the industrial revolution, 89, 96
innovations and inventions
of, 95–98
modern versus traditional,
93–94
Teilhard de Chardin, Pierre,
150
terrorism, 223
theft, 35–36, 38, 41, 187
Thomas, Elizabeth, 76–77
tithing, 173–177
Toffler, Alvin, 96
trade
electronic, 6, 18, 90, 249–
250
external, 68–69
free, 248
internal, 69
money and ease of, 12–13
as peace-making activity,
110–111
primitive money and, 64–
67
rise of, 116
specialization in, 14
transnational corporations,
125–126
and growth of world econ-
omy, 221–222

and structure of world
economy, 267
tribal societies
generosity and sharing
among, 76–80, 88, 90
gifting and, 74–75
identity in, 38–39, 41
markets in, 80–83, 89
modern, 89–90, 99–100
monetary management in,
139
and origins of money, 63–
65, 76–80
reactions to threats, 98–101
value of work in, 58
vulnerability of, 239
see also hunter-gatherers;
specific groups
Trobriand Islanders
generosity among, 78
gifting and, 74–75
True Value Units, 226–227

unconscious
archetypes in, 16–17, 156–
166, 176–177
collective, 158–161
dreams and, 147–152, 158
and healing process, 183–
185
and primal anxiety, 187
and psychology of money,
153, 183–185
United Nations, 121, 267
universal human, 152
Unlimited Wealth (Pilzer), 260
usury, 143, 248

value, adding, 15–16, 57–59
Veblen, Thorstein, 109

ABOUT THE AUTHOR

William Bloom was born in London in 1948. He has been a major figure for more than two decades on Britain's publishing and cultural scenes, devoting himself to the integration of new paradigms into traditional modes of thought and practice. In the 1970s he founded the Open Gate publishing imprint, one of the first to specialize in counterculture titles. He cofounded Advise, the first twenty-four-hour counseling service for immigrants in London. He then received a doctorate in social psychology from the London School of Economics, and also taught there. During the same period he earned his teaching certificate and spent nine years working with special needs teenagers and adults in an inner-city community college. He also helped pioneer a course in managing community organizations.

In 1988 he cofounded the popular Alternatives program of St. James Church, Piccadilly, in London. The program offers weekly lectures, workshops, and classes covering a wide range of alternative spiritual practices, such as tribal religions, spiritual ecology, meditation, metaphysics, new psychology, and science. The program attracts more than 10,000 people every year.

Bloom has taught regularly at Scotland's Findhorn Foundation for more than twenty years and is a member of their educational faculty. *Money, Heart and Mind* grew out of his research in the history of money and a three-year project in which he led "Money Game" workshops for individuals and organization.

His other books include *Meditation in a Changing World, Personal Identity, National Identity and International Relations* and *First Steps—An Introduction to Spiritual Practice.*